CAPTAIN LUCKLESS
*
JAMES, FIRST DUKE
OF HAMILTON
1606–1649

PLATE I

HAMILTON IN COURT DRESS
by Daniel Mytens

Reproduced by permission of His Grace the Duke of Hamilton and
Brandon and the National Galleries of Scotland.

CAPTAIN LUCKLESS

JAMES, FIRST DUKE OF HAMILTON
1606–1649

HILARY L. RUBINSTEIN

1975
SCOTTISH ACADEMIC PRESS
EDINBURGH AND LONDON

Published by
SCOTTISH ACADEMIC PRESS
25 Perth Street, Edinburgh 3

and distributed by
Chatto & Windus Ltd
40 William IV Street
London W.C.2

★

Clarke, Irwin & Co. Ltd., Toronto

ISBN 0 7011 2112 2

Printed in Great Britain by
Western Printing Services Ltd, Bristol

CONTENTS

GENEALOGICAL TABLES

LIST OF ILLUSTRATIONS

PORTRAITS

viii LIST OF ILLUSTRATIONS

MAPS

Dedicated to

BILLY

INTRODUCTION

"Captain Luckless"—the soubriquet applied to the first Duke of Hamilton at the end of his life by his enemy, the Marquis of Montrose—is a fitting epitaph for this maligned and misunderstood man. It is curious that Hamilton's eventful and enigmatic career should have been so studiously neglected by modern historians. For two decades he occupied a supremely influential place at the court of King Charles I, where he succeeded the assassinated Buckingham as royal favourite. The fact that he was the next heir to the throne of Scotland after King Charles, his sister, and their families, afforded him a unique position on the Scottish scene, and gave rise to his reputation as the arch-traitor. His importance went far beyond his role as the King's principal adviser on Scottish affairs, and he properly stands alongside Laud and Strafford as one of the key figures of Caroline politics.

I should like to thank all those who have kindly assisted me in the course of my research, and in particular the following: His Grace the late Duke of Hamilton, K.T., G.C.V.O., A.F.C.; Dr. David Mathew; Miss Doreen M. Hunter, Registrar of the National Register of Archives, Scotland; Mr. Robin E. Hutchison, Keeper of the Scottish National Portrait Gallery; Dr. Rosalind K. Marshall, Assistant Keeper, and author of a most readable biography of Hamilton's daughter; Mr. J. R. Maddicott, Librarian and Archivist, Exeter College, Oxford; Miss Margaret Brown, Reference Librarian, Hamilton Public Library; Mrs. Pamela A. Eddy of the Falmouth branch of the Cornwall County Library; Mrs. Elspeth A. Simpson of the Archives Department, University of Glasgow, and Mr. Robert M. Bartram of the George Peabody branch of the Enoch Pratt Free Library, Baltimore, U.S.A.

I owe a special debt of gratitude to Mr. Ian M. Parsons of the Scottish Academic Press, for his meticulous reading of my manuscript and many helpful suggestions. Finally, I must thank my husband, William, whose shrewd and perceptive insight into historical character and situations helped me immensely. His encouragement at every stage is much appreciated.

*Hamilton . . . could not contain himself within the
bounds of modesty and loyalty, nor could the
extraordinary favours heaped on him by his
sovereign withhold him from the forfeiture of his
allegiance.*

MARCHAMONT NEDHAM (1649)

*There is one good quality in this man, viz: that he
was born and that God made him; and another,
viz: that he is dead, and we must speak nothing
but good of the dead.*

RICHARD LLOYD (1665)

*[He was] a notable dissembler, true only to his own
ends, and a most excellent master in the art of
insinuation, by which he screwed himself so far into
his majesty's good opinion, that whoever undertook
the unrivetting of him, made him faster in it.*

PETER HEYLYN (1668)

*It seemed to me the greatest injustice in this world
that one who served his prince and his country so
long and so faithfully, and sealed all with his
blood, should . . . be deprived of the honour due to
his memory.*

GILBERT BURNET (1677)

Part One

THE MYSTERIOUS MARQUIS
June 1606 – December 1638

Better to stay in green Clydesdale by the
Falls of Corra, in that palace of thine.
THOMAS CARLYLE

CHAPTER I
EARL OF ARRAN

When James VI of Scotland became James I of England at the end of March 1603 and hastened south to claim his new inheritance, he left behind a poor and primitive country. The complaint a prominent Scot had made over forty years before, that he lived "in a corner of the world, separated from the society of men",[1] had not yet lost its validity.

Where in the previous century England had experienced an economic expansion and the rise of absolute monarchy based on an efficient centralised system of government, Scotland had been a divisive and feudal society, plagued by the squabbles of a highly powerful aristocracy having almost princely authority over tenants and vassals, and exploiting to its own advantage the long minorities first of Mary Queen of Scots and then of her son.

Although James VI, an unquestionably intelligent and astute man, had ruled wisely and for the most part well, trying hard to prevent the nobles' disputes by encouraging marriage alliances between the rival houses, his success had been more apparent than real, and he had been able to do little to curb their power. Yet never again would a faction of nobles challenge the crown by themselves; when they did, it was in cooperation with other elements in Scottish society. This was in no small measure due to James's policy, for he made it clear quite early in his reign that he would rule for all the people, and would not be the tool of any section of them.

For all this, Scotland at the beginning of the seventeenth century was still a semi-feudal society with no sizeable middle class, a land of about one million inhabitants, its nobles still fiercely jealous of their rights and influence. They were, as the King ruefully observed, "overfar first in greatness and power, either to do good, or evil, as they are inclined". Their greatest faults, he found, were three-fold: "to thrall, by oppression, the meaner sort that dwelleth near them, to maintain their servants and dependants in any wrong . . . and for any displeasure that they apprehend to be done unto them by their neighbour, to take up a plain feud against him; and, without respect to God, King, or Commonweal, to bang it out bravely, he and all his kin, against him and all his".[2]

The King had been the nobles' pawn throughout his youth, and his memories of their terrorism held him back from drastic measures to reduce their influence. These in any case he perceived to be unfeasible, and the most he could strive for was to court one powerful aristocratic faction and play it off against a rival.

If Scotland was a beautiful country, it was also a bleak and backward one, where tenant farmers held their lands on annual lease, eking out precarious livings and sharing their pitiful hovels with their cattle. Land hunger, in particular the famines of 1587 and 1594–98, had already driven thousands of Scots abroad—to the shores of the Baltic and to Ulster.

Lacking the economic self-sufficiency of England, and dependent for its livelihood on a few staple exports—oats, wheat, barley, salmon, timber, hides, and some coal—Scotland was "a land mainly devoted to supporting a struggling population, the small surplus of produce being employed in supplying the luxuries of life to those who could afford them".[3]

It was also a land of contrasts, perhaps less a nation than a combination of regions separated from each other by moor and mountain, and by clan and family loyalties, a land where the old conflict between Saxon and Celt had not yet been put to rest.

The southern Lowlands, rich in oats, wheat and barley, as well as good grazing pastures for sheep and cattle, and boasting newly discovered coal deposits, were mainly Anglo-Saxon and English-speaking, ruled by a few major families, among whom predominated the Stewarts, Dukes of Lennox, the Douglases, Earls of Morton and of Angus, and above all the Hamiltons.

Further north ruled two other major families, their power resting largely in the Highlands, and having sway over thousands of Celtic, Gaelic-speaking clansmen: the Campbells, Earls of Argyll, powerful in the west, and the Gordons, Marquises of Huntly, supreme in the north-east.

Below them came the nobles of the second rank—the Grahams, Earls of Montrose, the Erskines, Earls of Mar and later of Kellie, the Kennedys, Earls of Cassillis—whose main function had been to maintain a wary watch upon the hill country for the periodic incursions of cattle-raiding Highlanders, and also upon the Border for English invaders.

The Highland clansmen, over whom their chiefs still exercised virtual powers of life and death, were men of a tough, even savage stock, and would remain so until well into the next century. "As for the Highlands", wrote King James, "I shortly comprehend them all in two sorts of people: the one, that dwelleth in our mainland, that are barbarous for the most part, and yet mixed with some show of civility; the other, that dwelleth in the Isles, and are all utterly barbarous, without any sort or show of civility."[4] The Scottish Reformation of 1559 had not penetrated the Highlands; the clansmen were still overwhelmingly Catholic, and with their fierce patriarchal loyalties, their blood-feuds, their Gaelic speech and their romantic sagas, they had little in common with their countrymen in the Lowlands.

The harsh realities of Scottish life made for a hardy, industrious people, susceptible to the Calvinist doctrine of salvation preached by the Kirk since the Reformation. Inspired by John Knox and supported by most of the nobles, the Scottish Reformation, unlike its Lutheran counterpart in England, had resulted in the rise of no substantial class of new leaders. Essentially, it had played into the hands of the nobles, bent on dividing among themselves the spoils of the Auld Kirk. The Hamiltons, for instance, had gained the rich abbeys of Arbroath and Paisley.* "There are few revolutions recorded in history where the presence of self-regarding motives is so exceedingly obvious."[5]

Their concern to consolidate their wealth with new accessions of church property brought the nobles into constant conflict with religiously-motivated reformers, and although the reformed Kirk, like its Catholic predecessor, tended to assume responsibility for the social welfare of the common people, it exerted an austere tyranny over their everyday lives, and retained the formidable power of excommunication. Yet it was exceedingly popular by virtue of its national identity, its democratic form of government, and above all, the doctrine of the elect, which appealed to a poor hard-working population and gave the Scots a Chosen People concept. Such an outlook spawned many a narrow-minded zealot, and King James remarked that "ye shall never find with any

* The Abbey of Paisley had gone to Lord Claud Hamilton, who remained a Catholic.

Highland or Border thieves greater ingratitude, and more lies and vile perjuries, than with these fanatic spirits".[6]

Although the Auld Alliance with France which had existed since 1295 had weakened as a result first of the Reformation and then of the Union of the Crowns, by which the England against whom it had been aimed was no longer the enemy, a deep affection for France and a bitter distrust of England persisted. Indeed, a keen mutual dislike existed between Scots and Englishmen. Most Scots bitterly resented the withdrawal of their King to London, and many nobles—notably Huntly—purposely avoided personal contact with the English Court. For their part, the English objected to the influx into their capital of impoverished Scots of all classes, and fights and disputes between the two peoples were not infrequent. King James did his best to assuage the ill-feeling between them. The Englishmen, he told the Commons a year after his accession, "that doth not love a Scotsman as his brother, or the Scotsman that loves not an Englishman as his brother, is a traitor to God and to the King".[7] Such generous-hearted tolerance, however, could not be won overnight. The old feuds continued, and to the majority of Englishmen Scotland was still a despised and distant country, ruled from Whitehall and administered by James through the Scottish Privy Council: "here I sit and govern Scotland by my pen", he liked to boast. It was a land to which he showed no eagerness to return.

*   *   *

On Saturday, July 19th 1606, at Hamilton Palace, in the gently rolling countryside south-east of Glasgow, a son and heir was born to the seventeen-year-old second Marquis of Hamilton and his wife, Anne. The baby was given his father's name, James, possibly in honour of the King, whose birthday he shared.

The family into which he had been born ranked first among the foremost in Scotland. Almost certainly of Anglo-Norman origin, the Hamiltons attained prominence after the Scottish victory over Edward II at Bannockburn in 1314, when Walter Fitzgilbert of Hamilton, a Lanarkshire landowner and first known ancestor of the family, promptly surrendered Bothwell Castle, which he had been holding for the English, into the hands of Robert Bruce. For this he was rewarded with baronies and lands in Clydesdale,

West Lothian and Galloway. Six generations later, the family was ennobled when Sir James Hamilton of Cadzow was created the first Lord Hamilton, and became the husband of Princess Mary, daughter of James II of Scotland and his queen, Marie of Gueldres. As a consequence of this marriage the successive heads of the House of Hamilton stood in direct line to the Scottish throne, failing issue to the Stuart dynasty. This fact gave the Hamiltons a peculiar significance in Scotland: it strengthened the bonds of the various branches with one another, but it also incurred the bitter jealousy of their rivals and led to a perpetual scrutiny by their enemies. As David Mathew has so well expressed it:

> It was an erroneous but understandable notion that
> they were always waiting and that the successive heads
> of the family never gave a perfect loyalty to any
> sovereign, not to the Queen of Scots, nor in fact to her
> son, nor to her grandson. Their actions, or sometimes
> more especially their inaction, gave rise to the
> impression that they felt that circumstances might play
> into their hands.[8]

But suspicion of treachery was not the only trouble which beset the Hamiltons. They were afflicted, or so it was said, with a terrible melancholy, an inherent condition which drove two of them insane and tormented several others.[9] Yet for all their black moods and quirks of temperament, they prospered. Princess Mary added to their power by bringing the Isle of Arran, commanding the approaches to the Clyde, as part of her dowry, and her son, the second Lord Hamilton, created Earl of Arran in 1503, played a conspicuous part in national affairs during the minority of James V. But it was her grandson, the third Lord Hamilton, second Earl of Arran, who consolidated the fortunes of the family. Indecisive as he was, on the death of James V in December 1542, he was chosen regent of the kingdom and tutor to Mary Queen of Scots, then a babe aged six days. As such he was one life away from the throne, the acknowledged "second person in the realm", and self-styled "Governor and Prince of Scotland". In 1547 King Henri II of France paid him a singular honour by granting him a lucrative French fief, the Duchy of Châtelherault, an ancient town on the Vienne, some twenty miles north-east of

Poitiers, not for his life, as is sometimes stated, but "pour lui, ses hoirs et ayants cause, à perpetuité".[10] Seven years later, in 1554, he reluctantly resigned his offices in favour of the young Queen's mother, Marie of Guise.

Châtelherault's close proximity to the throne, his great following and immense possessions—he had further enriched himself out of the Reformation spoils—gave him such formidable power that his eldest son, the young and handsome James, Earl of Arran, was proposed in 1543 as husband to Mary Queen of Scots and in 1560 to Elizabeth of England. But Arran's bright star dimmed in 1562, when he became insane, and on Chatelherault's death thirteen years later his third son, Lord John Hamilton, became, in effect, head of the House. With his younger brother, the Catholic Claud, Lord Paisley, John became, after a stormy beginning and brief exile abroad, a firm adherent of Mary Queen of Scots, and on April 15th 1599 was rewarded by her son with the Marquisate of Hamilton. He died just five years later, on April 12th 1604, commending his "only and dearest son to his majesty's kind patronage and care".[11]

The second marquis, a boy of fifteen at his father's death, had been married to Lady Anne Cunningham, fourth daughter of the seventh Earl of Glencairn, in January 1603. Her family, Norman in origin and long important in south-west Scotland—the title was derived from a parish in Nithsdale, Dumfriesshire—had been among the principal architects of the Scottish Reformation, and Lady Anne, who brought her husband a dowry of 40,000 merks,* was herself a rigid Presbyterian.

Like most marriages of their time and class, theirs was not a love-match, and Hamilton was not faithful to his formidable little wife. A fine-looking man, charming, sophisticated, urbane, elegantly clad in the latest French fashion, he never lacked female admirers, and by Anna Stewart, the pretty young widow of Lord Saltoun, he had a daughter, Margaret.

At his succession to the marquisate he found his estates heavily encumbered by debt, but he had the good sense, not long afterwards, to write to King James at his distant Court in London, pledging his fidelity in the tradition of his ancestors, and requesting confirmation of his possession of Arbroath Abbey, one of the

* A merk was worth 13 shillings and 4 pence; a pound Scots was worth one-twelfth of a pound sterling.

church properties which Châtelherault had seized for his sons. "I thought, and ever shall think myself bound to your majesty beyond all the subjects of this kingdom", he declared in his winsome way,[12] and in May he was confirmed as temporal lord of Arbroath. He had enjoyed the first fruits of the King's favour, and there were to be many more. James liked handsome young men, and as early as January 1610, when Hamilton was visiting Venice, he was described as "dearly loved of his majesty".[13]

His estates were vast, extending from the region just west of Edinburgh through Clydesdale to Galloway. They boasted some of the richest lands in Scotland, where good mixed farming, corn and pasture were to be had in abundance, and there was also the occasional coal mine. Besides the ruins of Cadzow, which had been destroyed at the close of the wars of Queen Mary, and the house at Kinneil, Bo'ness, with its famed "parable room", he owned five major castles: his principal seat, Hamilton Palace in Lanarkshire, which Châtelherault had bought from the Dean of Glasgow in 1538; Avendale Castle and Strathaven Castle, both south of Hamilton; Bothwell Castle on the Clyde, reputedly the oldest and finest stone castle in Scotland; and Brodick Castle on the Isle of Arran. And so his heir, James, who came to be styled Earl of Arran on the death of his insane great uncle in March 1609, spent his childhood amid wealth and splendour, fully cognisant of his family's great position in Scotland and of his own potential importance. As time went on he was joined by three sisters, and by a brother, William, born on December 14th 1616.

In the spring and summer of 1617, the King, accompanied by the Duke of Buckingham, whom he appointed to the Scottish Privy Council in May, visited his native realm for the first time since his accession to the English throne. Observing the Marquis of Hamilton at several meetings of the Privy Council, he was immediately charmed by his captivating manner and undeniable good looks, and impressed by his apparent prudence and ability. At the end of July, as part of a series of visits to the great Scottish nobles, he spent two days at Hamilton Palace, and it was then that he invited Hamilton to come to England. Although admiration for the marquis was ostensibly James's reason for bestowing this mark of his favour on Hamilton, some detected an ulterior motive. "The King is becoming jealous of the great influence and power possessed by the Marquis of Hamilton in Scotland", reported a

foreign envoy. "Under a thin pretext he has desired him to come
and live near him in England, having chosen him to be a member
of the Council of State."[14] In August Hamilton was appointed to
the English Privy Council, and went to London with his elder
son, then aged eleven. His other children remained in Scotland,
and so did his wife, who managed his estates in his absence.

Himself a notorious womaniser, he soon became a favourite of
the homosexual King. His popularity was apparent almost at once.
"The Marquis of Hamilton is much made of by both his majesty
and Buckingham and carries himself very well and wisely",
wrote one courtier, and another, Sir Philip Warwick, writing
years later, remembered him as "a goodly, proper and graceful
gentleman" who "fed his own greatness and pleasure more than
[he] busied himself in intrigues and designs at Court".[15]

He prospered in England, and on June 16th 1619 the King
conferred upon him the English titles of Earl of Cambridge and
Baron Innerdale. The Earldom of Cambridge was a singular
honour, for hitherto it had been bestowed only on princes of the
blood. Then, in July 1621, after the King, as part of his attempt
to foist Episcopalianism upon an unwilling Scotland, had proposed the "popish" Five Articles of Perth,* he sent Hamilton to
Edinburgh as Royal Commissioner with the purpose of securing
their ratification by the Scottish Parliament. He succeeded, to the
deep gratitude of his sovereign. "Your provident and wise
carriage", wrote King James, "hath been highly commended to
us by all sorts of people, both ecclesiastical and lay."[16] It was the
high point of the marquis' career, but it cost him the goodwill of
many of his own countrymen, who regarded him as an apostate:

> O wretched Scot, when Cadzow turns thy King!
> Then may thou doole and dolour daily sing;
> For from the south great sorrow shall he bring,
> Therefore o'er Scot right short shall be his ring.[17]

His staunchly Calvinist wife, too, cannot have approved of his
part in a measure aimed against the presbyterian Kirk.

---

* The Articles required all to kneel when receiving Holy Communion;
private communion was to be administered to the sick; very ill and
dying infants were to be privately baptised; children of the appropriate
age were to be confirmed; Christmas, Good Friday, Ascension Day
and Pentecost were to be observed.

Meanwhile Arran, growing up at Court and at "Fisher's Folly", the splendid Elizabethan mansion outside Bishopsgate which his father had purchased from the Earl of Argyll, had become a sturdy, spoiled, solemn boy, the pride of his father, who lovingly described him to Buckingham as "your little servant James".[18] His leaving Scotland so abruptly had caused a break in his studies from which his formal education never completely recovered, so that while he developed an admirable command of language, his spelling, even by the lax standards of the day, remained atrocious. At the age of fifteen he was sent to Exeter College, Oxford, at that time a hot-bed of Puritanism, but with a growing reputation for scholarship. Its rector was the learned divine, Dr. John Prideaux, a Devonshire man of humble origins. Among his former pupils was Sir John Eliot, later to die in the Tower as an opponent of King Charles I. Most students at Exeter, a poor college until the Reformation, were of West Country stock, drawn mainly from the squirearchy of Devon and Cornwall. Why the Marquis of Hamilton chose to send his son there remains a mystery, but it might have been suggested to him by Buckingham, who had travelled on the Continent with Eliot, and was still his friend, though he would not long be. As a Scottish nobleman there, Arran must have been something of an oddity, yet Prideaux's reputation attracted an increasing number of foreign students, and another prominent Scot educated there—a few years previously—was Robert Spottiswoode, who long afterwards became Arran's enemy.

It is impossible to ascertain how much of Exeter's Puritanism rubbed off on Arran, for he was there less than six months. He entered on July 6th 1621, accompanied by his tutor, James Bale, a graduate of the University of Glasgow, and came down on December 14th of the same year, without, therefore, attempting a degree.[19] Why he left so soon is unclear. Perhaps King James urged Hamilton to remove his son from such dissentient surroundings; possibly the marquis, who was leaning towards the King's policy of a Spanish marriage for the Prince of Wales, and was even suspected of Papist sympathies himself, had second thoughts; most probably Arran was an idle scholar who successfully persuaded his father to let him resume life at Court.

Yet he was sufficiently attached to Exeter to present the college with some fine pieces of silver plate, and to use his influence to release some land north of the college for Exeter's expansion.

Then, too, he had befriended Prideaux enough to procure for him, two decades later, the Bishopric of Worcester. The college would always be glad to have been associated with him.

On coming down, he returned to London, where his father and Buckingham were devising their own plans for his future. Ever eager to advance the fortunes of his numerous relatives, Buckingham viewed Arran as a prospective husband for his niece Mary, daughter of William, Viscount Feilding, a Warwickshire gentleman of good but undistinguished family who owed his own rise to his marriage with Buckingham's sister, Susanna.

Buckingham was an upstart, and from that point of view little Mary was no fit match for Arran. So shameless was the favourite in seeking great marriages for his bevy of nieces that a doggerel asked:

> Hast thou no niece to wed, is there no inn
> Nor bawdy house t'afford thee any kin
> To cuckold lords withall?[20]

Yet his influence was so great that Hamilton persuaded himself of the desirability of the marriage. Thus, on the evening of Sunday, June 16th 1622, after supper, Buckingham's "little servant James", three days short of his sixteenth birthday, was married at Court in the King's presence to nine-year-old Mary Feilding.[21] The heir to a proud and princely Scottish house found himself wed to the daughter of a modest Midlands squire. It was a situation which Arran bitterly resented, and with which he never really came to terms.

Portraits exist by the fashionable Court painter Daniel Mytens of the bride at the time of her marriage, a brown-haired child with large dark eyes, wearing a feather head-dress and a ruff, and of the groom two years later, sullen and diffident in a black suit and scarlet hose and shoes with elaborate rosettes. Naturally, in view of the bride's tender age, no attempt was made to consummate the marriage, and after a perfunctory kiss the youthful pair were parted. Three months afterwards, in September, Lord Feilding was created Earl of Denbigh. The Villiers kinship wielded a formidable power, and young Arran believed himself their pawn. His suspicion was not without reason, for his marriage to Mary was quite an achievement, even for Buckingham.

In the meantime the Marquis of Hamilton had consolidated his position as one of the King's most valued courtiers. After his victory at the Scottish Parliament in 1621 it was widely rumoured that James was about to create him a duke along with Buckingham.[22] In 1623 he was appointed one of the commissioners to negotiate the terms of the marriage between the Prince of Wales and the Infanta of Spain, when proposals to give him a dukedom were renewed.[23] In March that year Arran, accompanied by his father-in-law, Denbigh, and others, travelled through France and across Spain to Madrid as part of Prince Charles' entourage. Hamilton was made a Knight of the Garter, and in May he was scheduled to receive the Infanta at Southampton. But the negotiations for the marriage broke down and Hamilton's hopes of a dukedom vanished.

Yet honours continued to accrue to him and his son. At the close of 1623 Arran was made a gentleman of the bedchamber to the Prince of Wales, and from then on he came into almost daily contact with the heir to the throne. "One would make believe", remarked the Earl of Kellie, himself a favourite Scottish courtier, "that it would be the best part of his portion with his wife."[24] Although Buckingham's influence was probably at work, it is possible that Prince Charles, a shy and stammering young man of twenty-three, had requested Arran's appointment as a result of a friendship between the two which had ripened in Spain. It is, indeed, unlikely that Prince Charles, who had come to share his father's infatuation with Buckingham, had paid much attention to Arran until about that time, for a six-year difference in age is a very wide gap in early youth, and would have precluded any real friendship between prince and courtier until Charles was in his twenties and Arran in his late teens. A few weeks later, at the end of February 1624, Hamilton himself was appointed to the lucrative post of Lord High Steward of the Household. In April he became a naturalised Englishman. All seemed set fair for both father and son.

CHAPTER II

RELUCTANT COURTIER

On Ash Wednesday, March 2nd 1625, in the early hours of the morning, the Marquis of Hamilton died following a violent seizure at Whitehall. His end was attributed to fever, though the sudden onset of the illness and the rapidity of his death made many suspect poison. He was only thirty-six and his body appeared strangely swollen and spotted.[1] It is not clear whether his heir arrived at his bedside in time to hear his dying wishes. Arran had been with the King's party, returning from a progress in the north of England, and had been taken ill himself at Chesterfield in Derbyshire. Growing steadily worse, he finally had to be left behind at Moor Park in Hertfordshire, home of Lucy, Countess of Bedford, a confidante of both his father and Buckingham. She was, indeed, no stranger to him, and at one time a marriage had been proposed between him and her niece, Anne, daughter of Sir Robert Chichester, but had met with vehement opposition from the girl's father.[2] He was now described as "dangerously sick" and there were fears for his recovery. But he is said to have managed to drag himself to Whitehall shortly before his father died.[3]

Amid the Court mourning, there were rumours that he had died a Catholic and that a Jesuit priest had administered the last rites.[4] Others, however, observed that he died "more subject to his pleasures and the company of women than to priests".[5] A post-mortem carried out by three doctors reported that he had died of an acute fever, and noted symptoms reminiscent of smallpox.[6] Three weeks later, on March 27th, King James himself died, of a tertian ague. The death of his other close kinsman, Esmé Stuart, Duke of Lennox, the previous year, had depressed him, and when he learned of Hamilton's death the already ailing monarch moaned: "If the branches be thus cut down, the stock cannot continue long."[7]

Now in his nineteenth year, the new marquis was a good-natured young man, considerate and compassionate as his father had been. He was pensive and introspective, and the expression on his dark features was often serious. Sir Philip Warwick has left us with a particularly vivid little pen-portrait of Hamilton as he was at this time. The second marquis, he says,

> had two sons, James and William, neither of them so graceful persons as himself, and both of some hard visage, the elder of a neater shape and gracefuller motion than his brother. However, I was in the presence chamber at Whitehall, when, after his father's death, he returned from his travels, and waiting upon the King from chapel with great observance, and the King using him with great kindness, the eyes of the whole Court were upon the young man. His hair was short, and he wore a little black callot-cap, which was not then usual, and I wondered much that all present, who usually at Court put the best character upon a rising man, generally agreed in this, that the air of his countenance had such a cloud on it that Nature seems to have impressed *aliquid insigne*, which I often reflected on when his future actions led him first to be suspected, then to be declaimed against.[8]

Young as he was, the stage seemed set for him to assume his place as a great figure at Court. On April 22nd it was agreed to grant him a pension of £2,500 a year out of the pretermitted customs, the amount his father had received.[9] On May 7th he played his first major official role since succeeding to his new titles, when with his younger kinsman, Lennox, he led the Scottish contingent at the funeral of the late King in Westminster Abbey. Almost a year later, on February 2nd 1626, he bore the sword at the coronation of Charles, who was dressed not in the customary purple but in white, a symbol of the purity and solemnity of the occasion and of his abhorrence of vulgar trappings. But it caused some criticism at the time, and was regarded by some as an "ill omen".[10]

Charles lacked the common touch, and his Court reflected this from the outset of his troubled and tragic reign: "he kept state to the full, which made his Court very orderly, no man presuming to be seen in a place where he had no pretence to be".[11] Soon the Court became known as the strictest in Europe, and as a result the King was a man respected and feared but not generally loved.

Almost totally dependent on Buckingham, and neglecting his little French bride, the dark-eyed vivacious Henrietta Maria, he became lonely and isolated.

If Hamilton had been a mere sycophant he could have become Buckingham's protégé, but he would not be manipulated, for he preferred to owe no obligations to the son of a Leicestershire knight and a former lady's maid. Although in the autumn of 1625 he had been on sufficiently good terms with his wife's uncle to accompany him on a diplomatic mission to Holland, the usually easy-going Hamilton was smouldering with resentment. He believed that Buckingham was trying to cheat him out of the pension that had been granted to him, and he made no secret of his distaste for the bride who had been forced upon him. As yet Mary, who was only fourteen, was his wife in name only, and the scandalmongers noted with relish that he was not inclined to make her anything more.

But he did have other grounds for concern. Sinister rumours were abroad: the suspicion that the late marquis had died of poisoning had not yet been laid to rest, and Dr. George Eglisham, a poet and life-long friend of the dead nobleman, and the only one of the three physicians not happy with the verdict of the post-mortem, had fled to Holland, and from there he had distributed a tract, *The Forerunner of Revenge*, in which he accused Buckingham of having poisoned both Hamilton and King James.[12]

This was not likely, though it was, of course, possible. An early attempt by Lord Howard de Walden, with whom the second Marquis of Hamilton did not get on, to sow dissension between him and Buckingham had failed, and the two men had been on cordial terms, sharing—though not equally—the old King's favour, sitting on the privy councils of both kingdoms, participating in many of the same schemes (notably the plantation of the New England colonies), joining their families in marriage, acting together in Court masques, and perhaps vying for the same mistresses. And yet towards the end of the marquis' life there does seem to have been some ill-feeling between them. Hamilton, conscious of his own ancient lineage, became jealous of Buckingham's meteoric rise and let slip in his presence a pointed comment about King James's new creations cheapening the peerage.[13] Furthermore, with all the lingering Francophilia of the Scot, he had grown more and more critical of Buckingham's war policy.

It was this last fact which lent an element of credibility to Eglisham's allegations.

If Hamilton did not believe that Buckingham had poisoned his father he cannot have remained unaffected by the rumours. At first he called for an inquest, and then, in the autumn of 1626 he withdrew to the estates he had inherited. He was bewildered by the talk of poison, and he needed time to forge his own contacts in Scotland, and still more to put his new property in order, for his father, by a combination of munificence and high living, had incurred many debts. And so he said farewell to Court, the King, and his virgin bride, and joined his mother, brother and three sisters in Scotland. Many were surprised to see him go. Noting the growing discontent in Scotland over the new King's religious policies, an astute observer commented that "the House of Hamilton has a large following, and it seems especially strange that the King should choose to handle affairs before receiving the Crown of Scotland". A little later he added that "people in general blame the King for allowing so great a personage to depart while affairs are in their present state and discontent at its zenith".[14] And here we have the first inkling of a rumour which was to follow Hamilton throughout his life, and which has plagued his memory beyond the grave—that, given the chance, he would seize the Scottish crown.

It was inevitable that his time was spent at first in acquainting himself with the rest of the Scottish nobility, and in inspecting his estates, meeting friends, neighbours and kinsmen—Glencairn, Abercorn, Melrose—as well as powerful dependents bearing the family name, important connections in the whole Hamilton alliance. As often as he could he explored, on foot and on horseback, the Lanarkshire countryside which he grew to love. He delighted in the chase at Cadzow, to the south of Hamilton, with its ancient oaks, the remains of the great Caledonian Forest, and its roaming herds of wild white cattle. Although he loved the green country of Clydesdale, he enjoyed above all the bewitching scenery on the Isle of Arran, and accordingly spent as much time at Brodick Castle as possible. Arran became, for him, a kind of paradise, and more than once during the years ahead, when he had come to view life almost as a series of trials, he looked back to the peace of the island with a painful yearning.

Yet even now he was learning what it meant to be a great

Scottish magnate. On July 14th 1625 he had acted as one of the
three witnesses to the King's letter of revocation, written at
Oatlands and despatched to the Scottish Privy Council, cancelling
all infestments and gifts of any kind granted by himself during
his minority or by his brother, Prince Henry, who had died in
1612, or by his father out of the property and revenues of Scotland, together with grants made by himself to the prejudice of
the royal domains.[15] On October 12th of the same year this document was superseded by a far more drastic Edict of Revocation
repealing grants made of crown property since the reign of Queen
Mary, and rescinding all dispositions of Church property into
temporal lordships.

It was his deep and sincere commitment to religion coupled
with his conception of Scotland as the lesser of his two kingdoms
which made him embark on this policy: to him it was wholly
just that former ecclesiastical property should revert to the Kirk,
and entirely right that the Kirk should be brought in time into
line with the Church of England. To him, as to most people,
Scotland was an obscure, unknown and inconsequential land.
"There was so little curiosity either in the Court or the country
to know anything of Scotland, or what was done there", Clarendon
explained later, "that when the whole nation was solicitous to
know what passed weekly in Germany or Poland and all other
parts of Europe, no man ever inquired what was doing in Scotland, nor had that kingdom a place or mention in any page of any
gazette, so little the world heard or thought of that people."[16]
For all that, it seems incredible that Charles should have been so
insensitive to the mood of the Scottish nobility.

Naturally, the Scottish nobles—including Hamilton, who like
his father before him was temporal lord of the Abbey of Arbroath,
which had some twenty-five parish churches in its charge—
bitterly resented this royal interference with the gains their
families had made out of the Reformation. They refused to
surrender their properties and powers, and on August 22nd 1626
the King instructed his Scottish Advocates, Sir William Oliphant
and Thomas Hope, to proceed with a "summons of reduction"
ordering the nobles to do so.[17] Over the next few months the
lairds and nobles affected by the summons held protest meetings
in Edinburgh. Their leader was a very distant Hamilton kinsman,
the Earl of Melrose, old King James's "Tam o' the Cowgate",

later Earl of Haddington, who urged Charles in vain to call a Scottish Parliament.

But Hamilton himself, mindful of his future relations with the King, refused to join the demonstrations. "We did expect no less from you", Charles wrote to him in December, "for you have reason to trust our favour more than any title you can have, and as we are very confident that no man shall be more careful than you for the advancing of our service, so be assured that we will be loath to see your estate harmed, and the more freely you give way to that which may import our goodwill we will deal the better with you."[18] The King had instructed his Advocates to prosecute Hamilton on the grounds that he "hath in possession some things justly belonging to us", but now he told them not to proceed with the summons because "we are confident of his affection to conform himself to our pleasure in these particulars and anything else that may concern our service".[19] On January 17th 1627 Hamilton was appointed one of the sixty-six Commissioners who were to sit from March until August and negotiate the surrender of the properties covered by the King's Edict.[20]

Meanwhile, the King's thoughts were never far from the marquis, his erstwhile companion and the son of his father's trusted friend. Charles would always find a place for him at Court, and looked forward to a time when he would return. He was not the only one. Hamilton's parents-in-law, the Denbighs, were understandably indignant at his studied neglect of Mary, who had now reached adolescence. In March 1627 Lord Denbigh travelled to Scotland to implore him to return to Whitehall. As he passed through the broad Hamilton lands he must have been impressed by the wealth of the young nobleman who had been forced to marry his daughter. Few Englishmen, then or later, fully appreciated the extent and significance of Hamilton's stature in his own country.

But the marquis was stubborn, and Denbigh's proposal that he join him in Lord Willoughby's naval expedition against the French would not induce him to leave. "The obduracy of youth", commented the Venetian ambassador with too much assurance, "is most easily mollified by the flames of glory and honour."[21] Indeed, for all the enchantment of his Scottish estates the restless young man longed to play a hero's part. Like many an introvert he dreamed of life as a man of action, but his temperament did not match his ambition, and an innate caution, mixed with indolence, restrained him. In any case, he was not yet ready to make his peace with the Buckingham connection, and Denbigh's mission proved fruitless.

On March 3rd 1627 the King issued a warrant from Newmarket appointing Hamilton, not yet twenty-one, to the Scottish Privy Council, "being credibly informed of the sufficiency of our right trusty and well-beloved cousin . . . and of his affection to our service".[22] At the same time he wrote "James" a touching personal note, making it clear that he for one believed Hamilton's avowed reasons for leaving Court, and showing the fondness that, even then, he had for his young kinsman: "I doubt not but your want forced you to leave me, but mine shall not hinder me to help yours."[23]

On April 3rd Hamilton attended his first meeting of the Privy Council, and three days later he surrendered to the Commission his relevant properties.[24] Thereafter, throughout the summer of 1627, he attended Council meetings with conscientious regularity. Dominating the executive, legislative and judicial processes of the government, the Council was responsible for the day-to-day running of the nation, and whoever controlled it in effect controlled the kingdom. Young as he was, the reality of Hamilton's position in the Scottish hierarchy and closeness to the King made his admission strongly desirable, and Charles had every reason to expect that he would loyally represent his interests: "We conceive that in anything that may concern us and the public good you will endeavour to give a good example unto others."[25]

With the passing of the months, however, Hamilton's attendance at Council meetings grew less frequent. Inevitably the Council was mainly occupied with mundane matters of administration— repairing highways, punishing criminals, settling civil disputes— and such affairs as the issuing of a commission to the Marquis of Huntly and others for the apprehension of a band of men who had failed to answer a charge of stealing "a brown chestnut coloured horse of seven years old"[26] were not destined to fire the imagination of a young man burning with unsatisfied ambition.

Perhaps his thoughts turned more frequently to Court, as the King's thoughts turned towards him. On January 1st 1628 Charles again wrote "James" an affectionate letter:

Having, as I hope, despatched your business, I must tell
you it was ill-luck and not ill-will that made it so long
a-doing, and likewise of the importunity of a house of
women for calling you hither. But it may be the company
of some where you are will make you give a negligent
ear to those that are here, yet I doubt not but when you
know (as these lines do assure you) that you cannot
come before you shall be welcome to your best friends
here, that your stay will not be long where you are.[27]

The marquis might have remained in Scotland indefinitely had
it not been for the assassination of Buckingham at Portsmouth on
August 23rd 1628, as he prepared to sail with his fleet to La
Rochelle for a second expedition against France. The nation was
jubilant at the death of "Spain's agent, Holland's bane, Rome's
friend",[28] and the murderer, Felton, was the hero of the hour.
But the King was shattered, and withdrew into himself. The duke
had been his idol from boyhood, the real ruler of Britain, and now
he felt himself quite alone. To Hamilton he offered Buckingham's
post as Master of the Horse, sending Lord Denbigh to him with
a message that read: "I look that you should be quickly here,
which again I assure you will be well done."[29] An amused Lord
Goring tried to be bawdy when he remarked that "the Mastership
of the Horse, it is thought, shall help to horse the Lady Marquess",
whilst another courtier wrote that it appeared that Hamilton had
been offered the post on condition that he "cohabit with his
wife".[30]

Hamilton's arrival in London was awaited with curiosity, for it
was well known that he was in no hurry to engage in sexual
relations with young Mary, and some wondered whether he would,
in fact, try to have the marriage annulled. He arrived on October
20th, and that very night, much against his will, he consummated
his marriage with his fifteen-year-old wife. The situation is
described exquisitely by a contemporary:

Monday week that night the Lord Marquis Hamilton
came to Court, where he lay with his lady that same
night. For the King would have it so, notwithstanding
the Marquis pretended his long journey of the same day
and his want of clean linen. Whereupon his majesty
commanded his own barber to attend him with a shirt,

waistcoat and nightcap of his majesty's, and would not
be satisfied till he had seen them both in bed together.
The Queen also sent him a posset* to welcome him.[31]

The King, indeed, was overjoyed to see Hamilton, who on
November 7th was officially appointed Master of the Horse,
though with a salary smaller than Buckingham's. As such he was
one of the most important figures in the Royal Household, and
to him alone fell the privilege of "riding at the King's stirrup".
Soon the name "James" became as recurrent on the King's lips
as "George" had been.[32] Although it is doubtful whether Charles
—who after what was perhaps a mild homosexual phase in
adolescence, had become positively uxorious—ever loved Hamilton
with the fervour with which he had loved Buckingham, Mark
Napier, looking across the span of two centuries, perhaps perceived accurately when he saw Hamilton as "the nobleman on
whom alone the King leant, and with a love surpassing the love
of women".[33]

Hamilton and his wife lived at first in apartments at Whitehall,
but when their family began to increase they moved into Buckingham's former residence, Wallingford House, between Whitehall
and Charing Cross, roughly where Admiralty Arch now stands.
They had first three daughters: Henrietta Mary, named in honour
of the Queen; Anne, named after the Dowager Marchioness; and
Susanna, named after Lady Denbigh. The births of three girls in
succession when an heir was required was not likely to inspire
Hamilton with much tender gratitude towards his wife. "I must
wish you much happiness with your little daughter", wrote the
Queen of Bohemia in April 1631, shortly after the birth of the
eldest, "though I see you are half ashamed you have one since
you tell nobody of it."[34] Three sons followed: Charles, Earl of
Arran, named in honour of the King; James, named after Hamilton's father; and William, named after Lord Denbigh. Of these
children, all but Anne and Susanna died young.

The marquis' marriage might not have been entirely satisfactory, but it seems possible that its unhappiness has been
overstressed. In later years, perhaps remembering his own discontent, he expressed the hope that his children would not be

* A hot drink of ale or wine in curdled milk often given to a bridal
couple.

forced to marry against their wills, yet there is no reason to suspect that his marriage was less happy than most of the arranged marriages of the period. Indeed, there is probably truth in Burnet's assertion that Hamilton reconciled himself to the match on account of Mary's physical beauty, dignity and gentleness.[35] He was certainly on good terms with his mother-in-law, Lady Denbigh, and his brother-in-law, Basil Feilding. For her part, Mary is said to have been "a most affectionate and dutiful wife".[36] Present at Court as a lady of the bedchamber to Henrietta Maria, and highly regarded by both King and Queen, she was nevertheless very much in the background, part of Hamilton's private life, of which we know relatively little. In love, as in most things, the marquis was an enigma.

CHAPTER III
CRY TREASON!

Scarcely had Hamilton settled into his court routine than he was forced to look beyond the seas, for the ordered calm of Whitehall was not undisturbed by the wars of religion in Germany, which had been pursuing their terrible course since May 1618, when a Protestant provisional government was set up in Prague in opposition to the ruthless yet well-meaning Catholic despot, Ferdinand, Archduke of Styria, who was elected King of Bohemia in 1617 and Emperor two years later. He was deposed in August 1619 and Frederick V, Elector Palatine, leader of the German Calvinists, was declared King of Bohemia in his stead. Frederick had married King James's only daughter, Princess Elizabeth, in 1613, and he and his supporters hoped that England would readily be persuaded to help their cause. But although many Britons—in particular many thousands of Scots—enlisted in Frederick's service, his father-in-law would not help him, fearing to upset Spain at a time when he was planning Prince Charles's marriage with the Infanta, and Frederick, good-natured, indolent, and indecisive, found himself in a perilous position. The Protestant Union, though pledged to defend the Palatinate, would not support his claims in Bohemia; Saxony, Hesse, Denmark and the Lutherans refused him assistance; the Dutch Calvinists gave him minimal financial aid, and Gustavus Adolphus, King of Sweden, who had recognised him as King of Bohemia, was too preoccupied in his war against Poland to intervene on his behalf. Meanwhile, with money from the Pope, a powerful army under Tilly, and the prospect of aid from Spain, Ferdinand's cause flourished, and in November 1620, Frederick's army, commanded by Christian of Anhalt, was utterly routed near Prague by Maximilian of Bavaria and Tilly. Frederick, the "Winter King", fled to the Hague with his wife and young family; Bohemia became a Catholic country, and Ferdinand wreaked a terrible vengeance on his opponents.

It was the end of Frederick's brief reign, but the war was only just beginning. Two months before his crushing defeat a large

Spanish force invaded and held the Lower Palatinate, and the ineffective Protestant Union crumbled the following year; only two German princes were prepared to defend the Palatinate, and Tilly swept all before him. The triumph of the Catholic cause seemed assured, but now foreign rulers, wary of the union of Spain and Austria, which greatly strengthened the Hapsburgs, decided to intervene. In 1624 King James, while officially continuing his policy of neutrality, allowed the Protestant general, Count Ernst von Mansfeld, to levy troops in England, although he hindered their effectiveness by refusing to allow Mansfeld to recapture Breda, which the Spanish had taken from the Dutch. Christian IV of Denmark and Gustavus Adolphus of Sweden similarly viewed with alarm the prospect of Hapsburg hegemony in northern Germany, and in May 1624 King Charles agreed to pay King Christian a subsidy of £30,000 a month, and in December of the same year Holland undertook to join England in subsidising the Danish King. But the squabbles between Charles and Parliament stopped the payment of these subsidies, and the Protestant cause suffered a setback once more. Gustavus Adolphus, whose operations in Poland prevented the Catholic Poles from making a diversion in northern Germany, failed to persuade his brother-in-law, George William of Brandenburg, to lend active help; several German princes, led by John George of Saxony, were reluctant to fight against the Emperor; France, alarmed by the Spanish occupation of the Palatinate, was too busy with the Huguenot revolt to intervene.

In these circumstances, Tilly and Wallenstein, a Bohemian Catholic appointed Commander-in-Chief of the Imperial Armies in 1625, occupied Lower Saxony. In August 1626 Tilly utterly routed Christian IV at Lutter, and a year later Wallenstein conquered Silesia and invaded Holstein (of which King Christian was Duke) with Tilly; Arnim, Wallenstein's second-in-command, seized Mecklenburg and then invaded Jutland; King Christian fled to the Danish islands, and by the end of October 1627 Wallenstein had subjugated the Danish mainland. The Imperial forces, encouraged, attacked the Baltic ports, but met with only partial success, and, alarmed by the designs of Gustavus Adolphus, made peace at Lubeck in May 1629.

But resentment was brewing over an edict issued by Ferdinand, in which he called for the restitution of all Church property secularised since the Peace of Augsburg in 1555, and John George of Saxony began to favour the possibility of a union of all Protestants against the Emperor.

On June 26th 1630, Gustavus Adolphus, who feared that the Baltic coast which Sweden had gained from Russia in 1617, and Sweden itself, were endangered by Ferdinand's Baltic policy, and who wished to defend Protestantism in Germany, so weakened by the Emperor's military successes, landed on the island of Usedom with an army soon numbering 45,000 men. He occupied Pomerania and seized Stettin, thereby securing a strong Baltic base. He had made peace with Poland in 1629, partly owing to the intervention of Richelieu, who hoped to secure Sweden's help in weakening Austria. But at first the German Protestants would not join him. They were afraid that if Ferdinand overthrew him as he had overthrown the King of Denmark, he would take strong vengeance on those who had supported him, and they feared that their own independence would be jeopardised if Gustavus was successful. Yet with the ending of the Danish and Polish wars, mercenaries of several nationalities were thrown out of employment and entered service in his new campaign, so that by the middle of 1630 there were 72,500 men under his command, of whom 38,000 were Swedes.[1] He enlisted a crack regiment of Scots under Lord Reay, chief of the Clan Mackay, which had served Christian IV with distinction, and he later used it in his most dangerous and critical enterprises.

Although many Englishmen believed that their country should materially aid the Protestant cause and show the Emperor that England's goodwill might be worth considering, the official English policy was still one of non-intervention. For no matter how popular Elizabeth of Bohemia was, no matter how widespread the sympathy for her and the Protestant cause, few at Court were prepared for England to plunge into war on her husband's behalf:

> Tourneys, masques, theatres better become
> Our halcyon days; what though the German drum
> Bellow for freedom and revenge, the noise
> Concerns not us, nor should divert our joys;
> Nor ought the thunder of their carabins
> Drown the sweet airs of our tun'd violins.[2]

But behind the scenes Sir Robert Anstruther and Sir Thomas Roe were hard at work, and Charles was understandably anxious to help his sister, without seeming officially to do so. He thus suggested to a willing Hamilton, "at that time pronest", by virtue of his age, "to a thirst of glory",[3] that he levy 6,000 volunteers for the army of Gustavus, with the help of Lord Reay, a German-speaking Scottish courtier named David Ramsay, and Farensbach, a Swedish agent.

Some observers thought that Charles, in delegating what they considered his responsibility to Hamilton, had not been fair to the marquis. This view was reflected in a play, *The Maid of Honour*, by the fashionable satirist Philip Massinger, published in 1632, in which a thinly disguised Charles makes a veiled reference to his official detachment from Hamilton's proposed expedition:

> . . . As I my lord,
> Before resolved you, I will not engage
> My person in this quarrel; neither press
> My subjects to maintain it; yet to show
> My rule is gentle and that I have feeling
> . . . . . We do consent
> That, as adventurers and volunteers,
> No way compelled by us, they may make trial
> Of their boasted valours.

And again,

> 'Tis well, and, but my grant is this, expect not
> Assistance from me. Govern as you please
> The province you make choice of; for, I vow
> By all things sacred, if that thou miscarry
> In this rash undertaking, I will hear it
> No otherwise than as a sad disaster,
> Fallen on a stranger; nor will I esteem
> That man my subject, who in thy extreme
> In purse or person aids thee.[4]

It was fitting, though, that the task of raising and leading such a volunteer force should fall to Hamilton, Elizabeth's nearest relative outside the Royal House of Stuart. From her brother she had gained a fond impression of the young man she hardly knew, who with his wife was to stand proxy for her and Frederick at the baptism of the little Prince of Wales in 1630. "I have not a kinsman I love better than I do you", she once wrote to him.[5] And Hamilton, at any rate, was a "good Protestant". In September 1622, when he was only sixteen, he expressed concern at King James's decision to release from prison recusants in England and Scotland. Bishop Williams had attempted to assure him that the King's action was intended to help, not hinder, the Protestant cause abroad, since it was hoped that reciprocal action would be forthcoming on the part of Catholics, and it was not to be inter-preted as a condonement of Popery.[6] Hamilton's precocious action was probably prompted by his fanatical and domineering mother, without his father's knowledge. In later years, though consistently hostile to Catholicism, he manifested a marked disinterest in forms of religious worship, and sympathised with John Dury in his attempts to reconcile Lutherism and Calvinism into a united Protestant creed. Despite his descent from the great Reformist family of Glencairn, and his own membership of the Presbyterian Kirk, he had no qualms about attending Anglican services with the King whenever and wherever it was expected of him. Religion was never a dominant factor in his life. Now, however, he felt strongly enough about the Continental wars to state in a letter to the Earl of Sutherland soliciting recruits that his German enter-prise was "undertaken for the liberty of the true religion".[7]

Acting on Charles's orders, Hamilton sent at the end of 1629 the Earl of Haddington's half-brother, Colonel Alexander Hamilton, a professional soldier who was to make his reputation as an engineer, to Gustavus with the offer of his services, and he later despatched David Ramsay of the Bedchamber to agree upon the terms of his commission, which stated that "whereas the illustrious and our sincerely beloved Lord James, Marquis of Hamilton . . . out of his zeal for the public good, and for acquiring eternal fame, hath resolved to dedicate himself and the fortunes and forces of all he is concerned in, for restoring our oppressed friends in Germany, and for that end hath offered to us . . . his fidelity and service, and that he will on his own expense gather a strength of six thousand men, and bring them over, as soon as may be, to any place we shall appoint".[8]

The commission was signed on May 30th 1630, the day after Hamilton had been made a Knight of the Garter on the occasion of Prince Charles's baptism at Windsor. It was felt that the Garter, as the highest honour in the kingdom, would increase his prestige in the eyes of his Continental allies. On March 1st 1631 he ratified the articles of the "mutual compact betwixt the most serene and mighty King of Sweden and me, for joining of our forces",[9] and in May he went to Scotland to levy volunteers, but owing to the large number of Scots already in foreign service, he could get only 400 men.[10]

Meanwhile, around the camp-fires of British mercenaries in Germany, idle gossip was circulating, idle gossip which quickly got out of control when it was repeated and embellished by Lord Reay, who was jealous of Hamilton, and resented David Ramsay's suggestion that he bring his regiment under the marquis's command. He claimed that Hamilton did not intend to bring his troops to Germany at all, but rather use them to seize the royal castles at Edinburgh, Stirling and Dumbarton, kidnap Charles and the royal children, send Henrietta to a convent, execute Lord Treasurer Weston and the adherents of Spain, and make himself King of Scotland.[11] It was later alleged by a spiteful Royalist pamphleteer that Hamilton's friends, including, incredibly, Reay himself, had drunk his health in the name of "James, by the grace of God King of Scotland", and that he would divorce Mary, then pregnant with her second child, to marry the adolescent Princess Palatine, eldest daughter of Frederick and Elizabeth of Bohemia.[12]

Claiming that this information came from Ramsay, Reay repeated it to his friend, James Stewart, Lord Ochiltree, whose father had in the previous century deprived the Hamiltons of the Earldom of Arran, only to be dispossessed of it again. This had left a legacy of bitterness between the two houses, and Ochiltree informed Lord Treasurer Weston of all he had heard. He alleged that Hamilton's messenger, Eleazer Borthwick, had substantiated the rumours, naming as his informant Robert Meldrum, said to have been a creature of the marquis.[13] Weston, whose daughter Anne was married to Hamilton's brother-in-law, Lord Feilding, hastened to Charles, and Ochiltree, ushered into the King's presence, told him: "Sir, we know the business but know not the time, therefore, sir, rather do or die."[14]

In the meantime Hamilton returned from his unsuccessful levying in Scotland, quite unaware of the allegations levelled against him. Weston warned Charles that he was too dangerous to be received alone, but the King disregarded this advice, and quietly informed the astounded marquis of what Ochiltree had said. He insisted that Hamilton spend the night alone with him in his bedchamber. It was a deliberate reproof to the young nobleman's enemies, and Hamilton always remembered it with gratitude.[15]

Anxious that his name should be publicly cleared, even though the King was convinced of his innocence, Hamilton insisted that the whole affair be thoroughly investigated and Reay and Ramsay be brought face to face. The subsequent examination showed that the Earls of Haddington, Roxburgh and Buccleuch were implicated in the alleged plot along with Hamilton, and Charles wrote to the Scottish Privy Council clearing them of all suspicion.[16]

Reay and Ramsay each charged the other with making the accusations against Hamilton, and Ramsay challenged Reay to single combat. The matter was referred to a court of chivalry, which ordered the duel to take place in Tothill Fields, Westminster, on April 12th 1631, with pikes, swords and daggers.[17] But the King postponed the appointed day until May 17th, and when the court of chivalry reassembled on May 12th both parties were informed that since Charles considered both of them culpable in some degree, though not guilty of treason, they should be discharged on condition that they kept the peace.

But for Hamilton's sake Charles was determined to make an example of Lord Ochiltree. He sent him to Edinburgh for trial, and he was closely guarded in the Tolbooth. His trial was postponed throughout 1632 and in May of the following year, when King Charles left London for his coronation in Edinburgh, he was transferred to Blackness Castle, to be "in close prison" until further notice. He paid a terrible price for slandering the marquis, and remained in captivity until 1652, when he was released, a broken man, by order of the Commonwealth.[18] As for Hamilton, those who cared about such things might have considered the supposed traitor well-named, for "James" signifies "a supplanter".

The dust did not quickly settle on the Ochiltree affair, and the suspicions it kindled surrounded Hamilton for the rest of his life. It hampered his recruiting, since for every would-be volunteer who dismissed the allegations as so much malicious talk, there was at least one other who gave them credence. As before, he was faced with general apathy towards the affairs of the Palatinate, and many veterans, mindful of the ill-treatment they had received under Mansfeld, who was ruthless and ambitious, were reluctant to re-enlist: "for although so far as the commander is concerned, there is a great difference, yet many believe that the enterprise will not prove very unlike it, because they do not know where they are to be led or how they will be employed, while in addition to this the English, who constituted the bulk of the force, do not like serving under a Scottish commander."[19]

Hamilton pitched his tents in Islington Fields and offered fourteen pence a day to every volunteer, but since men did not come forward in sufficient numbers he was forced to resort to the methods of the press-gang.[20] On June 19th, the marquis' twenty-fifth birthday, Charles sent identical letters to the lord lieutenants of twenty-six counties, with instructions to do their utmost to help the would-be general levy his target of 6,000 Englishmen. The countryside was to be scoured for the idle, the shiftless and the unemployed, and so desperate was Hamilton for men that those past their prime as well as able-bodied youths were to be rounded up. Thus Sir Robert Ducie, Lord Mayor of London, was commanded that "vagrants and masterless men" with whom "the city and suburbs are pestered" be pressed, while the administrative officers of the Company of Watermen were ordered to round up "divers lewd and unnecessary persons, and a great number more than can be employed" among the watermen, bargemen and fishermen on the Thames, and deliver them to Hamilton's lieutenants by July 8th, when the expedition was due to sail.[21]

But adverse winds prevented them from putting to sea on time, and on July 9th the King renewed his plea to the watermen. Two days later it was reported that 170 men had been pressed into service, but only eighty-three were actually enlisted: these comprised fishermen and bargemen and some accused of "lewd misdemeanours".[22]

On July 14th 1,500 pikes and corselets, 1,500 muskets, rests and bandoliers, and a reserve shipment of 700 bandoliers, were ordered to be delivered to the marquis, and finally, on July 19th, Hamilton, with Admiral Pennington aboard the *Bonaventure*, set sail from Yarmouth Road with 38 ships and 6,000 men.[23] He disembarked at Elsinore on July 27th, and was politely received by

Christian IV for a two-day stay, but offended his hosts by his strong disapproval of their drinking habits.[24]

Setting sail again on the 29th, he came to the mouth of the Oder at Usedom, where Gustavus had first landed, and on August 2nd and 3rd his forces disembarked. Hamilton himself left his ship on the 5th and on the 7th Pennington and the *Bonaventure* set sail for England. The marquis·and his men were sent by Gustavus into Silesia, and since they had come with only four months' supply of funds it was believed that the Swedish King had sent them so far away from the rest of his forces in order to compel Hamilton to find some way of raising money to support his troops entirely by himself.[25] The enemy was alarmed by a false report that he had in the region of 20,000 men, and Tilly, who at the end of August received reinforcements from Italy following the Peace of Cherasco, invaded Saxony and besieged Leipzig, was forced to leave some 6,000 or 7,000 more men behind in his garrisons than he would have done if Hamilton had not arrived. Gustavus, advancing to relieve Leipzig, utterly routed Tilly at Breitenfeld on September 17th.[26]

And then Gustavus came to Hamilton at Werben, beyond the Elbe, and "caressed him with the highest expressions of kindness",[27] asking him to request more money from Charles. It was not for nothing that the soldier-statesman of Sweden, tall, fair and masterful, was called the "Lion of the North", and at first he completely overawed the young marquis. But Hamilton's admiration waned as he began increasingly to distrust Gustavus, who ordered him to subordinate himself to the Saxon field-marshal, Arnim. Hamilton considered that this contravened the terms of his commission, by which he had been promised an independent command. He became aggrieved and restless, and his mood was not improved when he became allied later with the over-cautious Swedish marshal, Baner.[28]

Acting on Gustavus' orders he began to march towards Frankfurt, intending to guard the passes on the Oder, but en route from Stettin plague and famine claimed one-third of his army, reducing it to 4,000 men. One of his pages fell a victim to the plague, and rumours reached Whitehall that he, too, had died.[29] He antagonised the English under his command by insisting on beating the Scottish march, and fights broke out between the English and the Scots.[30]

In the midst of all these troubles he sent Alexander Leslie, a
Scot who made his military reputation in the wars, to Crossen on
the borders of Silesia with 500 men, and when the town fell to
the Emperor's forces, he sent Leslie an extra 100 troops and
transferred him to the relief of Guben. Just as Hamilton was
advancing on Glogau, the second largest town in Silesia, he
received orders from Gustavus to join him in Lower Saxony.

This irritated him still more, since he suspected that the
Swedish King wanted him to leave Silesia as it was one of
Frederick's territories and he did not wish Hamilton to come too
far within the Elector's sphere of influence. At first the marquis
contemplated disregarding orders, but the garrisons in Silesia no
longer acknowledged his authority, and he prepared to join the
attack on Magdeburg, the chief town of Lower Saxony, which
Pappenheim and Tilly had besieged and taken on May 20th when
some 20,000 of its inhabitants had been massacred and most of
its buildings burned.

He arrived on the outskirts of the town with only 1,500 of his
own men, for the rest had either died of the plague or famine, or
remained garrisoned in Silesia, but he had an additional 3,000
German foot he had managed to raise, and 1,000 Swedish horse.
But it was useless to storm Magdeburg, with its strong garrison
of 3,000 of the Emperor's best troops, and it was planned to
starve it into surrender; in these circumstances the only action
seen by Hamilton and his men were two minor skirmishes.

Meanwhile Sir Henry Vane, whom Charles had sent to Germany
to interview Gustavus about his attitude to the future of the
Palatinate and "enter into a league with the King of Sweden upon
emergent occasions",[31] arrived at Hamilton's camp with messages
from his master. The King, who had earlier missed Hamilton's
company when he was in Scotland, missed him badly now. "Your
absence neither makes me alter nor forget you", wrote Charles
from Hampton Court, "for you may be assured that my trust of
you is so well-grounded that it lies not in the power of anybody
to alter me from being your loving friend and cousin."[32]

Still trying to smooth over differences, Gustavus invited
Hamilton to sit in on the talks between Vane and the Swedish
representative, Gustaf Horn, and accordingly, leaving his army
under the command of Baner and Leslie, he left Magdeburg for
the Swedish camp at Frankfurt-am-Main. But Vane was not

happy about the proposals Horn put forward on November 9th. In return for restoring Frederick as King of Bohemia and Elector Palatine, the Swedes insisted that Charles agree to pay and maintain two regiments of horse and eight of foot for the duration of the war, that he agree to resist any Spanish naval attack upon Sweden, and undertake to conclude a formal alliance between England and Spain lasting several years. To crown all, Gustavus wanted absolute control not only of the conduct of the war but also of the terms of the peace, apart from a vague promise to take the hopes and aspirations of England into account.[33] Vane had neither the inclination nor the authority to accept these demands, and for the next two months negotiations were suspended.

In the meantime unwelcome stories of Hamilton's conduct had reached Whitehall. On December 14th Christopher Crowe, who claimed to have served under the marquis in Silesia, made a statement before Sir Richard Grosvenor in which he asserted that Hamilton had allocated his troops only one pound of bread each every four days, resulting in the deaths of many, who cried for food with their last breath, and that he refused them their pay, explaining that he had run out of money, while at the same time forbidding them to pillage. Only 100 men remained alive out of his original 6,000.[34]

Crowe greatly exaggerated the numbers lost, and although his story was substantiated by others, he paid dear for it. He was thrown into Newgate and kept on a starvation diet, without light or heat.[35] Like Ochiltree he learned the dreadful price of attacking the King's favourite, for the outraged monarch could not believe that the beloved Hamilton had failed. "You will find that I neither mean to forget or break my promises to you", he wrote to the marquis on New Year's Eve, "and that you will not be unlucky if you have but as good fortune in all your actions as is wished to you by [me]."[36] He did not know it then, but his faith in his favourite was to experience many more attempts to undermine it. Indeed, Crowe's allegations are reflected in the Swedish minister Oxenstierna's perhaps more reliable verdict on Hamilton's behaviour, for he blamed his mismanagement for the wasting away of the army, "which for want of knowledge in the marquis in military affairs, and of care to provide for them, perished".[37]

Vane's negotiations with Horn reopened in January, and he pressed Gustavus to give Hamilton a fresh army. But Gustavus

demurred. He had secured the line of the Main by capturing
Wurzburg and Frankfurt the previous autumn, and on December
20th he had taken Mainz, and by the capture of Mannheim on
January 8th he established his hold on the Palatinate. It seemed
now as if he was prepared to forego the restoration of the Palatinate
and betray the Protestant cause in exchange for Bavarian neutrality, which was agreed to on January 9th. He told Vane that he
could not guarantee to restore Frederick since he was unwilling
to commit himself to take up arms against Duke Maximilian. Yet
he made it clear that he was prepared to restore Frederick to the
whole of his inheritance in exchange for 12,000 men a defensive
alliance against Spain, and a subsidy from Charles of £25,000 a
month. Not surprisingly the negotiations broke down, for these
were terms which England obviously could not meet.[38]

It seemed to Hamilton as if Gustavus regarded Germany as his
prize, to do with as he pleased, and although the Swedish King
continued to treat him with marked politeness, he refused to
grant him a commission to raise fresh troops, and would not
compensate him for the money he had spent in the course of his
service, saying that he had not spent a penny out of his own
pocket because Charles had given him £100,000 for the enterprise.

In March Vane's negotiations began again, this time with
Oxenstierna, who was at the same time conducting equally abortive
negotiations with Frederick. Gustavus' brusque manner offended
both Vane (whose offer of a subsidy was finally accepted) and
Hamilton, who complained to Charles of his "excessive ambition
and intolerable pride".[39] Charles became noticeably cool towards
the Swedish King and learned of his subsequent victories with no
display of enthusiasm.

Denied a new command, Hamilton nevertheless continued to
follow Gustavus throughout the summer in the capacity of a
volunteer, but his heart was not in it, and he longed to return
home. In August he received a letter from the King:

> You must choose either to stay or come away. For the
> first, it were very honourable to do . . . if you had an
> employment, but neither having nor likely to have any
> hereafter, it were dullness not patience to stay any
> longer . . . therefore I have commanded Henry Vane to
> propose a new employment for you, which though I

think it will show there is no way unsought for to find
you an employment with the King of Sweden. It is that
you may be sent into the Palatinate, to assist the French
with so many men as my contribution will maintain,
which if it may be done, they promise to put the lower
Palatinate in my hands. This, though, I do not hold as
gospel, yet if this design might be put in practice, it
might certainly prove useful to my affairs: this being
denied (as I think it will) you have no more to do but
to seek a fair excuse to come home, which will be best,
in my opinion, upon the conclusion of the treaty
between Sweden and me, or if any rubs arise, that you
might be sent to clear it with me. So that upon the
whole matter my judgment is that if you cannot serve
me in the Palatinate . . . the best way is that you take the
first civil excuse to come home to [me].[40]

Hamilton was now completely exasperated with Gustavus, and
disillusioned with his spell of soldiering. Understandably, he
considered it beneath his dignity to continue any longer as a
volunteer, and he told Gustavus flatly that having been away from
his own country for fifteen months with nothing to show for it he
was at the end of his tether.[41] Gustavus admitted that he had
reason to be annoyed, but blamed everything on Vane. The
marquis perceived an opportunity to escape the enterprise once
and for all, and he asked Gustavus for permission to return to
England to iron out any misunderstandings which might have
developed between the Swedish King and Charles, and also to
look into the possibility of raising another 10,000 or 12,000 men.
This was a request which Gustavus could not refuse, and on
September 8th he granted Hamilton a new commission, and gave
him instructions for concluding the treaty with Charles. In
bidding farewell to the marquis, who had been of very limited
use to him, he feigned warm feelings of friendship, "telling him
that in whatsoever place of the world he were, he would ever
look upon him as one of his own".[42]

On September 24th Charles wrote to Hamilton from Hampton
Court: "it is not fit to stay any longer where you are, for the
impossibility of your employment there, and the necessity of
your business here, requires your return . . . you shall be no

PLATE II

JAMES, 2nd MARQUIS OF HAMILTON
by Daniel Mytens

Reproduced by permission of His Grace the Duke of Hamilton and
Brandon and the National Galleries of Scotland.

PLATE III

MARY, MARCHIONESS OF HAMILTON
by Van Dyck

Reproduced by permission of His Grace the Duke of Hamilton and
Brandon and the National Galleries of Scotland.

sooner come than welcome to [me]."[43] Hamilton needed no further prompting, and he made his way back to England through France, joining Charles at Newmarket races on October 18th.[44] Sixteen years later, in 1648, when he had taken up the sword a second time, in another place and another cause, the Peace of Westphalia brought the German wars to an end.

CHAPTER IV
ROYAL FAVOURITE

Although he returned to Court no conquering hero, Hamilton was undismayed. Convinced that his fifteen months' service abroad had proved him a competent soldier, he was full of military talk and anecdotes about Gustavus. He liked to joke that he had learned no German except for one proverb: "ein barmherziger Soldat ist ein Hundsfott vor Gott" ("a merciful soldier is a rogue in God's sight").[1] Men were quick to notice that the King was as fond of him as ever. Charles was not a man to abandon friends lightly, or because they had failed. "The professional soldiers here", a foreign envoy noted, "although the marquis is so closely united to his majesty by blood and favour, renew very openly the maledictions and complaints against him, taxing him with being the chief cause of the total loss and destruction of the force which previously left these shores under his command."[2] The complaints fell on deaf ears. It is probable that Charles never interpreted Hamilton's disastrous enterprise as the result of mere incompetence, but believed he had been the innocent victim of ill-luck or the machinations of his Swedish allies. For where Charles placed his confidence he placed it entirely. "He does not trust many, and when he conceives a good impression of anyone he does not let it fall", reported the Venetian ambassador. "He is accustomed to say that it is necessary to grant his favour in a single person, and to maintain him in it, as he would be attacked on all sides with calumny."[3]

At first, Hamilton's attributes in the eyes of a King who did not like "very confident men"[4] were his Scottish voice and his gentle disposition, which made him remarkably courteous, even to his inferiors.[5] Charles, despite an English upbringing, never lost the speech of his native land, and he took comfort in having Scotsmen around him, "who he thought would never fail him".[6] The phonetic spelling in Hamilton's letters betrays a marked Scots accent which life at the English Court hardly modified. Of his enduring kindness and affability there is little doubt. Even those who grew to distrust or despise him generally acknowledged this; it was his sincerity they questioned. "I was known to him and ever civilly treated by him", recalled Sir Philip Warwick, who doubted Hamilton's political integrity and believed that "naturally he loved to gain his point rather by some serpentine winding than by a direct path".[7]

It is a testimony of Hamilton's personal charm that throughout his life he was exceedingly pleasant to all, whatever their station. His behaviour in this respect appears to have been dictated by a genuine regard for the feelings of others, with the consequent desire to put them at ease. Indeed, his manners were so studied and perfect that they sometimes appeared old-fashioned to his contemporaries. Several years later, Sir Edward Stanhope marvelled that Hamilton still employed the custom of taking another by the hand, a gesture of courtesy "out of fashion at Court ever since blue coats, and swords, and bucklers were laid by".[8]

He was usually placid and almost always easy-going. Later, on one occasion, he described himself as "naturally passionate",[9] but if this was so, he succeeded in concealing it. It was difficult to provoke him, but this very lack of passion was interpreted as a lack of commitment, and caused many to believe that he was never in earnest. Although he could assume a grand manner, he was not naturally arrogant, and his tendency towards aloofness, noted by Clarendon among others, was less due to a haughty awareness of his high station than to a certain fondness for quiet meditation. He was melancholy—a trait which increased with time—and reserved. This gave him an inscrutability which confounded his enemies and irritated his friends. At the very end of his life he reflected that never "was I so in love with speaking, or with anything I had to express, that I took delight in it".[10]

Yet though not loquacious he was voluble, and he could, when he wished, be imposingly eloquent. A gift for words found its greatest outlet in his letters, and his ability to command a fine phrase impressed the King. Charles was moved by Hamilton's flattery and did not notice when it gushed with insincerity. Of all the Scots at Court, "no man", observed Clarendon, "had such an ascendant over him by the humblest insinuations, as Duke Hamilton had".[11] In his correspondence with the King Hamilton was always courtly and occasionally almost obsequious. Never, not even at the height of his power, did he flout prerogative and lounge in Charles's presence, or wear his hat before him as

Buckingham had done. There was a restraint and a formality about him which the King entirely approved of and appreciated, yet it was no more than Charles expected.

Gone, however, was the vaguely Puritan aspect of short hair and skull-cap, described by Warwick. Upon establishing himself at Court the marquis was not slow to adopt the dress and demeanour of a man of fashion. In Mytens's magnificent portrait, dated 1629, we see Hamilton wearing a silver court dress, holding his beaver hat and resting elegantly on a cane. His dark brown hair falls in love-locks on his lace collar. Only his face, swarthy and masculine, counteracts the image of foppery. In 1635 Van Dyck portrayed him with the King in a famous painting which now hangs in the Louvre. It depicts a peaceful pastoral scene, the occasion of a hunting party. Hamilton, symbolic of his role as Master of the Horse, is seen bridling the royal steed. Clad in a suit of russet satin, with his rather fine physique and dark complexion, he presents a striking contrast to the slighter, neater, fair-skinned King.

The most familiar portrait, however, is Van Dyck's fine study of the marquis in armour, painted when Hamilton was in the prime of his manhood and at the zenith of his influence. The impression is of a stocky, not unattractive man of dignified presence, already showing signs of the flabbiness which was to mark his later years. He stands a little self-consciously, firmly, almost defiantly, grasping his marshal's baton, this courtier who never once demonstrated the slightest military talent, but who persuaded himself and convinced his master that as a soldier he was inferior to none. In this, as in all Hamilton's portraits, a hint of irresolution is conveyed: he stares uncertainly out of the canvas, and although his is not a weak face, it is not a face of power.

Commenting on Hamilton as he was at this time, Sir Philip Warwick says:

> He had a large proportion of his majesty's favour and
> confidence, and knew very well how to manage both,
> and accompany the King in his hard chases of the stag,
> and in the toilsome pleasures of the racket, by which
> last he often filled his own and emptied his master's
> purse; and though he carried it very modestly and
> warily, yet he had a strong influence upon the greatest

affairs at Court, especially when they related unto his own country.[12]

From the beginning he did not get on with the Queen. Gay and mercurial herself, she preferred men less reserved and serious than Hamilton, and the frivolous, foppish Earl of Holland and the jocular and personable Harry Jermyn were among her favourite courtiers. She cannot have felt any warmth towards the marquis when he got Jermyn temporarily dismissed from Court and banned from her merry gatherings at Somerset House for making pregnant a cousin of Hamilton's wife, Eleanor Villiers, and refusing to marry her.[13] In later years a sordid little story was circulated. Apparently Hamilton, realising full well that the Queen disliked him, yet needing her support for one of his schemes, determined to win her over by blackmail. She often entertained Jermyn, later her Master of the Horse, alone in her apartments, and Hamilton, knowing this, persuaded one of her ladies, Mrs. Seymour, to conceal him in Henrietta's bedchamber shortly before Jermyn was due to arrive. Then, later, he stepped out of his hiding-place, surprising the two in an intimate but innocent moment. From then on, it is alleged, the Queen, fearing that Hamilton would make good his threat to reveal what he had seen to the King, acquiesced in his intrigues.[14] The story can perhaps be discounted, but certainly in future years Hamilton and Henrietta did collaborate on several matters of Court patronage, and together exerted their influence over a King too inclined to heed the opinions of others. It was not until much later that she came to suspect Hamilton's loyalty to her husband, and then she turned on him with bitter fury.

On May 17th 1633 King Charles left London with Hamilton, Lennox, Laud and a splendid following on the first leg of his leisurely journey to Scotland, where at last he was to be crowned. It had been almost thirty years since the Dunfermline-born sovereign had seen the native land he had left at the age of four, and the Scots had prepared a splendid welcome: "For many ages this kingdom had not seen a more glorious and stately entry", wrote a contemporary historian of Charles's arrival at Edinburgh on June 15th, "the streets being all railed and sandied; the chief places where he passed were set out with stately triumphal arches, obelisks, pictures, artificial mountains, adorned with

choice, and divers other costly shows."[15] The dignity of the
occasion was marred, however, by Hamilton's insistence that
5,000 merks and a purse containing "a thousand golden double
angels" which the citizens of Edinburgh had collected as a token
of their loyalty to the King, be presented to him by virtue of his
office as Master of the Horse.[16] What Charles, who was crowned
King of Scotland on June 18th, had to say about his favourite's
impudence is not recorded.

When the King returned to England Hamilton remained in
Scotland to administer the collection of a taxation granted by the
Scottish Parliament, and Charles allowed him to repay himself
out of it for the expenses he had incurred during his German
expedition. He was in Scotland again the following year to
examine the accounts of the Treasurer, Morton.[17] At the same
time two of his dependants, Sir James Leslie and Thomas Dalmahoy, were given the sole right to grant tobacco licences, for a
period of seven years, in a hopeless attempt to stamp out illegal
trafficking in the weed.[18] During these visits to Scotland he
arranged the marriages of his sisters* (including his illegitimate
sister, Margaret, who had an assured place in the family circle)
and found time to have his portrait painted by the fashionable
artist George Jamesone, sometimes known as the "Scottish Van
Dyck".

Whilst enjoying the bounty of the English Court, the marquis,
contrary to some interpretations of his life and outlook, felt his
Scottish identity deeply, and it is significant that he kept his
brother in Scotland, and when the time came, chose to send him
not to Oxford or to Cambridge, but to the University of Glasgow,
which the Hamilton family had helped to found in 1450, and of
which Hamilton himself was to become the first lay chancellor in
1642. Lord William registered in March 1630 at the age of
thirteen, but there is no record of his having taken a degree.
Later, Hamilton sent him to the French Court, a tradition for
young Scotsmen of noble birth, established in the heyday of the
special relationship between France and Scotland. It was, of
course, a tradition which the marquis had missed, and it is
perhaps an indication of his consciousness of the limitations of
his own experience that he gave his brother this opportunity.

* See Genealogical Table A.

It was natural that the legion of Scots at Court should look to Hamilton as their spokesman and patron. But it was easy, in view of his English upbringing, his English education, his English marriage, and his service abroad, to underestimate his deep stake in Scotland. He would never loosen his ties with her, and in any development north of the Border he would expect, and be expected, to play a predominant part. Ever since Châtelherault had been "second person in the realm" the Hamiltons were accustomed to leadership among their countrymen. In this they can be compared to their chief rivals, the Stuarts of Lennox, who, if Châtelherault's illegitimacy could be proved, would challenge the Hamiltons' claim to the Scottish throne.

The Stuarts of Lennox, holding a Scots and later an English dukedom, were superior to the Hamiltons in rank but not in influence. James, fourth Duke of Lennox (and from 1641 second Duke of Richmond) was six years Hamilton's junior, a quiet, gentle, fair-haired young man devoted to his royal master. Whereas Hamilton's anglicisation was superficial, Lennox's was total, for his Scottish ties were diffused by the English blood in his veins. His mother, Baroness Clifton in her own right, came from an old Huntingdonshire family, and his father had become a naturalised Englishman as early as May 1603. His wife, whom he married in August 1637 and deeply loved, was Buckingham's only daughter. She was therefore a first cousin of the Marchioness of Hamilton. His mother married, as her second husband, Hamilton's cousin and namesake the second Earl of Abercorn, a Catholic. It is doubtful, however, whether between Hamilton and Lennox there was anything beyond a formal cordiality. Although closely allied in blood, the two men differed in temperament and headed two rival houses. Hamilton was jealous of Lennox, who, for his part, distrusted Hamilton. His chief motivation was the King's interest, from which he never swerved. He hardly knew Scotland, preferring his country house at Cobham in Kent to his sprawling Scottish estates, which were bordered so menacingly by Campbell territory.

Unlike Lennox, Hamilton would never forget that he was, however much it appeared to the contrary, a Scot first and foremost. It is crucial for a better understanding of his subsequent career to understand from the outset his relationship with Scotland. He had an understandable love for her as his native land and that of his ancestors. But his ties with her were not primarily emotional. His estates and the bulk of his fortune were there, and thus ultimately his interests. He could not escape his heritage. Few in his own time realised this, the King least of all. It was in the end Charles's misfortune—and it was also Hamilton's.

The marquis was not prepared to advance the interests of his Scottish protégés at the risk of his own. Although he was among the most important figures at Court, he did not feel completely secure in the King's affections. That, combined with his instinctive wariness, made him keep a perpetual watch for potential rivals. And of no one, perhaps, was he quite so jealous as of the Earl of Montrose. This young man, six years younger than Hamilton, proud, spirited, accomplished, a spoiled only son with a self-confident ambition born of a highly imaginative mind and an early identification with the heroes of history, returned from his grand tour during the winter of 1635–36. Whilst on the Continent he had met Hamilton's brother-in-law, Basil Feilding, British ambassador in Venice, who had suggested that on returning to Britain Montrose should seek an introduction at Court from Hamilton. Montrose, whose father had been Chancellor of Scotland, was restless and ambitious, longing to serve the King in the loyal tradition of his house. Hamilton readily agreed to sponsor him, but warned him not to expect too much from a King who, deep in his heart, cared little for Scots and Scotland. He also warned Charles not to encourage Montrose, since he was pushing and ambitious, and his royal descent from King Robert II might give him high ideas.[19]

It was a childish ruse, but it worked better than Hamilton expected. Charles was polite but markedly cool to Montrose, extending him his hand to kiss, and then turning immediately to converse with the favourite who hovered at his side. Montrose returned to Scotland hurt and puzzled, and though in time he suspected that Hamilton had been responsible for the King's attitude, he had to wait many years for his revenge.

However, Hamilton soon found himself with a more welcome protégé, for towards the close of 1636 Lord William Hamilton returned from his sojourn at the French Court, a dark, thick-set, rather cumbersome young man of twenty-one, proud, personable, intense, and with wild oats still to sow. Hamilton at once sought for him a place in the royal favour. Failing to be given the coveted post of Master of the Horse to the Queen, which on

Goring's resignation passed to Jermyn, Lord William sulked, and threatened to return to France. But it was only a tantrum, and the ambitious younger son had to be content with the offer of Master of the Horse to the little Prince of Wales, with the promise of better things to come.[20]

The relationship between the two brothers was characterised by an abiding mutual affection, but it is best seen in terms of Lord William's hero-worship of Hamilton, and, until his marriage to an heiress, his financial dependence upon him. Having lost his father at the age of eight he had long been accustomed to relying on Hamilton for advice and consolation, and now to the impressionable youth, as yet unschooled in the ways of men, Hamilton, the great officer of the Court and veteran of Gustavus' campaigns, seemed wise and omniscient. There were many who, in time, came to see Lord William as the better man: "he was in all respects to be preferred before the other", wrote Clarendon, "a much wiser, though, it may be, a less cunning man, for he did not affect dissimulation, which was the other's masterpiece."[21] Although in later years the marquis' image tarnished in his brother's eyes, Lord William never quite relinquished his admiration for him.

Although he sat on the Privy Councils of both kingdoms (he had been appointed to the English Privy Council on March 8th 1633) Hamilton did not feel bound to offer advice merely for the sake of it. Policy relating to Scotland was left to his "sole counsel",[22] but apart from this, in affairs of state Laud and Strafford overshadowed him. Indeed, during most of this time he appears as indolent and introverted, interested only in Scottish politics and concerned for the most part with his financial aggrandisement and his collection of paintings.

Essentially a Laodicean, having little interest in religion or the supernatural, he was above all a materialist, one of the wealthiest noblemen of his time. He possessed an astute business sense which it would be tempting to ascribe to Scots canniness. He could drive a hard bargain, and pursued his financial schemes with a singleness of purpose which he did not display in other fields, and which was to make him, over the years, one of the leading monopolists of the age, symbolic of the power and greed which spurred on Parliament's hatred of the Court party. As Samuel Rawson Gardiner neatly put it, "he had his share in the good things which Charles had to give away".[23] Besides his stipend as

Master of the Horse 'and his royal pension of £2,500 per annum, he acquired over the years a number of lucrative sinecure posts: Lord High Steward of Hampton Court, High Steward of Portsmouth, Hereditary Keeper of Holyrood House. The gross rental from his lands amounted to well over £2,000 a year, and from the fief of Châtelherault he was entitled to an annual rent of 12,000 livres.[24] A contemporary estimate put the total value of his fortune at £300,000.[25]

His striving for monopolies was not unusual: it was common among leading courtiers, and his father had held a number of them. It was the zeal with which Hamilton threw himself into these activities which makes them noteworthy. "Marquis Hamilton is not easily taken off", a correspondent of Wentworth remarked, "especially when there is a glimmering of good profit to come in."[26] In 1634 he, Lennox, Stirling and Stirling's heir, Lord Alexander, were registered as patentees and members of the Council for New England, and over the next three years Charles worked closely with them and Laud towards the liquidation of the Massachusetts Bay Company, from which Hamilton hoped to obtain 10,000 acres of land.[27] In 1637, with Holland, Pembroke and Sir David Kirke, he received a grant of the whole province of Newfoundland, centre of a lucrative fishing trade.[28] Closer to home, he acquired lands in County Down and Leinster, and he was always keen to expand his influence in Ireland.[29] In 1637 he became licenser of hackney coaches for London and Westminster, and as many as he thought necessary for other places in England. The following year the Vintners' Company undertook to pay him £4,000 a year and £1,500 to two of his dependants as part of their fine for serving meat with wine at banquets, a practice not authorised in their charter. The way in which Hamilton hounded the Vintners, whose breach of contract was initially referred to the Star Chamber, reaching an agreement with Alderman Abell, master of the company, through a rather shady agent named Richard Kilbert, did him and the Court party little credit.[30]

Like the King, Arundel and Pembroke, he was an enthusiastic collector of works of art—paintings, statues, furniture—although the cynical could not help wondering whether he was motivated by their aesthetic merit or their potential market value. The majority of his paintings were of the Italian school and came directly from Venice, where his brother-in-law, Feilding, was

ambassador between 1634 and 1639.[31] Early in 1636 Feilding
sent Hamilton several paintings which the marquis complained
were overpriced copies, but he told his brother-in-law to continue
looking for good original masterpieces regardless of cost.[32] He
also instructed him to be on the look-out for anything which
might interest Charles; he had done this himself during his
service in Germany, when he had brought several statues in
Munich to the King's attention.[33] In the summer of 1637 he was
unlucky enough to receive a number of marble figures broken,
owing to poor packing, but he also received reports of a fine
collection belonging to Bartolemo della Nave, a wealthy Venetian
citizen, and passed them on to the King. "His Majesty, having
seen the note of della Nave's collection, is so extremely taken
therewith as he has persuaded me to buy them all, and for that
end has furnished me with moneys", he told Feilding. "So,
brother, I have undertaken that they shall all come to England,
both pictures and statues, out of which he is to make choice of
what he likes, and to repay me what they cost if I have a mind to
turn merchant."[34] The price asked was 20,000 ducats, but
Hamilton hoped to beat della Nave down to 12,000 (about £2,000
in the currency of the day). He himself would have been prepared
to spend no more than £1,500, but Charles was so delighted with
the prospect of owning them that he instructed Hamilton to
arrange to buy them whatever their price, and in the spring of
1638 Feilding bought the collection in bulk. It included works
by such masters as Correggio, Raphael, Tintoretto, Titian and
Veronese, and was a most welcome addition to the galleries of
London. After 1638, however, when the Scottish troubles began
as a prelude to Civil War, neither Charles nor Hamilton had
money to spend on paintings. In their new budgetary arrangements
armaments were given priority over ornaments.

CHAPTER V

SCOTLAND ABLAZE

The troubles which now began to boil in Scotland had been heating by slow degrees ever since the union of the crowns, when the King had deserted his Scottish subjects for his English Court, intending in time to reconstitute the two former enemies into one kingdom, with a common church and a common parliament. The mode of religion chosen, however, was the English one, and James was wise enough to shelve the rest of his plans after noting how adverse the Scots had been to the establishment of Episcopalianism in 1606, when he restored the bishops as one of the Estates, and particularly in 1621, when the Five Articles of Perth had been enacted (though not generally enforced).

The presence of their King on English soil disgruntled the Scottish nobles, who were left without their traditional lobbying-place, the Court. Despite his promise to visit his native realm every three years, James had returned to Scotland only once since 1603, and his son had been on the throne for eight years before he ventured north for "the most glorious and magnificent coronation that was ever seen in this kingdom".[1] By that time Scottish discontent had already reached a dangerous level: the young King's acts of revocation and his avowed intention of "drawing back into our Crown all the heritable offices", such as sheriffdoms, had alienated the nobles. In 1629 Hamilton had surrendered his hereditary sheriffdom of Lanarkshire in accordance with the King's demands, and in 1635 he had given up his rights to the Abbey of Arbroath as an example to the rest of the nobles who held temporal lordships, since they "do not venture to keep this sort of property when the chief of the nobility has surrendered his".[2]

In a further extension of his policy of Episcopalianism, Charles created a new diocese covering the area from the Forth to the Border, with its see in Edinburgh, and its first bishop, Wililam Forbes, was consecrated in St. Giles's Cathedral in 1634. The following year the Earl of Kinnoul died—"that old cankered gouty man", Charles had called him[3]—and was replaced as

Chancellor not by another layman, in the tradition which had evolved since the Reformation, but by John Spottiswoode, Archbishop of St. Andrews. Many of the younger clerics, in Scotland as in England, were turning to Arminianism* as a reaction against the rigid Calvinist doctrine of election, and as a result the whole structure of the presbyterian Kirk was threatened.

But it was not only religion which caused a rift between King and people. Secular issues loomed large in the list of Scottish grievances. The King had annoyed the city of Edinburgh by questioning the privileges granted in its charter of 1630. In 1631 he proposed that the Court of Session sit not for the customary two terms but only from October to April, and in 1636 he recommended that owing to the frequent changes of personnel in the town's government, with its resultant "inconsistency", there should be a "constant council".[4] The new system of taxation worked out in 1633 bore heavily on Edinburgh, which paid double the amount it had under the old system.

Even the coronation had upset the Scots. It had come so late as to seem a begrudging gesture to their national feelings, and the immense cost of the King's visit—Edinburgh alone spent £40,000 on it—with the resultant impoverishment exacerbating the other complaints which cast their shadow across the proceedings.

A heavy blow to Scottish pride was dealt by the King's penchant for tampering with the composition of the Scottish Privy Council, whose power and prestige had been steadily declining since his father's reign. King James had possessed the wit to make the Council's membership reflect the influence of the nobility, but shortly after his accession Charles excluded from it anyone who was also a Lord of Session, thereby removing some of the best legal minds in the country, and over the ensuing years he appointed a steady stream of bishops to the vacant places on the Council. The unintentional result of his meddling was a Council increasingly detached from the realities of Scottish political life, and over-prone to fickleness and intrigue. It was willing enough to obey Charles's commands, but it found itself more and more unable to carry them out. The real power in Scotland remained to a great extent outside it, and a man such as the Earl of Montrose, whose

* Jacobus Arminius, or Harmensen, (1560–1609), was a Dutch theologian who argued the existence of free will and thereby rejected the Calvinist notion of predestination.

father had been a councillor for over twenty years, saw no reason why he should be excluded from membership. The nobles were restless and purposeless, with a deep resentment of the King and of Hamilton, and in time they came to make the rest of the population as bitter as they were.

The supplication drawn up by William Haigh, and handed by Lord Balmerino to the Earl of Rothes in 1634 for presentation to the King, was indicative of the future mood of the Scottish people in its combination of secular and religious demands. It opposed the Five Articles of Perth and Arminianism, and showed uneasiness at Charles's manipulation of Parliament.[5] The King's mood was reflected in his contemptuous disregard of the supplication. "My lord, ye know what it is fit for me to hear and consider, and therefore do or do not upon your peril", he warned Rothes, who returned the document—unread—to Balmerino. Its author, Haigh, fled to Holland, but Balmerino was imprisoned and tried for treason. Yet there was nothing offensive in the tone of the petition, which declared itself "the humble supplication of a great number of the nobility and other commissioners in the late Parliament" and it was hardly the "scandalous, odious and seditious libel" described in the indictment.

The Scottish Estates, which had always been haughtily independent of the Crown, could not take kindly to the prosecution's statement:

> Albeit by the law of God and the laws of all nations the
> person of the supreme and sovereign prince is and
> ought to be sacred and inviolable, and he ought to be
> reverenced, honoured and feared as God's lieutenant on
> earth; and that all subjects are bound and tied in
> conscience to content themselves in humble submission
> to obey and reverence the person, laws and authority of
> their supreme sovereign; yet the said unhappy and
> infamous libel, in the first entry thereof, begins with an
> outrageous upbraiding and taxing of our sovereign lord's
> majesty of a point of injustice or indiscretion in our
> behaviour at Parliament, for putting of notes (as the
> said infamous libel alleges) upon the names of a number
> of our said subjects who did vote contrary to the Acts
> of our church government passed in Parliament, which

is a fearful thing in a subject, to pry into the gesture of
his sovereign in his supreme Court, and upon a gesture
without speech to infer a ground of exprobation and
reproach to the sovereign prince.[6]

And yet, for all this, the Crown was neither swift nor decisive
in its prosecution of Balmerino, and the trial dragged out from
the summer of 1634 until the spring of 1635, when he was convicted by a majority of one. But the King, after further delays,
decided to reprieve him, largely owing to the counsel of the
Earl of Traquair. This action, however, earned Charles and his
advisers more contempt than gratitude, for it was felt that they
dared not carry out the sentence in the face of Scottish opposition.
"The common people, avowedly, with high and uplifted voices,
were praying for Lord Balmerino, and for those that loved him
and his cause, and prayed for a plague to come upon them that
had the blame of his trouble."[7]

"My father knew the whole steps of this matter, having been
the Earl of Lauderdale's most particular friend", wrote Bishop
Burnet many years later. "He often told me that the ruin of the
King's affairs in Scotland was in a great measure owing to that
prosecution."[8] From then on Scotland moved towards the brink
of revolution, scornful of the bishops and bitter towards the
Court. Those Scots who did journey to London to pay their
respects to their King were uneasy at what they saw there: "all
that came down from Court complained of the King's inexorable
stiffness, and of the progress Popery was making, and of the
Queen's power with the King, of the favour shown to the Pope's
nuncios, and of the many proselytes who were daily falling off to
the Church of Rome."[9]

The resentment which had been simmering for so long finally
reached boiling point with the King's imposition, in the summer
of 1637, of Archbishop Laud's Service Book throughout the
Kingdom of Scotland. Charles and Laud, the son of a Reading
clothier, had underestimated the depth of anti-Episcopalianism
in the Scottish people, and on June 28th, the day appointed by
the Scottish Privy Council for the introduction of the Service
Book, two councillors, Traquair, the Treasurer, who pleaded a
previous engagement, and young Lord Lorne, who feigned sickness, excused themselves from joining the procession to St. Giles's

Cathedral for morning service and the first reading from the offensive Book. They thereby added the weight of their influence to the protest against the "pride and avarice of the prelates seeking to overrule the whole kingdom".[10]

John Stewart, Earl of Traquair, owed his rise to power and fortune entirely to his sovereign's favour, yet was not especially grateful and never repaid Charles with absolute loyalty. He was motivated largely by the chance of office, and was strongly suspected of growing wealthy out of the Treasurership by embezzling the funds. He was persuasive and voluble: one contemporary, fancying that he saw in his fine gift of expression traces of the Old Testament prophets, wrote of his "asiatic eloquence".[11] He later tried to check the flood of rebellion which his example had helped precipitate: "the matter went much further than he seemed to intend, for he himself was finally caught in the snare laid for others."[12]

As soon as the service in St. Giles's began, a riot broke out among the congregation, and abusive words flung at the Dean, Dr. Hannah, were followed by Bibles and folding-stools. The principal troublemakers were ejected, but during the rest of the service a great crowd demonstrating outside banged incessantly on the doors and hurled missiles at the windows. Similar displays of anti-Episcopal solidarity took place in other churches that day, and gangs in Edinburgh milled around the streets after the service, assaulting the King's supporters.

The Privy Councillors, who had anticipated some violent opposition for the past few months, resolved to meet in future not in the centre of Edinburgh, where their personal safety might be endangered as they passed through the grey narrow streets, but in Holyrood House. They declared the rioters guilty of treason and deserving of death, but they took the precaution of suspending the Service Book, and although they paid lip-service to royal authority they knew in their hearts that they were unable to enforce it.[13]

When the news of their cowardice reached the King, who was enjoying a summer's hunting at Oatlands, he was incensed, and appreciating the realities of the situation less perfectly than they, he commanded them immediately to restore the use of the Service Book and to punish those principally connected with the demonstrations against it. But the Council lacked the means to obey.

PLATE IV

HAMILTON IN ARMOUR
by Van Dyck
Reproduced by permission of His Grace the Duke of Hamilton
and Brandon.

JAMES STUART, DUKE OF LENNOX
by Van Dyck

PLATE V

WILLIAM, EARL OF LANARK (left) AND
JOHN MAITLAND, DUKE OF LAUDERDALE (right)
by Cornelius Johnson

They were unwilling to risk mob violence, and they had seen sympathetic ministers, brave enough to stick to their principles and use the Book, physically set upon by their angry congregations. The Bishop of Brechin, who conducted an Episcopal service with loaded pistols at his side, had a lucky escape from the wrath of the mob.[14]

Opposition to the Book had spread much wider than Edinburgh, for burghers, scholars, lairds and Lowland noblemen hastened to join this national movement cloaked in religious fervour. The white heat of Scottish resentment at the long years of impersonal government from Whitehall had finally caused the nation to boil over. The popular Duke of Lennox, who came to Edinburgh in September for the funeral of his mother, proved a well-meaning but ineffective mediator, and early in October Charles renewed his plea to the Council for firm action to disperse the demonstrators thronging the city. But finding that their faint-hearted attempt to do so led to the "rascally people of Edinburgh" rising "in such a barbarous manner, as the like has never been seen in this kingdom",[15] and roughly manhandling the Bishop of Galloway, who escaped with difficulty, the Council dropped all further pretence at resolute action. Traquair, the Lord Treasurer, was at his wit's end. "It becomes none better to represent these things to our master than yourself; for God's cause, therefore, do it", he wrote to Hamilton. "And seeing he will not give me leave to wait upon himself, let him be graciously pleased seriously and timely to consider what is best for his own honour, and the good of this poor kingdom, and direct me clearly what I shall do. . . ."[16]

The rebels now boasted some of the best minds in Scotland: Sir Thomas Hope of Craighill, the Lord Advocate, a staunch Presbyterian who secretly opposed the Service Book; Archibald Johnstone of Warriston, a brilliant, hard-working young lawyer half-crazed with fanaticism; Alexander Henderson, the intense and sincere minister of Leuchars in Fife; the Earl of Rothes, politically motivated, tough and shrewd; young Montrose, flamboyant and impetuous yet sensitive and entirely committed. The King was severely embarrassed by the Ship Money case, and his Scottish jester, Archie Armstrong, earned his dismissal by an unfortunate outburst: "Great praise to the King and little Laud to the devil!"[17]

Nevertheless, Charles stayed firm. He paid little heed to

Traquair, who came to London to report the troubles first-hand, and he rebuked the Council for their conduct, at the same time ordering them to issue a proclamation bitterly censuring the nobles who had opposed the Service Book.[18] The Council reluctantly published the document at Stirling, on February 20th 1638, and found to their consternation that the opposition's time had come. Hope refused to concur in the publication; Lorne, again taking the easy way out—he was not noted for courage— was absent from the official reading; and so were the bishops, afraid of mob violence.[19] How the rebels knew of the plan to issue the proclamation at Stirling was not quite clear, since the move had been given no publicity in order to reduce the likelihood of a demonstration. It is possible that they had been informed by Traquair himself, who two months earlier had declared that he would rather resign his office than accept the new liturgy.[20] If the crowds of demonstrators were great at Stirling they were even greater at Edinburgh two days later, when the proclamation was read again. Their ferocity and enthusiasm were kept at fever-pitch not only by formal protests but by inflammatory speeches by some of the leaders, including Montrose, who clambered on top of a barrel that all might see him.

"All sorts and qualities of people within this kingdom are commoved with the proclamation", Traquair warned Hamilton, "and truly, in my judgment it shall be as easy to establish the Missal in this kingdom as this Service Book." He added: "the not urging of the present practice thereof does no way satisfy them, because they conceive that what is done in the delaying thereof is but only to prepare things the better at a more convenient time, and believe me, as yet I see not a probability of power within this kingdom to force them, and whoever has informed the King's majesty otherwise, either of this Book itself, or of the disposition of the subjects to obey his majesty's commandments, it is high time every man be put to make good his own part." As far as the Treasurer was concerned, the bishops were not blameless:

> My condition at this time is hard; for as, upon the one
> hand I am persecuted by the implacable underhand
> malice of some of the bishops, so am I now in no better
> predicament with our noblemen and others, who adhere

to their course, and I may truly say, the bishop they
hate most is not more obnoxious to their hatred than I
am at this time. But I shall not foolishly give offence to
any, and if, in the prosecution of my master's
commandments, I offend, I must expect the protection
of my master, and the countenance of your lordship's
respect.[21]

Before Hamilton had received this letter the crisis in Scotland
had erupted into full-scale rebellion. On Wednesday, February
28th, in Greyfriars Kirk, Johnstone of Warriston read aloud a
document which he, Henderson and the Reverend David Dickson
had been preparing for weeks. This was the National Covenant,
in essence a call for a re-subscription of the Confession of Faith
which the boy king, James VI, had been forced to sign in 1580,
and which should have established Calvinism in Scotland for
good. The Covenant, however, was not a straightforward restate-
ment of the Confession: it protested against all that had been
done since 1580 to alter religion in Scotland, and defiantly vowed
to maintain the faith.[22] It was the focal point for all the grievances
of the nation, and after the nobles, the gentry, the ministers and
the citizens of Edinburgh had finished signing in Greyfriars
churchyard, copies of it were distributed throughout the Lowlands, and thousands more set their hands to it. The nation, in
Warriston's view, was wedded to God.[23] Archbishop Spottiswoode fled to England. The Council acknowledged itself powerless
to deal with the rebellion. Southern Scotland was in ferment.

We can never know how close the ties maintained between
Hamilton and the Covenanters were at this time, but he was
accused, both then and later, of encouraging the discontent for
his own ends. Certainly the Covenanters tried to make use of him,
along with Lennox and Morton, to carry their supplications to
the King.[24] It seems that he did act as an intermediary, by way
of a messenger, Eleazer Borthwick, by whom he "did encourage
us to proceed with our supplications".[25] Certainly he had little
interest in the ideologies of the struggle. His own attitude to
religion is probably reflected accurately in a speech he made
eleven years later: he was "not of a rigid opinion" and "differing
in religion does not move me", for "it is not this religion or that
religion or this or that fancy of man that is to be built upon, 'tis

but one that is right ... that comes from God, and the free grace of our Saviour".[26]

In March 1638 seventeen leading moderates, including Traquair, Roxburgh, Southesk and Lorne, chose Hamilton— "our very honourable good lord"—as the man most likely to present their points of view favourably to Charles: "because the business is so weighty and important, that in our opinion the peace of this country was never in so great hazard, we have thought fit to recommend the business to your lordship, according to your great interest in his majesty's honour and peace of the kingdom, may concur by your best advice and assistance at his majesty's hands to bring these great and fearful ills to a happy event."[27] The sentiments in this letter, carried to the marquis by his kinsman, Sir John Hamilton of Orbiston, the Justice Clerk, were spelled out at greater length in a message Traquair included with it. He stressed that throughout Scotland all manner of people were daily signing the Covenant. They were likely to be pacified only if the King would drop his proposal to establish the Service Book and Book of Canons in the northern kingdom, and would assure them that he would not, after all, introduce religious innovations there. Traquair added that "if the King, for the good of his own honour and service, may be moved to anything in this kind, I wish earnestly your lordship should not spare your pains in coming home, and undertaking to do his majesty's service; but except something of this kind be granted, I know not what further can be done, than to oppose force to force; wherein whoever gain, his majesty shall be a loser".[28]

It was apparent that a negotiator with the rank of Royal Commissioner would have to be sent to Scotland, and that he would have to be a Scot. Apart from Hamilton, only three men possessed sufficient power and prestige in the country to be considered, and all were ruled out. Lennox was unsuitable because of his close family connections with Catholicism: his mother-in-law, Lady Antrim, was a convert, and his brothers had been bred in the old faith. He was himself an Anglican, but current rumour had it that he was a secret Catholic.[29] Besides, his knowledge of the Scottish scene was limited, and though he might have inspired trust and respect, he was an untried politician, better left at Court.

The Marquis of Huntly, head of the powerful Gordon clan, was rejected on similar grounds. The "Cock o' the North" was officially an Episcopalian, but he was the son of Catholic parents, and Catholicism was widely practised and tolerated throughout his lands. Now in his late forties, he was an unknown quantity, for although he had been educated by King James alongside his own sons, he had spent his prime in Paris as captain of the Scots Guards, and had returned to Scotland only two years earlier, on the death of his father. Handsome and haughty, addicted to astrology and quick to take offence, he was a proud Royalist and very conscious of his family's ancient power. He was related by blood or marriage to his three major rivals: his grandmother had been Châtelherault's daughter, and he was said to have inherited his notorious indecisiveness from this strain of Hamilton blood; his mother, Lady Henrietta Stewart, was Lennox's aunt, and his wife was Lorne's sister, Lady Anne Campbell. But he had no political acumen and was a difficult man to work with. Moreover he was heavily in debt, particularly to Lorne. This made him the object of contempt and mockery: "three parts of his name is decayed", scoffed Rothes.[30] His appointment would have deeply antagonised the Covenanters and would have done no credit to the Crown.

Lord Lorne, heir of the old Earl of Argyll, and effective head of the Clan Campbell, had expressed concern over the Service Book, but had not yet revealed himself as a true Covenanter. Presbyterianism was rife in his territories and support for the Covenant overwhelming. His own position was thus very suspect. "He is a man of craft, subtlety and falsehood, and can love no man", his father is alleged to have once warned the King, "and if ever he finds it in his power to do you a mischief, he will be sure to do it."[31] Lorne was a few months younger than Hamilton, and his childhood had been lonely and bitter. He loathed his father and the old man's family by his second wife, an English heiress, and he had been brought up by the Earl of Morton, whose daughter he had married. He was wary and suspicious and in time would reveal a terrifying capacity for vindictiveness. Slightly built and softly spoken, with light-auburn hair and a noticeable cast in his grey-blue eyes, there was nothing in his manner suggestive of his awesome power and ruthless ambition. His contemporaries found him "gentle, mild and affable, gracious and courteous to speak to".[32] Shrewd and calculating, and something of a scholar, he was the greatest man on the Scottish Privy Council. His prime concern was the aggrandisement of his clan. His political arena was Scotland alone, and in this lay his strength, for he had none of Hamilton's cosmopolitanism, and his knowledge of Scottish affairs was sound and thorough.

But for the Commissionership Hamilton, though not ideal, was the only viable choice, and he was appointed on May 8th.[33] He was far from overjoyed at the honour thrust upon him. "The marquis, to the uttermost of his power, declined this charge", for he feared either to "offend those who least he would, either his bountiful and gracious master, or his mother country, wherein, after the King, his hopes were justly greatest."[34] As Hamilton later confessed, he accepted the employment "against his will".[35] For he remembered how the Scots had denigrated his father for his part in enacting the Five Articles of Perth, and he was desperately anxious not to be similarly reviled. He was already resented as an absentee Scot, and above all things he was concerned not to appear an apostate. In Traquair's despair he found a foretaste of his own anguish:

> I am in all things left alone, and, God is my witness,
> never so perplexed what to do. Shall I give way to this
> people's fury, which, without force and the strong hand,
> cannot be opposed? I am calumniated as an underhand
> conniver. Shall I oppose it with that resolution and
> power of assistance that such a business requires? It
> may breed censure and more danger than I dare venture
> upon, without his majesty's warrant, under his own
> hand, or from his own mouth.[36]

The new Commissioner was anxious also that his performance north of the Border in carrying out the King's instructions (which the two men hammered out at Whitehall on May 16th) should not jeopardise his position at Court. "In execution of all which, or what else your majesty shall think fit to command, it is most humbly desired that I may be so warranted, that the labouring to put them in execution may not turn to my ruin, nor hazard the losing of your majesty's favour, dearer to me than life."[37]

The only concession that Charles was prepared to grant his rebellious subjects was the temporary suspension of the Service Book, but he agreed to receive petitions concerning their grievances. In return he demanded that they entirely abandon the

Covenant and immediately surrender all copies of it. Hamilton was given authority to dismiss unsatisfactory or disloyal Privy Councillors and arrest anyone participating in public protests. He could also bribe the Covenanters one against another and break up gatherings by force. If necessary, as a last resort, he could preclude the Covenanting leaders traitors. "You shall declare that if there be not sufficient strength within the kingdom to force the refractory to obedience, power shall come from England, and that myself shall come in person with them, being resolved to hazard my life rather than to suffer authority to be condemned", Charles told him. "If you cannot by the means prescribed to us bring back the refractory to obedience, we do not only give you authority, but command all hostile acts whatsoever to be used against them, they having deserved to be used no other way by us but as a rebellious people." And he added: "for the doing whereof we will not only save you harmless, but account it as acceptable service done to us."[38]

Still, Hamilton's mind was in turmoil. He had little to gain and much to lose by his mission into Scotland. If he took a tough line with the Covenanters, resulting in a war in which they were victorious, he would be accused of provoking war in order to topple the Stuart dynasty, for it was undeniable that he had a vested interest in any dispute between the Stuarts and their Scottish subjects. If he sought a policy of reconciliation based on compromise—and compromise was at the basis of his nature—he would be accused by the Royalists of betraying Charles.

His chances of being able to persuade the rebels to abandon the Covenant and absolutely accept the royal proposals for religion in Scotland were almost nil. The most he could realistically hope for was to delay any showdown as long as possible, and perhaps build up a royalist faction in Scotland, giving Charles time to make adequate military preparations for a war against the Scots. And here we have the essential dilemma of Hamilton—how to reconcile the King's interests with his own. For where Charles was counting on the possibility of war to restore his power and establish Laudian ritual in Scotland, Hamilton was more inclined towards a solution acceptable to both the Episcopal bishops and the Covenanting lords, a solution warding off the ministers' threat to the balance of power and leaving his own interests in Scotland unthreatened. "God in his mercy direct us aright", he wrote to his mother, "and grant us good consciences toward him, loyal hearts toward our sovereign and pitiful ones towards ourselves and country."[39]

Only the grave illness of his wife prevented Hamilton from a total preoccupation with the Scottish troubles. Mary had contracted tuberculosis towards the end of the previous summer, and since then had grown perceptively weaker. Always pious, she now became obsessed with Catholicism, to which her grandmother, the old Countess of Buckingham, had been a convert. The defection of eminent ladies to the Roman faith was becoming something of a fad: "our great women fall away every day".[40] Mary's interest was probably encouraged by the Queen, and certainly by her Catholic cousin Olivia Boteler, wife of the ubiquitous Endymion Porter. Olivia brought her a steady supply of Catholic propaganda, and had an ally in George Con, Scots-born papal agent at Henrietta Maria's court, who visited Mary every day. Together they set out to save her soul, aware that she knew she was dying.

But the marchioness had second thoughts about conversion. She realised that such a step would seriously embarrass her husband, and she confided her feelings to him. Apathetic as he generally was towards religious sectarianism, Hamilton was no lover of Catholicism, and he bitterly resented the surreptitious efforts of Olivia and Con to tear his wife away from what he considered the true faith. Alarmed and angry, he sought advice from Laud, who sent the Bishop of Carlisle to remonstrate with Mary. "Little will it help you, my sister", taunted Olivia, "that the soul of that old man shall be with you in the devil's house."[41] But Mary would not be intimidated, and despite her inner conflict she remained a Protestant.

And then, in April, her condition rapidly deteriorated. On May 10th she died. The passing of one so young and lovely was mourned by the poet Edmund Waller:

> Her Bounty, Sweetness, Beauty, Goodness such,
> That none e'er thought her Happiness too much;
> So well inclined her Favours to confer,
> And kind to all, as Heav'n had been to her.
> The Virgin's part, the Mother, and the Wife,
> So well she acted in this spell of Life,
> That tho' few Years (too few alas!) she told,
> She seem'd in all things, but in Beauty, old.[42]

"There never lived a better nor a more religious creature", ran the tribute of her "sad and grieved" husband.[43] Mary was buried on May 12th in Westminster Abbey, alongside her grandmother, Lady Buckingham, who had died six years before.

On May 26th, a fortnight after her funeral, Lord William Hamilton was married at St. Anne's Church, Blackfriars, to Elizabeth, eighteen-year-old eldest daughter of James Maxwell of Kirkhouse, Lord Innerwick, later Earl of Dirleton. The bride's mother was French, and her father had been one of those Scots who had served James I and been retained by his son. Hamilton had arranged the marriage and negotiated the substantial dowry—£10,000 and Scottish lands—which freed Lord William from financial dependence upon him. "It was not without reluctance that he [William] was engaged that way, but his brother's authority over him was absolute."[44] The marriage proved a happy one, and in the course of the next ten years it produced six children.

Meanwhile Hamilton had rented in socage the manor of Chelsea for his children, who were too young to travel, to live in during his absence.[45] Immediately he had seen them settled he set out on his journey northwards. It was the last he would know of peace.

CHAPTER VI

'A KINDLY SCOTSMAN'

Although he was the only feasible choice, Hamilton's appointment as Royal Commissioner caused a stir in many quarters. Wentworth, doubting the marquis' loyalty, opposed it, and Laud too was hostile, believing that he lacked sufficient zeal and moral force to deal effectively with the rebels. Laud may have agreed with Bishop Williams, who declared that although he did not share the "vulgar opinion" of Hamilton, which held him "cunning and false", he did fear that he lacked "a head-piece".[1] Moreover, the declarations of Hamilton's formidable mother in support of the Covenant aroused misgivings about the loyalty of the marquis himself. It was widely believed that he would exploit the crisis for his own advantage, and attempt to disrupt the union of the crowns, leaving Charles with the English throne and appropriating that of Scotland for himself with the support of the powerful rebel leaders. "He [Charles] has sent the Marquis of Hamilton to try to gain them over", reported a Jesuit priest to his superior in France, "which most people think very strange, knowing how little affection he has for the King's affairs, and the authority he might have with that people, being descended from their blood royal, and a man fit for their designs."[2] Or, as the Venetian ambassador, Francesco Zonca, put it in one of his lively despatches:

> There is general astonishment at the King's confidence
> in the marquis, as the Parliaments of Scotland have
> already declared him the heir to that kingdom after the
> line of this King and it is not thought prudent to let
> him appear there in the present disturbances with power
> to appease them, on the ground that if he is as malicious
> as he is subtle, he might turn his arts to his own
> advantage, as the material is all there; he would find the
> people disposed to second him and the moment is
> inopportune for the King to stop him, because he has
> not the love of the people or the magnates, all being

most dissatisfied with the present government; so they
think his majesty might find it difficult to defend the
rest of his dominions. Such is the talk among the
great, and many will be glad to see it.[3]

But as Hamilton journeyed north, accompanied by Sir Thomas
Hope's son Alexander, one of his protégés, thoughts of a crown
were not on his mind. It was in a mood of confusion and depression
that, in compliance with Charles's commands, he ordered the
sheriffs of the English counties to ensure that throughout the
summer the local trained bands, whose primary purpose was to
be on call in the event of an invasion, assembled for military drill
at least twice a week.[4] If war proved necessary, the King's men
would have made a gesture of preparation.

He had already written to his tenants, requesting them to turn
out in force and meet him at Haddington on June 5th. Such a
gathering would enhance his position as Commissioner, but
threats from the Covenanters were to prevent it taking place. He
had also despatched Eleazer Borthwick to the rebel leaders,
advising them of his coming. At Newcastle, Borthwick met
Lindsay, Rothes, Henderson and others, who found that he "had
some private directions by tongue from the marquis, which
appeared also to be with his majesty's knowledge, showing that if
the supplicants would only crave such things as they might crave
by standing law, and go no further, it was like his majesty would
grant a General Assembly and a Parliament".[5]

They sent Borthwick back to Hamilton with a warning not to
take up his commission unless he could grant their desires in full,
otherwise "he would both return without doing any good, and
bring a great deal of hatred upon himself, if he were not able to
give them content".[6] He arrived at Berwick on the night of
Sunday, June 3rd, where he met Roxburgh, who, in frustration
and despair, told him of "the people's fury, the small probability
of doing good".[7] On the following day Lindsay and Lauderdale
assured him that they would never abandon the Covenant, that
they were determined to abolish the Five Articles of Perth, and
that they would force Episcopacy in Scotland to be non-existent
in all but name.[8]

All Scotland from Fife to Galloway was aflame with support
for the Covenant. A difficult task faced the Royal Commissioner

as he passed into his native country. At Dalkeith he met the Privy Council. It was not a comfortable experience. Most of the councillors scarcely concealed their sympathy for the rebels, and Sir Thomas Hope did not hesitate arrogantly to contradict the unschooled Hamilton on many points of Scottish law. Furthermore, he flatly refused to pronounce anything in the Covenant illegal. "He is no man fit to serve you", grumbled Hamilton, but warned Charles that "the time is not proper for his removal".[9]

As for the other prominent councillors, Lorne's attitude was still uncertain, and only Traquair, Roxburgh and Southesk (who was father-in-law to both Traquair and Montrose) could be counted on as Royalists. Even Huntly's loyalty could not be taken for granted. "He spake nought as we hear against our cause", gloated Dr. Baillie, Provost of Glasgow University and a leading Covenanter. "He carried himself like a Protestant."[10]

So critical was the situation that even at this early stage, before his negotiations had begun, Hamilton saw no grounds for optimism. On June 7th he informed Charles frankly that if he was to restore order in his northern kingdom he would have to invade her at the head of an army. In these circumstances he saw his own role in terms of playing for time. He believed that if the Covenanters could not force the King to bow to their demands they would forswear the royal authority by summoning their own Parliament and legislating on their own initiative. "Be confident", he added, "they, by God's grace, shall neither be able to do the one nor the other in haste, for what I cannot do by strength I do by cunning."[11]

But the Privy Councillors were not the only ones to meet him at Dalkeith. Also there were representatives of the city of Edinburgh, who officially invited him on to Holyrood. They readily granted his request to be formally received as Royal Commissioner, but they resisted his demand that the heavy guards the Covenanters had placed at the gates of Edinburgh and around the Castle be removed. It was feared that if this was done he would immediately attempt to seize the Castle for Charles. The arrival of a ship off Leith Roads, belonging to a private merchant and laden with ammunition, had led to rumours of a gunpowder plot to destroy the leading Covenanters, who now began to follow the King's example of buying up arms from northern Germany and the Low Countries in anticipation of a conflict. Lord Lorne finally used his influence to have the guards on the Castle removed, but a secret watch on the building was maintained by Covenanting patrols. Hamilton, who on June 9th moved to Edinburgh from Dalkeith, begrudgingly accepted this arrangement.

Not surprisingly, his good humour was running out. Not only had threats from the Covenanters prevented his tenants from meeting him, but the nobles and leading gentry of the country had similarly ignored his request to gather at Haddington. The King's Commissioner had been insulted, and perhaps more important to him, the head of the House of Hamilton had been ignored. Rothes came to mollify him, but only perverse pride and a dogged determination born of despair prevented him from turning back to Court in anger.

The situation was very different as he approached Edinburgh. "In his entry at Leith, I think as much honour was done to him as ever to a king in our country", marvelled Baillie.[12] The vast multitudes who crowded to meet him, however, were not jubilant well-wishers, but the Covenanting strength mustered in force. Some 60,000 people of all ranks had convened in Edinburgh to watch the Commissioner pass by, and as he rode across the flat sandy beach from Musselburgh to Leith he encountered a host of Covenanters, both clerical and lay, drawn up on each side of his path. In stony silence they cast stern looks at this richly dressed courtier astride his splendid horse, this renegade Scotsman who had come prepared, like his father before him, to impose the religious whims of a London-based sovereign upon his own unwilling people.

But suddenly a cryptic remark of Hamilton's had them agog with speculation. "Vos estis sal terrae", he murmured. "Ye are the salt of the earth." It was believed by some that he alluded to an old Scottish proverb, meaning it was they who "made all the kail salt", or were the cause of all the trouble.[13] It was not the first puzzling remark that Hamilton had made, and it would not be the last.

Over five hundred clergymen were there, conspicuous by their black cloaks and grim faces, and from their midst emerged William Livingstone, "the strongest in voice and austerest in countenance", intending to assail Hamilton with a speech. But the marquis would not hear him: "harangues in field were for princes", he told the minister, "and above his place, yet what he had to say he would hear it gladly in private." [14] They took him at his word, for scarcely had he installed himself at Holyrood House than Livingstone and a small deputation of earnest clergymen called on him. "Our Kirk", warned Livingstone, "is rent by schism, the worship of God is defiled by superstition, the whole kingdom in a fire, which is likely to consume all if it be not quenched." He added that he hoped Hamilton would prove "a worthy patriot, faithful counsellor, good Christian, and a compassionate member of your mother Kirk, mourning under manifold miseries, and shall reap the fruits of a sweet remembrance in after ages, and a wonderful peace and strong consolation when it comes to the breaking of the eye strings and giving of the last gasp". [15]

Hamilton treated them with the patient politeness characteristic of him. He assured them that the King was a convinced and true Protestant, and that if he had been mistaken, after all, in introducing the Service Book and Book of Canons, he had surely redeemed his error by his concessions, for as soon as Scotland was in a more reasonable mood, Charles would summon both a General Assembly and a Parliament. He advised them not to provoke war with the King, for they could not hope to win it; such a conflict would only wreak havoc and misery on Scotland. [16] The Covenanters were encouraged by his behaviour. "The marquis, in the way, was much moved with pity, even to tears; he professed thereafter his desires to have King Charles present at that sight of the whole country, so earnestly and humbly crying for the safety of their liberties and religion", wrote Baillie. "His Grace's countenance and carriage was so courteous, and his private speeches so fair, that we were in good hopes for some days to obtain all our desires. . . ." [17]

But when they learned that Hamilton intended to have the King's proclamation read at the Mercat Cross, their "good hopes" evaporated. They would hear of no proclamation until the offending books were abandoned, and some of the firebrands even talked of forcing Hamilton himself to sign the Covenant. Their attitude made him decide not to publish the proclamation, a wise move, since he was anxious not to cause any deterioration in the situation, but one which was interpreted as a sign of weakness. "It seemed to many that his instructions were of so many parts, that he had warrant to press every piece to the outmost, and then to pass from it, if no better might be, to the next."[18] Quite naturally, this made the Covenanters all the firmer in their stand.

Yet Hamilton did not shirk. "I shall leave nothing undone that can be thought, be it either by threats or bribes", he assured Charles, adding: "I do now humbly entreat to delay the taking of that course till you again be advertised, for if once more there be the least noise of ships and men to come, there is no hope at all ever to do anything but by total conquest."[19] Above everything, he was anxious to avoid a breach with his own countrymen.

Since his immediate concern was to undermine the Covenanting strength, he endeavoured to sow discord between the clergy and the nobles, by trying to woo the moderate nobles away from the extremists. With this policy in mind, on June 13th he met again with Rothes, for he knew that the earl's Covenanting zeal was dictated more by political than religious considerations. On Rothes he pinned the greatest hopes of a compromise, and he also wooed—with some success, since they admitted the King's concessions to be "fair"—his brother-in-law, Lord Lindsay of the Byres, the Earl of Cassillis, and Lord Loudoun, a powerful Campbell kinsman. His secret talks with some of the nobility, which were to arouse suspicion of his motives, at least temporarily allayed the Scots' headlong plunge into rebellion.

Charles approved of his manoeuvres, and on the day that Hamilton was meeting Rothes he wrote to him from Theobalds: "I cannot but approve your proceedings hitherto, for certainly you have gained a very considerable point in making the heady multitude begin to disperse, without having engaged me in any unfitting thing."[20] The following day a delegation of Covenanters came to the Commissioner with renewed demands for a General Assembly and a Parliament. Rothes informed him that "the people were more resolute", but on June 17th Hamilton informed the Covenanters that "he believed that during the present disturbance, it was an unfit time".[21]

But already Hamilton's natural propensity to bouts of depression was aggravated by his employment as Commissioner, and what looked hopeful to Charles from London did not appear so to him. He was constantly worried that if his negotiations failed the King would think badly of him, and he allowed himself to believe that he faced the possibility of assassination. He wrote to Charles in terms of extravagant despair. "God knows", ran one letter, "that if my life would appease them and settle royal authority I would willingly give it, and I shall not strive to preserve it for any other end than to serve you." And again: "it is your majesty's favours and letters that keep me alive, otherwise my heart would burst."[22]

Still he thought that Rothes, whose influence was wide despite his scattered, debt-encumbered lands, was worth purchasing, and after a Privy Council meeting he took the earl by the hand and led him into a bedchamber where they remained behind closed doors for two hours. He flattered Rothes, telling him that he considered him "much wiser and discreeter than any of the rest, and [one] who had given evident proof of his temperate disposition in the carriage of this business, and who had great power with the rest of the nobility". He went on to explain "how much it concerned him to endeavour the liberty of religion, which he so much valued, and of this nation [Scotland], having all his estate here...." Further, he begged the nobles to be "temperate, and not crave these things which the King could not in honour grant".[23]

"We were, and still are", replied the nobles, "so far from any thought of withdrawing ourselves from our dutiful subjection and obedience to his majesty's government, which by the descent and under the reign of one hundred and seven kings is most cheerfully acknowledged by us and our predecessors, that we neither had nor have any intention or desire to attempt anything that may turn to the dishonour of God or diminution of the King's greatness or authority; but, on the contrary, we acknowledge our quietness, stability and happiness to depend upon the safety of the King's majesty, as on God's vice-regent set over us for maintenance of religion and administration of justice."[24]

Meanwhile Hamilton had added another string to his bow, and had embarked on a policy designed to hurt Lord Lorne, whom he realised he could no longer keep officially uncommitted to the Covenant. He knew it was only a matter of time before Lorne declared his support of the rebels, and so he urged Charles to consider the territorial claims of the Earl of Antrim, who was anxious to regain some of the old MacDonald lands now controlled by the Campbells, the MacDonalds' hereditary enemies. "I cannot neglect the representing to your majesty that the Earl of Antrim may be of use in this business", wrote Hamilton, "for [he] is beloved by diverse of his name, and hath some pretensions to lands in Kintyre, Isles, and Highlands, and will no doubt repair to Ireland and bring such forces with him as will put those countries in that disorder, and chiefly if the Deputy can spare of any of the army there to join with him, as I hope that part of the country will do us but little hurt."[25]

Antrim, young, handsome and dashing, was married to Katherine, Buckingham's middle-aged widow, and had been at Court since boyhood. Years earlier he had offended the Hamiltons by refusing to marry Abercorn's daughter Lucy, to whom he was affianced. Such petty feuds did not matter to Hamilton: he would make use of almost anyone. But Antrim's schemes to reconquer his lands in Scotland were, contrary to Hamilton's expectation, opposed by Lord Deputy Wentworth, who suspected that the marquis might be supporting the MacDonald claims in order to acquire some Campbell territory for himself.[26] Wentworth, for all his own ambition, did not approve of Hamilton's bids for self-aggrandisement, and had earlier resisted his attempt to acquire some of the Londonderry Plantation in Ulster. Although the plan called for Antrim to invade Scotland and raise his clansmen when war broke out between the King and the Covenanters, and although Hamilton remained in contact with the MacDonalds throughout the summer, nothing came of it. Lorne learned of it and warned Hamilton that he would not stand meekly by if his lands were invaded.

In the meantime Hamilton warned Charles that if he declared war on the rebels they would exploit the King's troubles in England and win friends among his enemies there. But Charles left Hamilton in no doubt that he was reconciled to the possibility of a military solution. "I intend not to yield to those traitors the Covenanters, who I think will declare themselves so by their actions before I shall do it by my proclamation, which I shall not be sorry for, so that it be without my personal hurt of you or any of my honest servants, or the taking of an English place."[27]

The object was to gain time. "I will only say", wrote Charles on June 25th, in reply to Hamilton's warning, "that so long as this court is in force . . . I have no more power in Scotland than as a Duke of Venice, which I will rather die than suffer: yet I commend the giving ear to the explanation, or anything else to win time, which now I see is one of your chiefest cares, wherefore I need not recommend it to you."[28] Hamilton's hopes of an acceptable solution, of a compromise clothed in terms which

Charles might accept, vanished with the rise of the fanatical
Warriston and the radical extremists in the Covenanting ranks,
who forced the nobles to acquiesce in their decisions. The nobles
feared that if they did not do so they would see their position of
leadership eroded.

The marquis' policy had been applauded by many, not least
the Bishop of Ross, an uncle of Lord William Hamilton's new
wife: "the course your lordship keeps seemeth to be such as all
good and wise men must approve your lordship's wisdom and
loyalty."[29] But the policy had failed. Sterner measures were
required.

On June 24th Hamilton wrote to Charles urging him to speed
up his preparations for war. He offered him six cannon which he
had received from the Swedish government, and he also begged
leave to return to Court. "I have no hope that they will give up
the Covenant, yet it may be they will not so adhere to it as they
do now, therefore I do humbly beg leave to come up, it being the
only means left to hinder a present rupture."[30] With the Covenanters he now assumed a more aggressive tone. He threatened to
return in another "posture", which implied the use of force.[31]
Baillie says that he was "threatening us with the readiness of the
King's navy to set upon us with 10,000 land soldiers well-trained",
and that he also "spoke of the readiness of a Spanish army in
West Flanders to be employed where the King would direct".[32]

In order to gain more time and to work out another course of
action Hamilton proposed to the Covenanters that the negotiations
be suspended for three weeks. They agreed, on condition that he
return to England to try to convince Charles to grant a General
Assembly and a Parliament. Such an Assembly, Rothes assured
him, would be "indicted lawfully, with a large time, consisting of
two ministers and one lay elder, chosen out of every presbytery",
but no bishops.[33] Rothes considered it "fitting" for Hamilton to
return to Court, in order to "overcome difficulties".[34]

On June 29th Charles wrote from Greenwich, giving the
marquis permission to return, and warning him "to take heed of
how you engage yourself in the way of mediation to me, for
although I would not have you refuse to bring up to me any
demands of theirs to gain time, yet I would not have you promise
to mediate for anything that is against my grounds; for if you do,
I must either prejudice myself in the granting, or you in the

denying". He also told him to "leave any such encouragement to
these few that have not yet foresaken my cause, that they may be
assured (as well as I) that your up-coming is neither to desert
them nor it".[35]

In the same letter Charles ordered Hamilton to issue the royal
proclamation in its amended form before he left, and gave him
permission to recall the law courts into session. Accordingly, on
July 2nd the marquis called for the courts to re-open in the
autumn, and two days later he demanded that the Privy Council
sign the proclamation. This they did, and they also signed the
approbation giving it their support. Immediately afterwards, the
proclamation—and a promise that all who submitted to it would
be pardoned—were read at the Mercat Cross.

No sooner had they been read than Warriston delivered the
inevitable protest. That afternoon, bowing to pressure from the
rebel extremists, the privy councillors demanded that their signatures be deleted from the declaration approving the proclamation. Hamilton found that three or four councillors were
adamant in this and "would immediately fall off, if he gave them
no satisfaction".[36]

And then there reputedly took place an incident which has lent
weight to all the allegations of Hamilton's treachery. After the
Privy Council meeting he is said to have led Rothes, Loudoun,
Dickson and Cant through the state apartments at Holyrood to
the great gallery, where, well away from the councillors, who
remained in the audience chamber, he made a remarkable statement:

> My lords and gentlemen, I spoke to you before those
> Lords of Council as the King's Commissioner. Now
> there being none present but yourselves, I speak to you
> as a kindly Scotsman.* If you go on with courage and
> resolution you will carry what you please, but if you
> faint, and give ground in the least, you are undone. A
> word is enough to wise men.[37]

This conversation can never be proved. Guthry, Bishop of
Dunkeld, who related it decades later, maintained that it was
originally reported by Cant, one of those present.[38] Others have

* i.e. probably in the sense of a "fellow-Scotsman".

pointed out that if it really had taken place it would certainly have figured in the charges Montrose brought against Hamilton several years later.[39] Yet there does seem to have been an allusion to it in the charge which claimed that Hamilton spoke disrespectfully of the King, and encouraged the Covenanters to persist in their defiance.[40]

Perhaps the marquis hoped that by his encouragement the Covenanters would be moved to commit such acts of extremism that Charles would be justified in making war on them. Like all weak leaders, Hamilton vacillated, but it is possible that on this occasion he did have his master's interests at heart. Charles had, after all, given him considerable leeway at the start of the negotiations—"I give you leave to flatter them with what hopes you please, so you engage me not against my grounds."[41]

CHAPTER VII

THE GLASGOW ASSEMBLY

The sudden departure of Hamilton for Court took most of the Covenanters unawares. Some were amused:

> My lord your unexpected post
> To Court, made me to miss
> The happiness which I love most,
> Your lordship's hands to kiss.
>
> But though with speed you did depart
> So fast ye shall not fly,
> As to untie my loving heart
> Which your convoy shall be.[1]

But for others less light-hearted his departure gave rise to anxious speculation, since his conduct had savoured of ambiguity. "My Lord Commissioner has so carried himself from his coming to his going that he has made us all suspend our judgment of his inclination, whether it be towards us or our opposite. . . ."[2]

At Whitehall, however, he found the Court generally satisfied with his handling of affairs, even though it had met with no success. Secretary Windebank praised his "very great services" and even Laud conceded his "prudence".[3] On July 14th, in earnest talks with the King at Oatlands, he proposed that Charles renew the Confession of Faith of 1580, on which the Covenant was based, and in which he saw nothing contrary to the continuation of Episcopacy. Such a move, he argued, would take the wind out of the Covenanters' sails.[4]

Charles, who had, of course, long since decided on war, and was arming Hull and Newcastle, agreed to the proposal as a temporary measure, and Hamilton returned to Scotland at the beginning of August bearing the King's lengthy set of instructions, drawn up on July 27th. He was to use all the means in his power to cajole the Council into signing the Confession, but to prevent Charles losing face he was not to put the issue to the vote unless he was sure of carrying it. If he succeeded in persuading the councillors to sign it—and for that matter even if he did not, since he was only playing for time—he was to proceed with preparations for a General Assembly, even if the Covenanters themselves rejected the Confession. But he was to see that the Assembly met no sooner (and preferably later) than November 1st, although its location was left to his good judgment: "for the matter of indicting, you must be as cautious as you can, and strive to draw it as near as may be to the former assemblies in my father's time."[5] He was to ensure that the bishops be allowed votes in the Assembly, and try to arrange that the Moderator himself be a bishop. Although the Service Book and Book of Canons were suspended, he was to uphold the hated Five Articles of Perth and protest against the abolition of Episcopacy and resist all encroachments on the power of the bishops. At the same time he was to discourage the bishops from taking their places at the Privy Council table until the times were less troubled. For all this, "notwithstanding all these instructions . . . you are by no means to permit a present rupture to happen, but to yield anything though unreasonable, rather than now to break".[6]

Hamilton arrived at Holyrood on August 10th, with his religious adviser, Dr. Walter Balcanquall,* and immediately found himself the centre of controversy. During his absence in England several Covenanting leaders, notably Montrose, Henderson, Dickson and Cant, had gone to Aberdeen in an attempt to browbeat the citizens into signing the Covenant. They had not been very successful, for Aberdeen, in the heart of Huntly's territory, was a stronghold of Episcopalianism. Only about twenty Aberdonians had signed the Covenant, and the Covenanting ministers had been forbidden to preach their sedition in the city's churches. A series of exchanges had taken place between Henderson, Dickson and Cant and a number of loyalist clergymen from Aberdeen, in which the three Covenanters complained that under pressure from Hamilton the Scottish Privy Council had rescinded the act of the approbation of the last Proclamation, and had destroyed the "subscribed missive" which was to be sent to the King.[7]

It had not taken much time for the story to circulate that Hamilton had torn up the act. The Council, says Baillie, "did not rest till they had gotten back that subscribed act, and rent it in small pieces".[8] To make matters worse, Henderson, Dickson and

*Dean of Rochester, and later of Durham.

Cant had charged that the marquis "was contented and well pleased with the explanation of the Covenant which was presented to me [Hamilton], as a humble supplication of the noblemen and other Covenanters".[9] In a fury, Hamilton took steps to counter the rumours in a manifesto he issued from Holyrood: "I do aver upon mine honour, that I never said so, I never thought so", he declared, and denied "any ground for their opinion of my acceptance of that declaration, unless they call receiving accepting, and that was not in my power to refuse." He blamed the rumours on those afraid of a peaceful settlement of affairs in Scotland, who were trying to "raise in my royal and gracious master a jealousy of my slackness in my King and country's service, that so might I be called back *re infecta*". And yet,

> notwithstanding this personal wrong offered to me, his
> majesty's High Commissioner, I will carefully, cheerfully,
> constantly go on with this great business wherewith he
> hath entrusted me, which as I pray God that it may
> prosper under my hands, so I praise God that he has
> given me so cheerful and willing a heart to go on in it,
> that if my life could procure the peace of this torn
> Church and kingdom to the contentment of my royal
> master, and comfort of his distracted subjects, he who
> knoweth all things, knoweth likewise this truth. It is
> the sacrifice of the world in which I would most glory,
> and which I would most sincerely offer up to God, my
> King and country.[10]

Colonel Alexander Hamilton, who had been associated closely with him in Germany, had also incurred Hamilton's displeasure, but he strenuously denied saying anything against the Commissioner:

> And that I may begin with that which hath least colour
> of truth, namely that I should have reported to many
> ministers and others that your lordship was satisfied
> with the Covenant in your heart. This is so far from
> any appearance of verity that both your lordship's self
> and all your friends with whom I spoke on that subject
> can witness that it has been my greatest regret to find
> your lordship so averse and contrary to it as the
> bishops themselves could be no more. . . .[11]

Over the next few days Hamilton was distant and uncommunicative, fearing that anything he said might be further misinterpreted. He refused to see his mother altogether, since her well-publicised sympathy for the Covenanters had greatly embarrassed him and incensed the King.[12] "I am infinitely traduced and left by many of my nearest friends", he complained, "and likewise by some that I have much obliged."[13] On August 13th, when some of the Covenanting leaders approached him in the hope of learning what had transpired during his talks with Charles, he sent them away, telling them bluntly that they would have to wait until he had spoken with the Privy Council on the following day.[14]

The Council had just received a letter written by the King on July 30th, informing them that the Covenant "being not subscribed by royal leave and authority . . . must needs be null in itself, and very prejudicial to the ancient and laudable government of both Kirk and Commonwealth".[15] Hamilton now informed them of Charles's decision to call a General Assembly and a Parliament. "We have", he said, "all cause to bless God and thank his majesty for it, such is his tender care for this poor distracted kingdom, that he will leave nothing undone that can be expected from a just prince to save us from ruin."[16]

He told the Covenanters much the same thing on August 15th, and sent a delegation of Privy Councillors to the Estates to decide between themselves who should be eligible for membership of the proposed Assembly and what matters should be brought before it. The Covenanters, hearing of this attempt to "prelimit" the Assembly, ordered that the presbytery of Peebles, about twenty-five miles south of Edinburgh, should begin choosing its delegates straight away.[17] On August 17th Hamilton presented them with a list of eleven demands, based on his talks with the King, which he insisted they agree upon before the Assembly met. These, says Baillie, "were very evil taken by us all", but perhaps the main opposition came with regard to the eighth, which demanded that "bishops and other ministers who shall attend the Assembly, may be sured in their persons from all trouble and molestation", and the ninth, which insisted that "the commissioners from presbyteries be chosen by the ministers of the presbytery only, and that no lay person whatsoever meddle in the choice, nor no minister without his own presbytery".[18] The

Covenanters warned him that if he persisted in trying to force these demands on them they would merely call their own Parliament and Assembly, but they agreed to his request for twenty days' grace, during which he would return to Charles for further talks.[19] A master of nothing if not of compromise, Hamilton reduced his eleven demands to two: that no laymen should participate in the selection of delegates, and that the Assembly should not presume to determine things established by acts of Parliament. His main concern, indeed, was to save the Assembly from lay control, for Rothes had already told him that a "free assembly" should include two ministers and one "elder" from each presbytery, yet the second Book of Discipline stated that elders should be "ecclesiastical persons".[20] When his demands became known the Estates renewed their threat to call an Assembly without the King's permission, but Hamilton called their bluff by refusing to return to Oatlands for further talks, staying on instead in Scotland as a private citizen. The Covenanters were not yet in a position for war and dared not force a breach.

So on August 25th he set out for Court again, promising to return by September 21st. Arriving at Oatlands once more, he warned Charles that a conflict was inevitable unless he was issued with more flexible instructions, and unless the King himself signed the Confession of Faith.[21] Hard on his heels came the Bishop of Ross, who implored Charles not to call an Assembly, but the King would not listen to him, and on September 9th he worked out a more acceptable set of instructions for his Commissioner. The marquis was given authority, at his own discretion, to revoke the Service Book, the Book of Canons, and the Five Articles of Perth.[22]

Though he now had more scope for bargaining, it was in a mood of deep personal anguish that Hamilton returned to Scotland. His heir, Charles, aged four, was lying dangerously ill at Chelsea of "a most malignant fever", one of those unexplained childhood diseases of the seventeenth century, and his two other sons were "weak and sickly".[23] His fear for their lives aggravated the depression he already felt over the course of the negotiations. The calm collected minister had, in the last few weeks, become emotional and excitable, sensing an assassin behind every arras and in every alleyway. It is not surprising that when he stopped off at Ferrybridge to meet the bishops—and give the Archbishop of St. Andrews £2,500 to resign the Chancellorship—he stayed only long enough to snatch a few hours' sleep. He was unsociable at supper and left early the next morning before the rest of his party were awake.[24] "God grant me as much strength and ability to go through with it as I have loyalty", he wrote to Charles from Holyrood, where he arrived on September 17th, "for never poor man had a heavier burden lying on him than for the present is undergone by [me]."[25]

Early on September 21st he informed the Covenanting leaders of the King's revised proposals; predictably, they welcomed the plans to call a General Assembly and a Parliament, but were opposed to the renewal of the Confession of Faith. That afternoon he informed the Privy Council that Charles definitely wished to renew the Confession. They received the news in sullen silence, and Hamilton called upon Traquair, always an able speaker, to give him moral support. Some of the councillors agreed to subscribe the Confession but most insisted that it be put to the vote. The meeting finally broke up at ten, with Hamilton demanding that they reach a decision by next morning.[26]

There was to be no sleep for the Commissioner that night. Until the early hours he was consulting his advisers and trying to persuade one councillor after another to support the Confession. At daybreak he was approached by Rothes and a group of Covenanting nobles who begged him to postpone the decision until the following Monday. In the interim, they said, they would show him good reasons why the plan to renew the Confession be dropped. At seven that morning he invited them to a further meeting of the Council, but they left angrily after three hours, realising that there would be no postponement: the Council unanimously decided to subscribe the Confession. For the Confession had called the councillors' bluff: no good reason could be advanced against it. They rose at four in the afternoon, having decided to call a General Assembly for November 21st and a Parliament for May 15th. The next day the Proclamation of Grace was read at the Mercat Cross, to a background of heckling by Covenanters bent upon hindering subscription of the Confession. All Hamilton could do was persuade the Council to pass a censorious motion labelling protest sedition. That same day he, Traquair, Roxburgh, Mar, Lorne and others put their names to the Confession.[27]

On September 24th he wrote Charles an account of these events, particularly praising Traquair, Roxburgh and Southesk, who had supported him with a fervour beyond their "accustomed courage".[28] "Be confident", he assured Rothes on the same day, "that my endeavours have, and do tend to no other end, but to the glory of God, the honour of his sacred majesty, and the preserving from ruin of this poor distracted kingdom."[29]

The violence of the opposition to the King's latest concessions alienated many moderates, but the Covenanting extremists believed that the King had a trick up his sleeve.[30] Dissension was apparent in the Covenanters' ranks from the ministers, who did not wish to see the tyranny of the King and bishops replaced by that of the nobles, and in the elections now taking place for delegates to the Assembly they bitterly contested the claims of lay elders. The ministers declared that "they would not agree to any protestation made against the King's declaration, except they considered it, and first read that intended protestation, since they saw no necessity for it",[31] and the protest was issued without them.

If Hamilton thought that a reaction against the Covenant was imminent in Scotland he was disappointed. Only in Aberdeen, where his commissioners obtained 12,000 signatures, was there any great support for the Confession of Faith, now called the "King's Confession", and only 16,000 signatures were forthcoming for the whole country.[32] Those he had selected as commissioners to obtain signatures included such Covenanting sympathisers as Rothes, Lindsay and Montrose, and crypto-Covenanters like Hope and Lord Lorne, who was soon to succeed his father as Earl of Argyll. This was very puzzling to Charles: "why", he asked, "have you mingled the protesters with my good subjects as commissioners?"[33] Hamilton's reasoning was that this would give these men a chance to prove their loyalty, since they could hardly oppose a document they were pressing others to sign. "But above all my chief end was to satisfy the vulgar people . . . they seeing the names of the prime Covenanters in the commission, it was the readiest means to effect the same."[34] It was perhaps a misreading of human nature, for Hamilton had no guarantee that the commissioners would carry out conscientiously the task entrusted to them.

Though the King expressed faith in his "dexterity and diligence",[35] the marquis was not overly optimistic. "My chief concern tends now only to prepare myself to make the nullities of this Assembly appear", he explained, "and if need shall be at the very first sitting thereof to dissolve the same, though it is not to be expected that they will obey, yet my leaving of them cannot but make their proceedings ineffectual, and give your majesty the juster grounds to take exception at them . . . I am confident [that] . . . by protesting in your majesty's name against the proceedings in the said Assembly, [I shall] preserve authority from being overthrown and make appear to all honest and indifferent men that your majesty is willing to secure religion though you will not permit sovereignty to be trampled on."[36]

The visions of a frenzied woman, Margaret Mitchison, who announced that God had told her that the Covenant had been drawn up in Heaven, and the revelations of Abernathy, an ex-Jesuit who claimed that the King had approved a Scottish liturgy formulated in Rome, had whipped the religious fervour of the people to fever pitch, especially in Edinburgh. For the Commissioner events had taken a sinister turn: "I know well it is chiefly monarchy which is intended by them to be destroyed, and I cannot say but that it hath received so great a blow as it can never be set right till the principal actors have received their just punishment, which cannot be great enough for their faults, but this cannot be done without a powerful force, which cannot be raised here until such time as the people's hearts be unpossessed by their fears of innovations in religion."[37]

Hamilton's suspicions were not, perhaps, unfounded, for Rothes reportedly babbled that "if we were rid of this King, we would never have any other, and if he will not give us way in what we expect we will take our own way, but yet we will not take arms against the King, unless he come in upon us".[38] Spurred on by the fanatical Warriston, many Covenanting leaders were now convinced that there could be no compromise with Charles. In such circumstances the Commissioner was seen as an unnecessary intermediary. Indeed, Hamilton cannot have failed to feel threatened by the talk among the more zealous Covenanters, who had begun to envisage a Scotland governed on the lines of Holland, where the nobles ruled hand in glove with the Calvinist clergy. Such an idea would have suggested itself to a man like Hope, whose mother was Dutch, and to those Scots who had seen service in the Low Countries.

Dumbarton Castle had been secured and fortified, but the Earl of Mar, whom Hamilton found arrogant and unreasonable, first refused, and then agreed (on payment of £2,000) to surrender the keys of Edinburgh Castle into the Commissioner's hands.[39] The King was stepping up his preparations for an armed invasion of Scotland, and on October 22nd he ordered Wentworth to send over five hundred troops from the Irish army to garrison Carlisle.[40]

The marquis was at his wit's end. "The people in their part are still mad", he reported to Huntly, remote in his castle of Strath-bogie, near Aberdeen, "and continue in the same courses they were in." He regretted that the Royalist ministers in the north were unwilling to come to Glasgow because of the threat of intimidation, and he urged the Gordon chieftain to persuade them to come, pledging himself to guarantee their safety. "The truth is, his majesty will not consent nor is it fitting [that] your lordship should be out of the north till we see how this Assembly ends, which I am most confident will not be well."[41]

Only nine of the fifteen judges at the Edinburgh law courts would be pressed into signing the King's Confession, and Sir Thomas Hope refused Hamilton's command to defend the right of the bishops to exist, on the grounds that it would be contrary to his conscience and the will of God. With characteristic insolence he reminded the Commissioner that only Parliament had power to dismiss him from his post as Lord Advocate, and Hamilton could do no more than order him to stay away from Glasgow for as long as the Assembly lasted.[42] Apart from Dr. Balcanquall—"a most useful servant"[43]—he could count on the support of only a handful of clergy. "My hope of effecting anything that is good in this Assembly is almost vanished", he confided in a letter to Huntly on November 11th, in which he complained of "the malice of this mad people" against the bishops. The main concern of the Assembly, he felt sure, would be the abolition of Epis-copacy.[44] This letter presented a sharp contrast to the optimism he expressed the next day, when he told Charles that shortly "the best and greatest part of the ministry will be on your majesty's side".[45] On November 16th Hamilton left Edinburgh for Glasgow.

Glasgow, a town of about two thousand inhabitants, was in the heart of Hamilton's territory and could fairly be expected to be under his control. Indeed, the University had signed the

Covenant only begrudgingly. The town was booming and increasingly prosperous—"the inhabitants (all but the students of the college which is here) are traders and dealers"[46]—and engaged in a busy trade with Ireland, France and Norway. But it was also solidly Calvinist. Its citizens based their lives on the doctrine of the elect and adhered strictly to the observance of the Sabbath. As the Covenanters gained support in Glasgow and elsewhere in the south-west, Hamilton's influence had declined. He had, indeed, been villified in the pulpits. Now the lesser nobles of purely local interest, paying lavish lip-service to the Kirk, were in the ascendant, and gangs of their retainers, armed with pistols and daggers, swaggered about the streets, intimidating the less zealous.

In these circumstances Hamilton might have raised his tenantry to disperse the Covenanting bands. But most had refused to sign the King's Confession at his bidding, and he dared not test their loyalty further. He had already forbidden the carrying of unusual weapons and it was anathema to him, as head of Scotland's most powerful family, that he had seriously lost face in his own district. In any case, he deliberately avoided a clash, for he had no wish to precipitate a conflict in Scotland before Charles was ready to crush the rebellion.

Apart from Samuel Rutherford and James Sibbald, two stalwarts, the ministers from Aberdeen, who would have lent the royal cause valuable support, were too frightened to come to the Assembly, blaming their absence on impassable roads. The bishops, too, were intimidated by the ferocity of the Covenant's supporters, and relied upon Hamilton's protection while they were shut up in Glasgow Castle. They were accused of all kinds of sins—of Popish sympathies, arrogance and pride, of Sabbath-breaking, simony, avarice, drunkenness and whoring. "Some of them", noted Hamilton, "have not been of the best lives."[47] A prostitute's claims that her baby's father was the Bishop of Brechin received wide publicity. The bishops wished to abandon the plans for an Assembly, fearing that their cause would only be done untold harm, but their suggestions met with no sympathy from the King—"I utterly dislike them, for I should hurt my reputation by not keeping it"[48]—and were ignored by Hamilton, who intended to challenge the legality of the Assembly on the grounds that the bishops were prevented from sitting.[49]

The Assembly opened on Wednesday, November 21st, amid

pandemonium. Noisy crowds milled outside the Cathedral, and those that could jostled their way inside it, and at the sides of many of them gleamed the blades of dirks and daggers. There were two hundred and forty delegates: one hundred and forty-two ministers and ninety-eight lay elders.[50] Hamilton sat on a canopied chair of state, and a little below him were ranged his six assessors. Argyll, as Lorne had now become, Lauderdale, Roxburgh, Southesk, Traquair and Sir Lewis Stewart. Their function was to advise the Commissioner: they could not vote on any of the Assembly's motions. Nearby sat the members of the Privy Council. It was noticed that Hamilton strode to his chair with an attitude worthy of a prince. A small table in front of him was reserved for the Moderator and Clerk of the Assembly, who had yet to be chosen. At a long table below that sat the nobles and lairds representing the Presbyteries, and on each side of them were five or six rows of benches occupied by ministers and commissioners of the royal burghs. Facing Hamilton, but far removed at the other end of the hall, was an elevated platform, where the eldest sons of peers sat. Above, in the galleries, sat the spectators, many of them women.[51]

After his commission had been read out in Latin, Hamilton made his opening speech. "The making of long harangues is not suitable either with my education or profession", he began, "much less with this time, which now after so much talking ought to be a time of action." He reminded his listeners of the King's concessions, assuring them that "he hath seriously considered all the grievances of his subjects". If the King's wishes were enacted in the Assembly, then Charles would be prepared to consider their desires.[52]

Even those who had come prepared to criticise were impressed by Hamilton's conduct over the next two weeks. "I take the man to be of a sharp, masterlike expression; loud, distinct, slow, full, yet concise, modest, courtly, yet simple and natural language [sic]: if the King have many such men, he is a well-served prince", ran Baillie's tribute. "My thoughts of the man, before that time, were hard and base, but a day or two's audience did work my mind to a great change towards him, which yet remains, and ever will, till his deeds be notoriously evil."[53]

"Accordingly we met", reported Hamilton to Charles the next day, "and truly, Sir, my heart was never sadder than to see such a sight, not one gown amongst the whole company, many swords, but many more daggers. . . ." He found them to be "a great and confused multitude, and I will add a most ignorant one, for some commissioners there are who can neither write nor read, the most part being totally devoid of learning, but resolved to follow the opinion of those few ministers who pretend to be learned, and those be the most rigid and seditious Puritans that liveth". In these circumstances, he saw no grounds for optimism: "what then can be expected but a total disobedience to authority, if not a present rebellion . . . which I would not so much apprehend if I did not find so great an inclination in the body of your Council to go along their way, for believe me, Sir, there is no Puritan minister of them all who would more willingly be freed of Episcopal governance than they would whose fault [it is] that this unlucky business is come to this height." [54]

So great was the popular passion that he feared mob violence and the old spectre of assassination: "this one suit I have to make to you (if it be true which I hear is intended) that, if they seize on me and those few of the Council who are faithful to you, that your majesty neither regard us nor consider our danger, but take just vengeance on your rebellious subjects." [55]

The first session of the Assembly had opened with a sermon—drowned by the din from the floor and public galleries—by one of the few loyalist ministers there, Dr. John Bell of Glasgow, who had been selected by Hamilton. Immediately afterwards the Covenanters had demanded in vain that a Moderator be selected. [56] They renewed this plea on the following day, but Hamilton insisted on reading the King's letter to the Assembly first. They refused to let him read the bishops' formal protest at their exclusion, and they thwarted his attempts to challenge the legality of the Assembly, voting that the election of a Moderator and a Clerk should top the agenda. They rejected outright his request that his six assessors be allowed to vote in the Assembly, and thus Charles was left with a single vote in the proceedings—Hamilton's—whilst the city of Edinburgh had two. In the face of Hamilton's opposition—he refused to vote on the issue—Alexander Henderson was chosen Moderator, and on the following day, November 23rd, Warriston was selected as Clerk. He celebrated the occasion by praying aloud that Christ's prerogative triumph over all earthly prerogatives. [57] The delegates seemed all set to bring the bishops to trial.

On November 26th the controversy of the legality of the elections was raised, but Hamilton's protests were rudely dismissed.[58] Events were fast reaching a crisis, and now the course was clear. The time had come to dissolve the Assembly.

Hamilton was plunged in the deepest gloom. Perhaps never had his spirits sunk so low. Reviewing the events of the last few months, he considered himself a failure: his tenants had disobeyed him, the masses had affronted him, the ministers had reviled him, the Assembly had contravened his wishes and most of those who mattered on the Council and in Scotland had deserted him. What few allies he had could not be counted on. Both Traquair and Roxburgh had assured him that they supported Episcopal government, and although he made use of them and urged Charles to do so, he did not trust them. Haddington's loyalty was half-hearted. Apart from Huntly, those who might be expected to continue in their fidelity to the crown were nobles of the second rank, of limited power and limited influence: Dalziel, Findlater, Kinnoul, Lauderdale, Linlithgow, Perth, Southesk. At Whitehall those jealous of Hamilton were busy trying to discredit him in the eyes of the King. It constantly haunted him—despite all the assurances to the contrary—that the way he had handled affairs might cost him his sovereign's favour. His private life offered little solace. His wife was dead, his sons were dying, his mother openly opposed him, and so did two of his brothers-in-law. Feeling thoroughly alone, all optimism spent, convinced that an assassin was about to strike, he sat down to write what he believed might be his last letter to Charles.

It was a remarkable document. "Yet so unfortunate have I been in this unlucky country", it ran in part, "that though I did prefer your service before all worldly considerations, nay, even strained my conscience in some points, by subscribing the negative confession,* yet all hath been to small purpose, for I have marred my end, in not being able to curb the insolency of this rebellious nation, without assistance from England, and greater charge to your majesty than this miserable country is worth." The sense of failure was paramount. "As I shall answer to God on the last day, I have done my best, though the success has proven so bad, as I think myself of all men living most miserable, in finding that I have been so useless a servant to him to whom I owe so much."

* The Confession of Faith.

Two descriptions of the key figures of Scotland which Hamilton gave to Charles because "you should know your officers and counsellors, of whom I shall write without spleen or favour", are particularly memorable. They are of his two main rivals, Argyll and Montrose. "The Earl of Argyll is the only man now called up* as a true patriot, a loyal subject, a faithful counsellor, and above all, rightly set for the preservation of religion", he explained.

> He must be well looked to, for it fears me, he will prove
> the dangerousest man in the state. He is so far from
> favouring Episcopal government that with all his soul
> he wishes it totally abolished.

As for Montrose, he was not to be taken seriously. The chief trouble-makers, Hamilton considered, were Rothes, Balmerino, Lindsay, Lothian, Loudoun, Yester and Cranstoun. "There are many others as forward in show, amongst whom none are more vainly foolish than Montrose." The great hero of the Covenanting movement was thus dismissed in a single sentence.

For the most part, the rest of the letter consisted of advice for Charles on subjugating Scotland, for "it is more than probable that these people have somewhat else in their thoughts than religion". In his dejection and disappointment, the marquis now fancied that he had been drained of all love for his native land. "If I keep my life (though next Hell I hate this place) if you think me worthy of employment, I shall not weary till the government be set right, and then I will forswear this country." His final thoughts were for the children he thought would soon be fatherless:

> I have now only this one suit to your majesty, that if
> my sons live, they may be bred in England, and made
> happy by service in the Court, and if they prove not
> loyal to the crown, my curse be on them. I wish my
> daughters be never married in Scotland.

He did not forget Lord William, since Mary's death the chief object of his affection. "I humbly recommend my brother to your care."[59] As Isaac D'Israeli remarks in his incisive little study of Hamilton, perhaps never has a frustrated politician penned a despatch so reminiscent of a last will and testament.[60]

* i.e. "described" or "regarded".

Early next morning Hamilton informed the Privy Council of his intention to dissolve the Assembly. The meeting in the Chapter House went on for two hours. In reply to Argyll, who asked whether the council was to have any say in deciding whether or not the Assembly was a lawful body, he curtly explained that he wanted only their support for an action which had already been decided.[61]

Having left the Council in no doubt as to his next move, he then prepared for his final confrontation with the Assembly. His intention to declare the proceedings illegal had been learned already by the Covenanters, even before he had revealed it to the Council. The delegates sat prepared for a crisis, and some of them had locked the cathedral's doors and made off with the key. He found them debating whether or not they were a free assembly in spite of the absence of the bishops. The arguments were predictably one-sided, and when the issue was about to be put to the vote, Hamilton rose. Two conflicting emotions, he told them, had welled up inside him: "joy, in making good what hath been promised by his majesty", and "sorrow, in that I cannot make further known his majesty's pious intention". And then he delivered his attack. "You have called for a free general assembly; his majesty hath granted you one, most free on his part and in his intentions; but as you have handled and marred the matter let God judge whether the least shadow or footsteps of freedom can be discerned in this assembly. . . ."

He condemned the fixed elections and the presence of lay elders. "Neither ruling elders nor any minister chosen commissioner by ruling elders can have a voice here, because no such election is warranted, either by the laws of this Church or kingdom, or by the practice or custom of either . . . there being more lay elders giving votes at every one of these elections than there were ministers, contrary to the Book of Discipline. . . . How can these men now elected be thought fit to be ruling elders who were never elders before?" On this point Hamilton was adamant. "By what law or practice was it ever heard that young noblemen, or gentlemen, or others, should be chosen rulers of the church, being yet minors, and in all construction of law thought unfit to manage their own private estates, unless you will grant that men of meaner abilities may be thought fit to rule the church, which is the house of God, than are fit to rule their own private houses, families and fortunes?" He claimed that many of the lay elders were in danger of excommunication from the Kirk, that some were anti-monarchist trouble-makers who had been sent down from the University of Glasgow, that some had been expelled from Ireland, and that yet others were presumptive outlaws. "What a scandal were it to the reformed churches to allow this to be chosen a lawful assembly, consisting of such members, and so unlawfully chosen", he fumed. The time had come to dissolve the Assembly. "I know that all my master's commands are justifiable. . . ."[62]

The Moderator than rose, and tried to rebut Hamilton's charges. "What is Caesar's or what is ours, let it be given to Caesar", he declared, "but let the God by whom kings reign have his own place and prerogative, by whose grace our King reigneth, and we pray may long and prosperously reign over us."

"Sir", replied the Commissioner, "ye have spoken as a good Christian and dutiful subject". Encouraged, Henderson continued in earnest. "Indeed, we take this to be a free assembly indicted by his majesty, and we trust that all things in it shall be so moderate, that the word of God and reason shall seem to proceed in everything", he said. "We are hopeful that such a righteous King as ours needs nothing but to have a clear truth pointed out before him, and when he sees it, he shall fall in love with it."[63]

After Henderson—who Hamilton admitted to have been "wise and discreet"—had resumed his seat, several noblemen rose, each intent on proving that the Assembly had a right to sit. The most notable was Argyll, who had all along been the cynosure of the Assembly. Although he had no right to speak, since he was not a delegate, he now lent his quiet voice in defence of the Covenanters. "I have not striven to blow the bellows, but studied to keep matters in as soft a temper as I could, and now I desire to make it known that I take you all for members of a lawful assembly and my honest countrymen." He was followed by Rothes, who maintained that if Hamilton left "we must protest that your grace has departed without a just reason".

But now the marquis turned his trump card. Perceptively agitated, he produced papers—which he flung at Warriston and ordered read out—which he claimed to be the secret instructions sent out to each presbytery on how and whom to elect.[64] "I must remove my person", he told them,

for my estate is not so dear to me as my reputation and
fidelity to my master. . . . I have laboured as a good
Christian, loyal subject, and kind countryman for the
good of this kirk, laying aside all private considerations
. . . for I desire to serve God, my King and my
country. But a weighty business is laid on the back of a
silly* young man overcharged with a toilsome business,
and unable to bring it to such an end as I would.

With tears in his eyes he dissolved the Assembly. "I make a
declaration that nothing done here in this Assembly shall be of
any force to bind any of his majesty's subjects, and I in his
majesty's name discharge this court to sit any longer."[65]
    Amid the ensuing uproar Hamilton rose, and with the coun-
cillors, including Argyll, stalked towards the door. But it was
locked, and as he waited for it to be prised open, he was forced to
listen to Henderson's thunderous challenge: "it becometh us not
to be discouraged when we seem to be deprived of human
authority". Similar sentiments were voiced by David Dickson—
"if we be silent and pass from this Assembly, now shall the will of
God be demonstrated to our King in points controverted . . .
therefore we must proceed"—and as Hamilton finally left the
hall, it was to the accompaniment of the earnest voice of the
young Lord Erskine, passionately regretting that he had not yet
signed the Covenant and begging to be allowed immediately to
do so.[66]
    Argyll had joined the other councillors in following Hamilton
out of the cathedral, but both he and Almond excused themselves
from joining him and the Privy Council in the chapter-house
shortly afterwards. Addressing themselves to the King, the
councillors paid tribute to Hamilton:

Never servant did with more industry, care, judgment
and patience go about the discharge of so great a trust.
And albeit the success has not answered his desires,
neither yet his extraordinary pains . . . yet his deservings
herein merit to be remembered to posterity.[67]

Despite this, Hamilton was so unsure of the loyalty of all the

* i.e. in the sense of "inexpert".

councillors present that he did not ask them to sign the proclamation dissolving the Assembly until the next morning, after he had sounded them out, and then several councillors followed Argyll's lead in disassociating themselves from the Commissioner's action.

On the following morning, also, Hamilton sought out Argyll. What he said to the Campbell chief must remain a matter for conjecture, but it seems reasonable to suppose that the marquis pressed Argyll to endeavour to restrain the extremists in the Assembly. Hamilton was sufficiently aware of Argyll's influence and shrewdness to try something of the kind. He cannot have been happy at the potential threat Argyll posed not only to the Stuarts but to the power of the Hamiltons in Scotland. At any rate Argyll remained in Glasgow, yet he had not signed the Covenant and unlike other late converts he made no attempt to do so.

The Commissioner himself departed for his house at Hamilton, accompanied by some of the bishops, who were afraid to stay in Glasgow. At the marquis' request Charles had agreed that £10,000 be distributed among them. A few days later he moved on to Holyrood, where, he complained, he suffered "infinite affronts".[68] On December 7th Charles wrote from Whitehall, approving the dissolution but warning Hamilton to "take care that your coming away do not cast things so loose that the honest men of my party do believe that you leave them as in a case desperate, or at least that by your absence they be denuded of advice and protection". He ordered him to "take good order that your absence do neither dishearten nor prejudice my party".[69]

Hamilton did his best by the King's commands. On December 17th he issued a proclamation, which he ordered to be read throughout the land, declaring all those who continued to sit in the Assembly traitors and reiterating Charles' intentions to preserve the established religion in Scotland. He also tried to reassure those still hostile to the Covenant by writing them letters designed to strengthen their resolve. Huntly, for one, received weekly missives of encouragement.

Meanwhile the Covenanters, learning that on Hamilton's orders ammunition and a month's supply of provisions had been sneaked into Edinburgh Castle, began a virtual siege of the garrison. And now the strain of the last weeks began to tell on the Commissioner.

A short illness induced by anxiety delayed his departure for Court. He had striven to serve his sovereign, and in doing so had come into conflict with the mass of his own countrymen. It posed the essential dilemma of Hamilton: there was too much at stake, either way, for him to lose.

Part Two

A NOTABLE DISSEMBLER
January 1639 – December 1643

The prince who relies upon their words, without having
otherwise provided for his security, is ruined; for friend-
ships that are won by awards, and not by greatness and
nobility of soul, although deserved, yet are not real, and
cannot be depended upon in time of adversity.

MACHIAVELLI

CHAPTER VIII

FIRE AND SWORD

When Hamilton arrived at Court on January 5th he was received with all the honour and friendship which Charles was accustomed to bestow on him, no matter how futile his advice, how fruitless his actions. "[His] credit and power with the King", noted the Earl of Northumberland, "is thought to be much increased since his late employments into Scotland."[1] Rumours of his infidelity died away. Now the marquis assured his attentive master that only if he approved the Assembly's decision thus far, and allowed them to be enacted as law, would war be avoided.

It was obvious that Charles was at present in no position to wage war, and would not be until March at the earliest. In England the long period of inactivity had led to complacence, so that even the most belligerent spirits held back, and in Scotland the only hope of support for royal policy lay with Huntly and his Gordons, a fighting force no more than 2,000 strong. Many Royalists professed to fear Hamilton and Court intrigues, whether real or imagined, more than the actual Scottish war plans:

> We feared not the Scots from the
> Highland nor Lowland,
> Though some of their leaders did craftily
> brave us,
> With boasting long service in Russia
> and Poland,
> And with their fierce breeding under
> Gustavus.
>
> Not the tales of their combats
> more strange than romances,
> Nor Sandy's screwed cannon did strike
> us with wonder;
> Nor their kettle-drums sounding before
> their long lances,
> But Scottish Court whispers struck
> surer than thunder.[2]

For their part, the Covenanters were not impressed by the list of great names ranged against them, as the following ballad shows:

> The Devil, the Pope, the King of Spain,
> The Jesuit, the Arminian,
> Lewd Laud with his cursed incantations,
> Queen Mother, incendiary of all nations,
> Treacherous Huntly! Grand Dunbar,
> The miscreant match of Hell, Traquair,
> Ambitious-hearted Lauderdale,
> Sole hazarder for the front seal;
> Douglas, the Pope's patriot,
> Drunken Menstrie,* that copper Scot,
> The mighty Marquis Hamilton,
> Whose land was bought with two of ten,
> Spottiswoode, chief president of bribes,
> Scandal of Justinian's tribes. . . .[3]

Moreover, it was painfully evident that the King's opponents in England sympathised with his enemies in Scotland. The play *The Valiant Scot*, in which the Covenanter stood in the flimsy guise of William Wallace, was applauded by the London theatre-goers as much for its message as for its presentation, and in many a City ale-house, no less than in many a Puritan dining-room, men were wishing the Scots well in their struggle for religious liberty.[4]

Hamilton had the wit to realise that in such circumstances caution was required: resolved as he and Charles were on war, they could not risk it yet. But the marquis advised the fortification of Newcastle, an open and vulnerable target for a Scots attack, and as winter gave way to spring the war plan proceeded. An army of 30,000 horse and foot was to be raised, and Charles would lead it in person. Berwick was to be garrisoned with 2,000 men under Sir Jacob Astley, and Carlisle, as we have heard, with 500 under Lord Clifford. A fleet would be sent to the Firth of Forth, from whence it would cruise off the Scottish coast to interfere with trade and land troops at loyalist Aberdeen. Indeed, Charles toyed with the idea of sending Hamilton to the Highlands in

---

* William Alexander, Earl of Stirling.

command of 5,000 men who would join up with Huntly's forces under the Commissioner's supreme command. Such an army, it was argued, would secure the north of Scotland and then sweep southwards as the royal army advanced, so that the Covenanters would be faced with an enemy on two fronts. Antrim would land on the coast of Argyllshire with over 10,000 men, ostensibly to enforce his claims on Kintyre, but really to contain the Campbells, whose fighting strength was reputed to consist of some 5,000 men. At the same time, Lord Deputy Wentworth would come over with the Irish Army, and Hamilton offered him the Isle of Arran as a base, with provisions and the support of the Hamilton tenants—"such naked rogues as they were".[5]

Early in February Charles named his officers: his selections were not all of the best. The Earl Marshal of England, Arundel—whose notions of warfare were somewhat outdated—was nominal Commander-in-Chief. The Earl of Essex, a professional soldier who had seen service under the Dutch and who was at least competent, was appointed Lieutenant-General of the Foot. His Puritan connections made him a prudent choice in view of the mounting Protestant criticism of Court policy. By contrast, the appointment of the Earl of Holland to command the Horse was unwise and unpopular, since in listening to Henrietta's pleas on behalf of her favourite, Charles had antagonised Arundel and Essex, who saw no reason why command of the Horse should not be their joint responsibility. But the Queen was recovering from the birth of the short-lived Princess Katherine, her seventh confinement, and one which had nearly taken her life; the King could refuse her nothing.

Hamilton seems to have acquiesced in Holland's appointment, if only because no important cavalry operations were anticipated. Understandably, his own appointment in charge of the fleet deeply annoyed the Lord High Admiral, Northumberland, who resented being passed over by one who, as Hamilton was the first to admit, knew nothing of the sea and ships. Charles himself silenced the marquis's protestations of ignorance by informing him that the veteran sailor Pennington would accompany the expedition as vice-admiral.

Huntly, now officially Lieutenant of the North, was instructed to be strictly on the defensive unless he was so seriously provoked or royal authority so grievously affronted that he could not avoid a confrontation. It was feared that if a conflict broke out before Charles had reached the Border, Huntly and his forces would be overwhelmed.

Meanwhile Charles despatched letters to the Lords Lieutenants of the counties, instructing them to levy men; and to the nobility, requiring them to meet him at York on April 1st. Armaments were in short supply, and shipments from Holland were found to be largely defective; the men conscripted from the shires were ill-trained and badly armed, and many were downright mutinous. Added to these difficulties, money was scarce. The prolonged stay at Court of the Queen's widowed mother, Marie de Medici, following a rift with her son, Henri II of France, had all but drained the Exchequer, and Charles could raise only £200,000. To make matters worse, Edinburgh and Dumbarton Castles fell to the Covenanters, under Leslie, late in March, and the Earl of Dorset was not slow to blame Hamilton for this turn of events. The Commissioner, he thundered at a full meeting of the Privy Council, deserved nothing less than to lose his head.[6]

Charles finally left London on March 27th and arrived at York on April 1st. Hamilton remained at Whitehall in order to superintend the naval preparations, though he lacked the expertise to carry out his task efficiently, and it was not until the end of April that he set sail with his eight warships and twenty colliers. He found the soldiers he was transporting able-bodied and well-clothed, but many of their arms were defective and few were trained: he estimated that of the 5,000 only 200 had ever handled a musket. "I was never a great undertaker, and now to promise much, considering who they are that goeth with me, were madness, yet this much I will say, I shall be able to make a great diversion, and keep them in perpetual alarms", he wrote from the cramped cabin of his flagship, *The Rainbow*, lying in Yarmouth Roads, adding, in the histrionic way he sometimes employed, "If I do not vex them, hang me at my return."[7]

For days the weather was wet and windy, and it was not until April 29th that the fleet reached Holy Island, the craggy outpost off the bleak coast of Northumberland. There Hamilton received the King's written instructions to issue a proclamation in Edinburgh offering pardon to all who laid down their arms within eight days and "proceed with fire and sword against all those that shall disobey the same".[8] The King looked forward to a "merry

meeting" with his admiral in Scotland, but told him to "think
not of the north until I have done some good in the south".[9]

On May Day Hamilton's fleet entered the mouth of the Forth
and anchored in Leith Roads. Immediately the procession of
sails hoved into view, the Covenanters on the coast lit beacons to
warn him away. The fishermen of Fifeshire and East Lothian,
watching his manoeuvrings with sullen suspicion, drove away his
landing parties searching for water. The next day his men landed
at two small islands in the Forth—one regiment of 1,500 under
Sir Nicholas Byron on Inchkeith and two of 3,000 combined,
under Sir Thomas Morton and Sir Simon Harcourt, on Inchcolm.
They dared not approach the mainland, and the Covenanters
vowed to refuse them water even if it meant poisoning all the
wells in the area.[10] The most irksome behaviour of all, perhaps,
was that of Hamilton's mother, that "notable virago",[11] who had
already cast her lot with the rebels. Not for Anne Cunningham
the embroidery needle when God's cause was at stake. She had
been busy raising a troop of horse—most of its members Hamilton's own tenants—bearing the motto "For God, the King,
Religion and the Covenant". Now, hearing of her son's approach,
she rode at their head from Kinneil to Leith, armed with pistols
and daggers, and threatening to kill him if he stepped ashore.
She had—or so the rumour went—silver bullets specially prepared
for the purpose, since lead bullets could not pierce the magic
armour of the Devil's agent.[12] The Covenanters were amused,
and there were merry whispers that "the son of so good a mother
could do them no harm".[13]

But her conduct not only made Hamilton a laughing-stock: it
embarrassed and infuriated the King. He had promised Lord
William Hamilton—who badly wanted the Earldom of Dalziel—
the Earldom of Dunbar, but when news of the old marchioness'
activities reached his ears he tore the patent up in anger.[14] However, his pique subsided sufficiently for him to create Lord
William Earl of Lanark on March 31st 1639. Perhaps he felt that
it would be unfair to punish the young man for his mother's
errors.

Meanwhile Hamilton, on his second day at anchor, sent ashore
a servant, Andrew Cole, with a letter addressed to his "loving
friends", the Provost, Magistrates and Council of the City of
Edinburgh, requesting them to behave as "loyal, dutiful and good

subjects" and obey the proclamation "so that, by your good example, the rest of this kingdom may do the like, which will be a means for you to redeem his majesty's favour which you have justly lost".[15] But Cole was turned back at Leith, and Hamilton, growing increasingly irritated, adopted a different tone. He commanded the Clerk of the City Council to issue the proclamation in the King's name at twelve noon on May 5th at the Mercat Cross. The order was disregarded, but the unfortunate admiral, believing it would be carried out, ordered the fleet's cannon fired to mark the triumphant moment. He and his fleet had become the butt of derision:

> The Rainbow was to man a sign of peace:
> This doth portend much blood—no sign of grace.
> God's Rainbow stayed the floods—O greatest wonder!
> This threats to burn us all with fiery thunder.
> What grief!—that he who hoped to grace our land,
> Should, to destroy it, in his Rainbow stand!

wrote a zealous minister, Patrick Hamilton, and several lines more.[16]

"You will find it a work of great difficulty and of vast expense to curb them by force, their power being greater, their combination stronger, than imagined", he warned Charles.[17] It was no wonder that he was dissatisfied with the whole naval enterprise. His scope for initiative was limited, for he could do nothing until the King had crossed the Border. His men were forced to send to Holy Island, the nearest friendly base, for provisions, since the Scots on shore repeatedly refused his request for fresh victuals, and told him that if he wanted water he would have to fetch it himself.[18] A smallpox scare among his troops had proved unfounded, but now there loomed the new danger of scurvy. His mother refused to meet him, and the local traders insolently rejected his request for a roll of cloth to make him a new suit. It particularly rankled with him that the Covenanters were using various English noblemen, including the Earls of Newcastle, Essex and Holland, as intermediaries with the King—"I do not write this to put jealousy in your majesty but methinks it is strange."[19] Like his father before him, he had paid the price for the favour of a King who reigned from London: he had lost the goodwill of his own countrymen. That which he most dreaded had come to pass, and

Argyll and a band of marauding Campbells crossed from Kintyre to Arran and sacked Brodick Castle. They remained in control of the island for several years.[20] Montrose stormed Aberdeen, browbeat Huntly into signing a modified version of the Covenant, and sent him to Edinburgh as a virtual prisoner. Such was the fate of the King's Lieutenant of the North.

On May 9th about fifty leading Covenanters, including General Leslie, Argyll, Balmerino, Rothes, Eglinton, and Hamilton's brothers-in-law, Lindsay and Montgomery, wrote to him explaining that they would not obey the proclamation since it entailed abandoning the Covenant, but they promised that if a Parliament was to be held, as they had long desired, he would find them "humble, good and dutiful".[21] The Commissioner's answer—in a letter to Rothes—was an icy rebuke. Their refusal to publish the proclamation constituted "a liberty taken to yourselves which never any loyal subjects assumed in any monarchy", he charged. The proclamation was not illegal, as they claimed, he protested, and their allegation that the King had persistently refused to consider any of their petitions was sheer nonsense, and designed to justify their "unwarranted actions" before the ordinary people of Scotland.[22]

Rothes' reply was equally cold. "It was far from my expectation, or your grace's oath and promise, that you should ever come in any chief command against your native country", he observed. "I hope you conceive that this navy and army upon the borders, and the invasion threatened in the west, do sufficiently warrant our preparations to defend these places and divert such danger."[23] "It is true", Hamilton answered, "knowing my own inability, I neither desired, nor indeed willingly did accept, the conduct of an army against this nation, but my backwardness proceeded not out of desire not to be employed against such in this country as were disobedient, but that his majesty might have found many more able to have served him, but since he hath been pleased to trust me, I will not deceive him." He added, "that can never be called violence which is only to suppress rebellion."[24] It was a desperate attempt to justify himself in the eyes of the Scots.

He had already been approached by Southesk and others, who implored him to tread carefully, since the Covenanting fervour was too strong to be easily allayed. Now, despairing of getting the proclamation published, Hamilton sent many copies of it for distribution throughout the land. Angry letters from Covenanting noblemen continued to bombard him, and his brother-in-law, Lindsay, told him candidly that they would die rather than abandon the Covenant, and boasted that their infantry was superior to the King's.[25]

On May 17th Charles wrote from Newcastle commanding his admiral not to fight until the royal army had appeared on the Border (which would take another eight days) unless the whole Covenanting army pressed down upon him in the meantime. And so the only activity the fleet could undertake was the harassment of local fishing boats and the seizure of Scottish merchant vessels.[26] Hamilton himself had embarked on his accustomed game of playing for time, pretending to negotiate with the rebels on terms approved by Charles. Only if they would lay down their arms and quietly disperse, surrender the royal castles and the houses of loyalists which they had seized, could a treaty be considered. If they would express deep regret at offending Charles, and seek his pardon, their stand against the bishops and their proceedings in the Assembly might be considered in the next Parliament, to be deemed just or unjust, as the members thought fit.[27]

"If I do not my part, then let me be hanged at my return", Hamilton told the King in a letter reminiscent of his despondent despatch prior to the dissolution of the Glasgow Assembly. "This my duty and allegiance ties me to, and over and above that, so powerfully do I hate this rebellious nation, as I had rather lose my life than not in my own particular be revenged on them. . . ." Yet he was aware of the general opinion of his conduct in both the King's and the Covenanters' ranks: "Though I am confident your majesty doth neither take me for a traitor or a coward . . . I know there will be those that will infer that my not entering into greater acts of hostility than I have done was a fault, and so labour to take that part of your majesty's favour from me which without any merit of mine you have been graciously pleased to confer."[28]

He did nothing to dispel his reputation for treachery by the secret talks he had with some of the Covenanting leaders in his clumsy attempt at reaching a solution acceptable to both sides. Well-meaning though indiscreet, he tended to emphasise the cloak and dagger aspect of these negotiations by meeting the rebels in remote spots at night. It was widely believed that he met Argyll's henchman, the Earl of Loudoun, at midnight on the links of Barnbougall for a conference lasting two hours, though it may have been merely that he ran aground there when pursuing a Covenanting merchantman too closely, and while waiting to be set afloat had left his ship to go searching for water with some members of his crew. At any rate, when this charge was flung at him several years later he denied it vigorously.[29]

But even more detrimental to his reputation was the episode involving Lord Aboyne. Huntly's eighteen-year-old second son, bent on raising the Gordons to release their chief, had appeared before Charles on May 3rd, imploring him to order Hamilton to deploy some of the English troops under his command to aid the Royalists in Aberdeen and Banff. This the King agreed to do, and sent his admiral a letter by way of the young lord, instructing Hamilton not to burden him with monetary expense, since he had already strained his finances, yet "as for what assistance you can spare him [Aboyne] out of the forces that are with you, I leave you to judge", adding, "if, with the countenance and assistance of what force you have, you may uphold my party in the north, and the rest of those noblemen I have sent to you, I shall esteem it a very great service."[30]

It seems fair to say that, with the best will in the world, Hamilton could have given Aboyne little practical assistance. He could not aid him financially, and his two regiments had already left for Berwick where they would join the main body of the royal forces. Forgetting the heroic daydreams of his own youth, he was peeved by Aboyne's buoyance and impetuosity. "I wish the Lord Aboyne was a little more stayed", he complained to Charles.[31] He might even have perceived Aboyne as a threat to his own place in the King's affections; as always, he could brook no rival. Yet he managed to conceal his feelings, and welcomed the young man aboard *The Rainbow* in Leith Roads with feasting and drinking, firing the cannon at every health, a custom he had learned in Denmark. But owing to the shortage of victuals he could not entertain him for long and sent him north with one ship, a limited supply of ammunition, four small pieces of artillery and a few field officers under the command of Colonel William Gunn, to whom, unknown to Aboyne though it is not clear why, he gave £500, and to whom, with some difficulty, he managed to persuade Aboyne to subordinate himself. He could make as much noise in Aberdeen as he wished. "I do not see any great service that he can do you in these parts", he told Charles sourly, "considering the abilities of the young man."[32] In all probability, he could hardly have furnished Aboyne with more military equipment than he did, and the King had specifically instructed him not to involve him in debt; yet it was widely reported that Gunn was a secret Covenanter, and that Hamilton had purposely associated him with Aboyne in order to betray the Royalist cause in Aberdeen.[33] The hapless admiral "committed so many palpable errors in the execution of his charge", wrote a Gordon sympathiser, that he aroused suspicions that he was doing his best to ensure a Royalist defeat.[34]

Rumours might abound, but the King was well pleased with the marquis's behaviour: "I would think myself a happy man if I could be as confident in the faith, courage and industry of the rest of my commanders and officers as I am of you."[35] Hamilton had some blunt advice to offer him: "it is now time for your majesty to speak like yourself, and to declare the heads of them traitors."[36] The Covenanters were seriously thinking of sending a delegation to Charles with an outline of their grievances, and demanding two noblemen—of whom Hamilton would be one—as hostages for their safe-conduct, but this idea was abandoned owing to the opposition of Argyll and Rothes, who considered it insolent and provocative.[37] The Scots had by now almost completely by-passed Hamilton as an intermediary, and were addressing themselves more and more to English noblemen. As Argyll wrote to the Earl of Holland at the end of May: "always if you love his majesty or the peace of his dominions, it is time to inquire where the fault lies, that as we must live by our own faith, let us not die by another's error, but let your own knowledge and no sinister information direct you both to advise and execute for his majesty's service."[38]

Clearly his own countrymen had little faith in Hamilton, who now sought to poison Charles's mind against his English rivals by hinting that they were traitors: "better it were for your service that they were declared Covenanters than to lay in your Court and betray you." He also tried to end the communication between the noblemen concerned and the Scots by advising Charles to command them to tell the Covenanters in no uncertain terms that they had no sympathy with them.[39]

The King ignored these suggestions, but on June 4th he

informed Hamilton that "I set you loose to do what mischief you can do upon the rebels for my service with those men you have, for you cannot have one man from hence".[40] But just two days after Hamilton had received this message he was in possession of another, summoning him to the royal camp at Berwick for negotiations with the Covenanters, and he arrived there on Friday, June 7th. The following Tuesday, when the Commissioners from the two sides met—Coke, Vane, Holland, Essex and Arundel on the Royalist side and Rothes, Loudoun, Dunfermline, Henderson and William Douglas, Sheriff of Teviotdale, on the other—they were joined unexpectedly by Charles, Lennox and Hamilton. Here Rothes made to blackmail the King, by threatening that if he persisted in trying to maintain Episcopacy in Scotland, the Covenanters would set out to destroy it in England.[41] As for Hamilton, he joined Morton in remonstrating passionately with the Scottish Commissioners, and yet his "way was yet so ambiguous that no man understood him, only his absolute power with the King was there clearly seen".[42] But if he opposed the Covenanters in public, he did also in private. Warriston, eavesdropping outside the royal tent, overheard him tell the King that if he gave way to their demands for annual general assemblies he might as well say farewell to his "three crowns", for if the Covenanters were granted this concession they would go on to demand others, which would ultimately lead to the overthrow of the monarchy not only in Scotland but in England and Ireland as well.[43] Advice of this sort did not win for Hamilton the reputation of loyalty; rather, his enemies, both then and later, maintained that he told Charles to resist the Covenanters so that they might all the more resolutely defy him.[44] It was even suggested that he made a dishonest profit out of the naval expedition, by pocketing all but £2,000 of the £13,000 Charles gave him for expenses.[45]

True to his love of intrigue and his anxiety for compromise, Hamilton suggested to Charles that since he could not abolish Episcopacy or give way to the Covenanters until times more advantageous to him, he could at least win the rebels over by favourable promises. The King refused to ratify the proceedings of the Glasgow Assembly, as the Covenanting negotiators insisted, but agreed to call a new Assembly and ratify its decisions in a Parliament. On June 18th, a week after the opening of the Berwick talks, an agreement was reached, and the resultant treaty signed in Lord Arundel's tent. The new Assembly was to convene on August 6th and Parliament to meet in Edinburgh on August 20th. Charles would come to Scotland to open Parliament in person. For their part, the Covenanters agreed to disband their forces and deliver up the royal fortresses they had occupied and the ammunition they had captured, restore any appropriated Royalist property to its owners and not attend meetings or convocations.[46] Although Charles was fully aware that the new Assembly he had granted would reintroduce the acts of its predecessor at Glasgow, he knew that in some respects he had outwitted and impressed the Scottish delegation during the course of the Berwick negotiations, and they were forced to concede the depth of his legal knowledge.

On June 20th, Hamilton, as Royal Commissioner, left Berwick for Edinburgh, where four days later he had peace officially proclaimed, and received the keys of the Castle on the King's behalf. By his own unwavering opposition to the Treaty of Berwick, he had become "odious" to the Covenanters,[47] and the King's declaration, since then, of the "pretended" General Assembly, had so incensed them that already, in the few days following the peace, an uneasy atmosphere was apparent. When Hamilton went to install Ruthven of Ettrick as Governor of Edinburgh Castle, he was harassed on his walk from Holyrood along the Cannongate by hundreds of jeering demonstrators who forced their way into the Castle with him, and hurled abusive cries of "Traitor!" at him and called upon him to "Stand by Jesus Christ!"[48]

CHAPTER IX

TOWARDS ANOTHER WAR

On July 5th Hamilton handed Charles a memorandum warning him that since the Covenanters clearly did not intend to disband their army he would either have to grant their demands in full or fight a new war, and if the second and more likely course was taken he would have to summon an English Parliament in the hope that it would grant him the necessary funds. In Hamilton's mind the essential dilemma was "whether it be fit to give way to the madness of the people, or of new to intend a kingly way?"[1]

Always indifferent to the Church and churchmen, he now urged the King to abolish the rank of bishop, holding this sacrifice necessary if order was to be restored in Scotland. Here, of course, he reckoned without Charles's obstinate but completely sincere belief in Episcopacy. And yet by accepting Hamilton's memorandum in essence the King did seem to be heeding the anti-treaty philosophy of his most trusted adviser. Indeed, the Scottish commissioners had already begun to circulate a paper in which they maintained that Charles had said things which indicated a modification of many of the conditions of the treaty.[2] It was even rumoured that he had ordered the treaty to be burned by the common hangman.[3]

Meanwhile the King had requested Loudoun to send fourteen of the leading Covenanters to meet him at Berwick, and he ordered Hamilton back to Scotland as Commissioner. This is what the marquis had most been dreading, and on July 8th he sent the King an impassioned plea, begging to be relieved of his office:

> The hatred that is generally carried me, and in
> particular by the chief covenanters, will make them
> (hoping thereby either to ruin me, or at least make
> my service not acceptable) stand more peremptorily on
> these other points of civil obedience, which your
> majesty aims at, than they would do to one that is less
> hated. Since they are the same men I have formerly

> treated with, they cannot but find these particulars,
> which I have often sworn and said your majesty would
> never condescend to, will now be granted: therefore
> they will give no credit to what I shall say thereafter,
> but will still hope and believe that all their desires will
> be given way to, thinking, as they have often said, that
> I had power to condescend to more, but would not,
> that I might endear myself to your majesty, and be
> thought a deserving servant, in procuring more than
> you was [sic] content to accept of. [4]

As always, he feared the enmity of his own countrymen. Such
was the "rage and malice" of the Scots against him that he had
been advised not to return in the role of Commissioner if he
valued his life. He was afraid that Charles would punish his
assassins, thus ending any prospects of peace in Scotland. He
warned the King that if he continued to be employed as Commissioner the Scots would come to believe that Charles intended
to rule Scotland by means of a Commissioner, but if another were
appointed, this would not appear so, because the continuity
would be broken. Above all, he dreaded the consequences of
failure in his role, of losing the King's favour. [5]

Reluctantly, Charles agreed to appoint another as Commissioner, and the honour fell upon Traquair, who was not keen
to go. [6] On July 12th and again on the 15th he reported to Hamilton,
who was sharing the King's quarters at Berwick, [7] and who had
permission to answer all but the most involved of Traquair's
letters without consulting his master, telling him of the Covenanters' attitude towards the King's request that fourteen of
them meet him at Berwick. There was a rumour that they might
be in danger if they came. [8] On July 16th six leading Covenanters
including Montrose, Rothes and Warriston, arrived at the royal
headquarters, and it was now that Hamilton and Charles entered
into an extraordinary and misunderstood arrangement, lending
the marquis the role at once of peacemaker and of spy, but more
often making him appear in the eyes of Covenanters and Royalists
alike as a traitor. For on July 17th Charles issued him with a
secret warrant:

> We do by these presents not only authorise, but require
> you to use all the means you can, with such of the

Covenanters who come to Berwick, to learn which way
they intend the estate of Bishops shall be supplied in
Parliament; what our power shall be in ecclesiastical
affairs; and what farther their interests are. For which
end, you will be necessitated to speak that language,
which if you were called to an account by us, you
might suffer for it. These are therefore to assure you,
and, if need be, hereafter to testify to others, that
whatsoever you shall say to them, you shall neither be
called in question for the same, nor yet it prove
anyways prejudicial to you; nay, though you shall be
accused by any thereupon.[9]

Hamilton took full advantage of this warrant by ingratiating
himself with the King's opponents north of the Border, and
regaining some of his old influence in Scotland. From Loudoun
and Lothian he learned that the Covenanters planned to abolish
Episcopacy in the next Scots Parliament and intended to alter the
method of introducing legislation by the Lords of the Articles, as
a step towards limiting Parliament's power.[10] He seems also to
have discovered that they were bent on obtaining freedom of
worship for the Puritans in England; biennial, or at least triennial,
parliaments, and that they wanted the fortresses of Scotland to be
under the control not of Charles alone, but of the King and the
Estates. They were also insisting that the Privy Council and the
judiciary be selected by Parliament.[11] Such innovations struck
Hamilton as sinister and subversive.

On July 20th the six Covenanting representatives were dismissed
by Charles and returned to Edinburgh with a list of his grievances.
Dunfermline, Loudoun and Lindsay, meanwhile, travelled to
Berwick to try to explain their position to Charles. But he would
not see them. In the circumstances he had abandoned any idea of
going to Edinburgh to attend the opening of the General Assembly
or of Parliament. Indeed, like Hamilton, he viewed another war
as inevitable. "Come when you will", he had already written to
Wentworth, "you shall be welcome."[12]

The object, again, was to win time. Traquair would wait upon
events, seeing the proposed Assembly and Parliament through,
with leave to agree to almost anything and make use of almost
anyone. Charles, realising that he could do nothing to weaken

the Covenanters' stand, returned to London, arriving at Whitehall on August 3rd. Hamilton seemed as indispensable to him as before, and shared his bedroom for the rest of the year. It was a singular honour for the marquis, for it indicated the King's protection and favour.

Traquair's commission was signed on August 6th, and six days later the Assembly opened in Edinburgh. In essence it turned out to be a repetition of the Glasgow Assembly: Traquair, who implied that he came as Hamilton's spokesman—"I can act nothing but the part of an echo"[13]—and who was, in fact, being prevailed upon by Lennox to avoid "anything that may give the Covenanters cause of suspicion of what [the King's] intentions are",[14] proved as powerless as the marquis in preventing the flood of legislation approved by the delegates, and within a week they had voted to abolish Episcopacy and had rejected the King's religious policy out of hand.

Hamilton was not unduly worried; his concern was that time be gained for the King's military preparations. "It matters not much how many informalities or illegalities be in your proceedings", he reminded Traquair, "so it causes not a rupture".[15] On August 16th his brother-in-law, the Covenanting Lord Lindsay, wrote to inform him that Traquair was indeed proving a good servant to his King, and most unsympathetic to the Covenanters.[16] Hamilton, clumsily groping for time, still playing the conciliator, still fumbling in the role of spy, yet above all seeking for himself the goodwill of his countrymen, sent Lindsay a faint-hearted reply from Whitehall four days later. He regretted that his brother-in-law's letter and Traquair's did not agree, since the latter complained of the behaviour of the Assembly, but he hoped they would receive the King's reply as they "ought", he said. He lamented that despite all his efforts on the King's behalf many Royalists considered him "the pernicious man", yet he was confident that in time they would come to appreciate his loyal conduct.[17]

On August 30th the Scots Parliament met, and, guided by Argyll, just managed to push through a proposal that in future each estate would elect its own Lords of the Articles, the group responsible for initiating legislation. The lairds and burgesses together would elect sixteen members and the nobles eight: the King was thus divested of any influence.[18] Even more damaging to royal authority was the decision to impose a general tax to provide funds for the Covenanting cause, and the demand that only Scotsmen be appointed to command the royal castles with the approval of the Estates. Furthermore, the perplexed Traquair had been unable to quash the Assembly's demands that all male Scots be made to sign the Covenant.

It had become apparent to Charles that the prospect of a peaceful settlement was fast disappearing, and on September 22nd Wentworth arrived at Court. He had voiced suspicions of Hamilton, and his solution to the Scottish problem, indeed, would have included no room for the marquis, since he believed that the governor of a vanquished Scotland should be an Englishman— preferably himself.[19] Naturally, any move to create a Lord Deputy of Scotland must, in the marquis's view, be based on the premise that the appointee be not only a Scot, but a Scot of overwhelming stature in the country, and this could only mean the head of the House of Hamilton. On these fundamentals the two ministers were diametrically opposed.

At the end of October Charles ordered Traquair to prorogue the rebellious Scottish Parliament, but the opposition was too formidable, and all that the Commissioner could do was gain a brief adjournment until November 14th whilst he consulted with the King. The Scots, meanwhile, sent Dunfermline and Loudoun to Whitehall to present their case to Charles, but he refused to hear them on the grounds that their commission had not been signed by Traquair. They felt that they had been shabbily treated by the "junta"—the members of the English Privy Council committee with responsibility for Scottish affairs, consisting of Hamilton, Wentworth, Laud, Windebank and Juxon—and the King's attitude kindled their discontent. He instructed Traquair to suspend the Scottish Parliament until June 2nd 1640, and only after he had done so was the hapless Commissioner allowed to return to Whitehall to deliver an account of his progress to his master.[20]

On December 5th the English Privy Council formally conceded the necessity of war, and Wentworth, supported by Hamilton, advocated the calling of a Parliament. Before that, however, he would himself summon an Irish Parliament to vote money for the Scottish campaign, and thereby provide the English with a good example. The Privy Council undertook to advance Charles a loan of £200,000, but beneath their optimism lurked the uneasy fear that Parliament might refuse to grant the necessary war funds and the certainty that, if it eventually did agree to do so, it would be in return for the redressing of its many grievances. It would extort from Charles a terrible price for its favours. Moreover the major cities, London in particular, were Puritan in their sympathies and had little love for the Court party. They would be unlikely to grant the required money.[21]

The Council of War for the coming assault on Scotland was appointed on December 30th, and included Hamilton, who was again entrusted with the navy, Wentworth, Vane, Windebank, Northumberland, who was made Commander-in-Chief of the royal forces, Conway, who was given the cavalry command, and the indefatigable veteran Sir Jacob Astley.[22] Apart from Hamilton these were men whom Wentworth, the dominant figure in these war councils, could trust: he got on particularly well with Northumberland. The war plan now hammered out was similar to that proposed earlier. Whilst Northumberland would advance to the Border and invade southern Scotland, Wentworth's 6,000 Irish troops would land on the west coast of Scotland near Ayr, and Hamilton's squadron would blockade the coast and divert the Scots' attention by disembarking troops in the north-east, probably in the Gordon country around Aberdeen, which would serve to rally the loyalists as it had done in the previous expedition. At the same time, Berwick and Edinburgh Castle were ordered to be secured and strengthened, and arms and ammunition were ordered for the coming hostilities.[23]

On January 12th Wentworth achieved a long-standing ambition when he received the Earldom of Strafford, that part of Yorkshire where his lands chiefly lay, being simultaneously promoted from Lord Deputy to Lord Lieutenant of Ireland. He and Hamilton bore little love toward each other, as the appointment of the new Secretary of State showed. For in the meantime the septuagenarian Sir John Coke had been dismissed as Secretary owing to his failing powers, and the Earl of Leicester, Northumberland's brother-in-law, expressed strong interest in the vacant post. His candidature was firmly supported by Strafford, but Hamilton, abetted by Henrietta Maria, pressed the claims of Sir Henry Vane, Comptroller of the Household, with whom Strafford had recently quarrelled over the title of Raby, Vane's family seat, which had once belonged to the Wentworth family. To Vane's bitter indignation Strafford had sought for his son the courtesy title Viscount Raby. As a result the Court had tended to split into two factions, the one supporting Vane and the other Strafford. A wave of outraged sympathy temporarily surrounded the Comptroller, who on February 3rd 1640 was made Secretary of State. Ambitious as he was, he felt no gratitude to the Queen and Hamilton, whose intrigues had gained him a post for which he was not suited, and he afterwards complained that the marquis had procured it for him in order to embarrass him.[24]

Then, on February 21st, the old Earl of Stirling, Secretary of State for Scotland, died at his residence in Covent Garden, and Traquair made it clear to Hamilton that he was expecting to be appointed in Stirling's place.[25] But Charles, ignoring his claims, made a double appointment: Sir James Galloway and the Earl of Lanark were to be joint secretaries, residing at Court to receive the King's instructions on Scots affairs. Lanark was to have special responsibility for the Scottish Privy Council in England.

Hamilton's satisfaction with these appointments was soured by the obvious discontent he felt at the prospect of again engaging in war against his own countrymen. How much greater would be the "rage and malice" of those who had vented their wrath against him as Commissioner. Still, he stumbled on along the path destiny had marked out for him, urging that Edinburgh Castle be strongly garrisoned in order to isolate the chief town from the rest of the kingdom, and on one occasion he stepped in personally to ensure that a shipment of armaments came safely into the Castle.[26] "I care not", he told Lindsay, who had warned him that "unavoidable ruin" would be his if he took up arms against his fellow Scots, "for I have laid my account long since, and am resolved on the worst that can befall me." But he added, "nothing can grieve me more in this world than to be sent in any hostile manner against my friends, kindred, and country". He told Lindsay that without the King's favour he could not bear to live in England, and he attempted to rationalise his command by pointing out that if he was not in charge, someone abler would be, to the greater disadvantage of the Scots. Yet he still hoped for a peaceful solution by which "the effusion of much Christian blood will be saved, the country preserved, Scotsmen esteemed valiant, just and loyal, not only in this Kingdom but through all Europe". To encourage his brother-in-law to reconsider his position, he informed him that the King was ready to confer on him the Earldom of Crawford in exchange for his loyalty. In closing this letter, which was ratified by Charles, Hamilton described himself as "now much troubled".[27] He had need to be.

On February 20th Dunfermline and Loudoun had come to London for consultations with the King, but he had again refused to see them, and they had stayed on in the Capital. Then, in April, Loudoun was seized and imprisoned in the Tower on a charge of treason. As early as May 1639 the Covenanters had been thinking seriously of seeking the aid of Louis XIII of France in their dispute with Charles, and one of their messages had been intercepted by Traquair. Deeply subversive, it not only requested Louis's intervention, but was addressed "Au Roy"—"to the King".[28] Its signatories included Montrose, Rothes, Lord Montgomery and Loudoun, the only one in a position to be instantly arrested. The affair was to become an integral part of the case against the Scots which Charles was to present to the English Parliament, due to meet on April 13th. Extremely angry now, he impetuously ordered Loudoun's summary execution. This alarmed Hamilton, who with Sir William Balfour, governor of the Tower, hastened to the King's bedchamber and implored him to revoke the hasty sentence for fear of the inflammatory effect it would undoubtedly have on the Scots. Hamilton had frequent interviews with Loudoun inside the Tower, the most notable lasting from two in the morning until four in the afternoon, and on the strength of these talks he managed to persuade Charles that Loudoun could be bought and was worth purchasing. So on June 27th he was released, having agreed to move among the Covenanters as Charles' spy.[29] Hamilton's part in gaining Loudoun's liberty roused once more the suspicions of the Royalists; they began to watch him carefully.

When the new Parliament (in which Lanark sat as member for Portsmouth) met on April 13th it refused to grant the twelve subsidies the King asked for, in return for the renunciation of Ship Money, until he had redressed its grievances, and the Parliamentary leaders, flaunting their contempt in his face, opened negotiations with the Scots. Enraged, Charles dissolved Parliament on May 5th, after only three weeks. Not only had Strafford advised him to make use of Irish troops, he had also tried to get Spanish help. But Spain, like Parliament itself, France, the Vatican and the City of London, refused to lend Charles funds and he levied Ship Money again. Acting on Strafford's initiative, the Privy Councillors rallied round, and lent him nearly £200,000 out of their own pockets. Realising that it was expected of him— especially as he was under close scrutiny of the Royalists— Hamilton lent the King £10,000 in cash and a further £8,000 in gold; in the four years between 1638 and 1642 he loaned his sovereign almost £30,000 in cash, including, incredibly, £15,000 in 1641, when his relations with Charles were not at their best.[30]

At the end of April Hamilton was faced with troubles of a more personal kind: the death of his eldest son and heir, Charles, Earl of Arran, a sickly little boy aged five, who appears on a Van Dyck canvas in the guise of Cupid. His two other sons had already succumbed to the perils of seventeenth-century childhood, baby William in December 1638 and toddler James in April 1639. However much the marquis may have grieved privately, he appears to have kept his feelings very much to himself. Perhaps, in that hazardous age, he took his bereavements philosophically. But it is possible that this melancholy man with his tendency towards fatalism believed that these deaths were an indication that his brother was destined to succeed him, and may explain, in part, why he took no second wife.

His failure to remarry is certainly puzzling. As a nobleman with young children and an important household he would have sur- prised no one if he had married again after a decent period of mourning. But a certain piety and cynicism in Hamilton's nature may have determined him not to marry again. He may well have been influenced by a fond remembrance of Mary, considering remarriage a betrayal of her. His attitude to women is unclear. Burnet hints that he was seduced by "bewitching but deceiving charms" without specifying their nature, and tells us of the "foolish pleasures of sin" which long "possessed too great a room in his thoughts".[31] His father had been licentious, and so, too, was his brother for a time, but although he himself fathered an illegitimate daughter, Mary,[32] if he had many love affairs they have remained his secret.

His remaining a widower particularly chagrined his mother, whose dearest wish was that he remarry. "There is one thing that I would beseech him to above any earthly thing", she declared in her will, drawn up in November 1644, ". . . make choice of some good woman to match with, that, if it please the Lord, his father's house might stand in his person."[33] Although the question of his remarriage became crucial after the deaths of his sons, he was content that Lanark should succeed him.

CHAPTER X

BETWIXT KING AND KIRK

"Hamilton", observed the Earl of Northumberland to the Earl of Leicester on May 21st, "is most absolute at Court",[1] but by the mid-summer of 1640 he was a most unhappy man. The secure world which he had known for so long, yet never entirely taken for granted, had fallen apart. Whichever way he looked he saw the signs of ruin. He, Laud, Strafford and Cottington were marked men, for the King's opponents in England and Scotland were working in collusion to bring them down. By striking at the ministers, they were striking at the King. Hamilton's many reasons for despair are still best described in the words of Clarendon:

> The Marquis of Hamilton, if he had been weighed in the scales of the people's hatred, was at that time thought to be in greater danger than any of the other, for he had more enemies and fewer friends in Court or in country than either of the other [Strafford and Cottington]. . . . He had more outfaced the law in bold projects and pressures upon the people than any other man durst have presumed to do, as especially in the projects of wine and iron . . . the entire profit of which always reverted to himself and to such as were his pensioners. He had been the sole manager of the business in Scotland till the Pacification, and the most visible author of the breach of it. Lastly, the discoveries between the Lord Mackay and David Ramsay, wherein the marquis was accused of trying to make himself King of Scotland, were fresh in many men's memories, so that he might reasonably have expected as ill a presage for himself from those fortunetellers as the most melancholic of the other.[2]

On August 16th Charles, who had been spending the summer at Oatlands, summoned a meeting of the English Privy Council and announced his intention to leave immediately for York to be with his army. Hamilton, who had reservations about the war plans, questioned the advisability of this since the underpaid army was showing signs of disaffection, and he argued that the defence of Newcastle could be completed without the King being in the north. Although most councillors tended to agree with this, Strafford forcefully supported the King, suggesting, however, that he delay his journey for a few days until the Border had been secured.[3] Accordingly, he set out for York on August 20th, accompanied by Hamilton, Lennox, Holland and Pembroke. Strafford followed four days later.

Once again Hamilton showed himself to be an inadequate commander. He had been ordered to send ships to Ireland to convey the 6,000-strong army in Ulster to the coast of Ayrshire, but he deliberately failed to do so. Though Strafford and others were aghast at his inaction, he had good reasons for doing nothing. He well knew how bitter would be the Scots' reaction if Irish troops were used against them a second time, and Loudoun had written to warn him that Argyll had plans to send 10,000 troops from the west of Scotland across to Ulster at the first sign of the Irish army preparing to disembark.[4]

Hamilton, indeed, was in close contact with Argyll, and together they put before the Covenanting leaders a controversial proposal. It was that so long as the national emergency lasted Scotland should be partitioned into two regions, and that Argyll would have military control of the territory north of the Forth, while Hamilton would have identical powers in the territory south of it. This scheme had to be abandoned almost at once, mainly owing to the Covenanting army's distrust of Hamilton, who was, after all, the King's commander, and it aroused suspicions that the two noblemen were seeking to exploit the Scottish situation in their own interests, rather than aiming at a victory for either King or Covenant.[5]

Partly as a result of this, Montrose and seventeen like-minded nobles and gentlemen met that August at the Earl of Wigtons' residence at Cumbernauld, some thirteen miles north-east of Glasgow, and signed a pledge—known as the Cumbernauld Bond—to advance the "public ends" of the Covenant in opposition to the "particular and indirect practising of a few", by which they meant Argyll and Hamilton, though they did not name them.[6] Apart from the partition plan, the former had outraged

moderate opinion by his unnecessary violence towards clans and
families traditionally hostile to the Campbells (in particular the
Stewarts of Atholl and the Ogilvys of Airlie) whilst ostensibly
waging war on behalf of the Covenant.

Elsewhere, Montrose had a sharp warning obviously directed
at Hamilton:

> And you great men—if any such be among you so
> blinded with ambition, who aim so high as the Crown—
> do you think we are so far degenerate from the virtue,
> valour and fidelity to our true and lawful sovereign, so
> constantly entertained by our ancestors, as to suffer you,
> with all your policy, to reign over us? Take heed you
> be not Aesop's dog, and lose the cheese for the shadow
> in the well. [7]

Meanwhile, on August 20th, as the King began his journey
northwards, the Covenanting army, headed by Leslie, and with
Montrose conspicuously to the fore, crossed the Tweed at Cold-
stream and marched into England. By-passing Berwick, which
was heavily fortified, they advanced rapidly towards Newcastle,
threatening to burn all the collieries there unless the city yielded.
The commander of the garrison, Lord Conway, determined to
hold the Tyne at all costs, sent 3,000 of his best troops to guard
the ford at Newburn, some five miles to the west of Newcastle.
There, after less than two hours' fighting, they were routed, and
the following day, August 30th, the Scots entered the abandoned
garrison. [8]

This humiliating defeat, the swiftness of which surprised even
Leslie, caused consternation in the royal headquarters at York.
Again Hamilton came under heavy criticism for his failure to
send ships to Ireland, for if the Ulster army had been on Scottish
soil it would have diverted Leslie's rear. Foolishly, he did not
offer any explanation of his conduct, and rumours of treachery
exploded again. He was in an unenviable position, derided by all
sides.

The royal defeat at Newburn gave rise to the very real and
alarming possibility that his victorious countrymen might persecute him, along with Traquair and others, as an incendiary. For
on June 9th 1640 the Scottish Parliament passed an ominous
act: "all bad counsellors who instead of giving his majesty a true

and effauld counsel hath given or will give information and counsel to the evident prejudice and ruin of the liberties of this Kirk and kingdom should be exemplarly judged and censured."[9] It was not an empty threat, for a few months later the Committee of Estates summoned seventy-five noblemen, bishops, gentlemen and others to answer before Parliament for "their misinformations and seditious stirring up of his majesty".[10] There was no reason for Hamilton to be confident that next time their victims might not include him.

Yet south of the Border the outlook was even grimmer. There he faced the possibility of impeachment by an enraged Parliamentary opposition for his part in urging Charles to go to war the previous year. Indeed, some of the zealots were muttering that he should be brought to trial for stirring up mischief between the two kingdoms. At the same time, he faced the possibility that the English Royalists might interpret the failure of his whole Scottish policy since 1638 as treason, and try to prove it such. The outspoken Lady Devonshire, a middle-aged expatriate Scotswoman who had known him since his childhood and was one of his closest friends in London at this time, had more than once hotly rounded on him and called him a traitor. Her words reflected what other Royalists were thinking; they were not lost on him, and he carried the sound of them to his grave.

His reputation was further impaired by the wild ravings of a certain Crichton, a servant of the Bishop of Ross. On September 2nd 1640, meeting a Dr. Kipping, his physician, in an alehouse near the Old Bailey, Crichton babbled that he was in a position to know that Hamilton was "the archest traitor that ever betrayed any king", that he "lays claim to the crown, notwithstanding that, besides the King's children, the Prince Palatine be nearer in blood than he", and, furthermore, that he "has scouts abroad to hear what men say of him, fearing to be discovered".[11] Believing it his duty, Kipping hastened to Secretary Windebank to report what he had heard. The accusations were hardly new, but repeated and rehashed as they were, it was not surprising that in time all but the most sceptical came to credit them with a modicum of truth, and even Charles himself could not remain unaffected for ever.

Everywhere the writing was on the wall. A current rhyme mirrored the mood of the people:

Laudless Will of Lambeth Strand,
And Black Tom, tyrant of Ireland,
Like fox and wolf did lurk,
With many rooks and magpies,
To pick out good King Charles his eyes,
And then be Pope and Turk.[12]

Hamilton counted among the "rooks and magpies". He, Laud
and Strafford were Charles's most influential and most hated
ministers, and after the dissolution of the Short Parliament in
May, a placard-waving mob shouting anti-Episcopal slogans had
marched menacingly through London, howling for the blood of all
three of them.[13] Since that time, Hamilton had tried to persuade
Strafford and Laud to leave the country, but the former had been
"too great-hearted to fear" and the latter "too bold to fly",[14] and
Cottington had drifted more and more into Strafford's confidence.
Hamilton, remarked the Earl of Northumberland, who frankly
despised him, "seems to keep an interest in them all, but he
deceives the world if he hath kindness to them or anybody else".[15]

Groping after self-preservation, Hamilton found himself, little
by little, forming an uneasy alliance with the King's enemies.
The temper of the times made this inevitable, for Hamilton
understood much better than did Charles the realities of Scottish
politics and the precariousness of his own position in both kingdoms. He feared Argyll north of the Border and Pym south of it,
and somehow he would make his peace with both of them.

It proved easier for him to come to terms with the Scots, for
initially Charles had been able to protect him and Traquair from
their fury by telling the Covenanters that he would "not be
averse" to granting some of their demands if they "desist from
troubling" the two noblemen.[16] For a time, in fact, it was Montrose's turn to be alarmed when it was discovered that he had
been in secret communication with the King. No one knew
for certain how his letters came to light, but many held Hamilton
responsible, alleging that he searched the King's pockets at night
after he was asleep, and sent copies of the letters to the Scots'
camp at Newcastle. While he was certainly in close touch with the
Covenanters at this time,[17] the culprit may have been William
Murray. Whatever the source of this embarrassing disclosure,
Montrose was only temporarily nonplussed, and he quickly

asserted his right to communicate with his King, who also defended the correspondence. The complainants—Argyll chief among them —were silenced.

In the meantime, on September 2nd, Rothes had sent a petition to the Secretary of State, Lord Lanark, requesting that peace negotiations be opened, and three days later Lanark replied, in accordance with the King's instructions, that Charles would seek the advice of the English peers who were summoned to a Great Council at York on September 24th. But soon there were rumours of a Catholic revolt in Ireland and reports that Spanish troops would land, putting all Englishmen and Protestants to the sword. This scare spread across England and reached the troops at York. Throughout the summer it had been apparent that a sizeable portion of English opinion favoured the Scots, and welcomed the war which would end Laud's ecclesiastical tyranny and the Papism of the Queen. Many liberal-minded peers were of this opinion, including the Earls of Hertford, Bedford and Essex, and Bristol spoke for all of them. The Scots refused to come to York as long as Strafford, whom they regarded as their principal foe, was there, and it was clear that they hungered after his fall, if not his death. They believed that he would do all in his power to prevent a peace treaty, which, after all, would end the policy which he had followed for the past eleven years. The Great Council broke up at the end of October, by which time an armistice had been signed with the Scots and a writ sent out for a new Parliament. Until peace was concluded the Covenanting army was to occupy the six northernmost counties of England, and receive £860 daily. Meanwhile, commissioners from both sides, who had been meeting at Ripon, left for London so that Parliament could be consulted as to the final terms of the treaty.[18]

The Scots commissioners promised not to press their cases against Traquair and Hamilton, who had been appointed colonel of the King's personal regiment of 1,500 foot, and by December 1640 Baillie was happily writing that both noblemen, out of a mixture of gratitude and lingering anxiety, "both do us all the good they can, and would amend bygones by fair play now, to eschew the storm of incendiaries, if it were possible".[19] In Hamilton's case it was possible, for by the end of January 1641 he had succeeded in having the list of incendiaries reduced to five names—Traquair, who had become something of a scapegoat,

Dr. Balcanquall, Sir John Hay, Sir Robert Spottiswoode and the Bishop of Ross. "The marquis rules all the roost, and is much commended by all."[20] He had worked hard for his security: he had repeated the procedures he also used towards the King's English opponents and had promised rewards to those among the leading Covenanters who might prove moderate if given the chance of office. Rothes and Loudoun were those he concentrated on, and the winning of Argyll was his ultimate goal. This strategy not only helped to preserve him: it also held out the sinister hope that a Royalist party might be built up in Scotland.

Meanwhile Hamilton, the hated monopolist and embodiment of Court privilege, had not been idle in England. Within the space of two months he would see ministers broken and the Court cease to exist as a political force. Charles was powerless to prevent these events. Now Hamilton grovelled before the Parliamentary party for its favour—it was the only way he could avert its wrath from himself. He concentrated his efforts on those Opposition peers who, although they professed disillusionment with the Court and ostentatiously shunned it, might nevertheless be won over by the promise of preferment and personal gain. Hamilton was in a position to hold out such bait, for his power over Charles was as strong as ever.

On November 3rd Charles opened the Long Parliament, and four days later John Pym, in a vehement speech, launched an all-out attack on those responsible for the kingdom's ills, in particular the Arminian clergy (this meant Laud), those who encouraged the King to show favour to Papists (this meant Windebank), and those who allegedly were plotting to alter the form of government to a despotism, for the achievement of which it had been planned to bring an Irish army into England (here, of course, he meant Strafford). He had been aiming at the Lord Lieutenant for months, and on November 11th the impeachment was served on "the greatest enemy to his country and the greatest promoter of tyranny that any age has produced".[21] Strafford was hurried away to the Tower, and Laud followed three weeks later; Windebank, thoroughly alarmed, had already fled to France, and was presently joined there by Lord Keeper Finch, who on December 21st was charged with treason for his part on the Bench in the Ship Money case.

With the removal of these ministers, Hamilton's contemporaries were observing sourly that he had "at this time the sole power with the King".[22] For some time he had not been on speaking terms with the Queen,[23] but early in the new year he found an unwitting ally in her, and in March and April 1641, both before and during Strafford's trial, he held secret talks with Bedford, Pym and Saye and offered advancements in return for Strafford's life. The Queen saw herself in the role of a Lady Bountiful, from whom the proferred honours would come. The immediate outcome of the marquis' overtures to the Opposition peers, and concurrent negotiations with the King, was reached in February when Bedford (who had been ambitious enough to hope that Hamilton would marry one of his daughters), Essex, Saye, Mandeville and Hertford were brought on to the Privy Council.[24] His rival, Lennox, was ousted from his post as Warden of the Cinque Ports, which passed to Holland's Puritan brother, the Earl of Warwick.[25] By procuring these appointments, Baillie noted, Hamilton was "thoroughly reconciled to the English".[26] Yet the victory these noblemen seemed to have won over the King and Court was more apparent than real. Charles had, in essence, conceded practically nothing, since the advice of the new councillors was as little heeded after their appointments as before. Hamilton's gain was equally illusory, for his proposed impeachment had merely been postponed until Strafford was out of the way.

Strafford's trial opened on March 22nd in the austere surroundings of Westminster Hall, which had been built by William Rufus in 1097 and rebuilt by Richard II three centuries later. Broken in health, prematurely aged, stooped and ashen-faced, his head protected from cold draughts by a snug fur cap, the prisoner as the weeks progressed evoked sympathy and a begrudging admiration for his spirited defence even from those most ill-disposed towards him. He had been charged with high treason—not against the Crown but against the People of England, a difficult thing to prove. But Secretary Vane's son Harry, a sectarian extremist, found and read his father's minutes of Privy Council meetings, including that of May 5th 1640, wherein Strafford had advised King Charles: "You have an army in Ireland you may employ here to reduce this kingdom." He had most certainly been referring to Scotland, and his plans to land the Irish army in Ayrshire were well known, but there was nothing in Vane's notes to indicate that. It was therefore possible to argue that, given his anger at the behaviour of the Short Parliament and the King's opponents in general, he had been advocating the invasion of England, and the younger Vane, perceiving this, copied it out and sent it to Pym, who wrote it out again, to protect his source.

There is no reason to suppose that Hamilton actively worked for the end of Strafford, as was often suggested, but at the same time it is certain that he did little, apart from his bargaining with the Opposition peers, to impede his fall. On April 5th he was called as a witness and testified that Strafford's remarks at the Privy Council meeting referred to Scotland, not England, and he intimated that the Lord Lieutenant's propensity for the calling of a Parliament was something of an *idée fixe* which bored his fellow councillors.[27] In outlook and temperament he had nothing in common with the mighty minister whose difficult, dominant personality and uncompromising policy were summed up in his motto, "Thorough". Along with Holland, Hamilton had escorted Strafford to the steps of the throne when he was admitted to the Order of the Garter on September 13th 1640, which was intended to demonstrate the King's faith in the persecuted Lord Lieutenant. But Strafford viewed Hamilton with a mixture of haughty disdain and grave distrust. Now that the earl was deeply in debt, there were many who, recognising Hamilton's lust for financial aggrandisement, considered him a dangerous enemy waiting impatiently to get his hands on Strafford's interest in the Irish revenue from the tobacco farm, for it was known that in July 1637 he had offered Strafford £10,000 for the monopoly of importing tobacco into Ireland.[28] For all his own financial schemes, Strafford had always looked disapprovingly on Hamilton's profit-making ventures, particularly when they encroached upon Ireland. On the other hand, Robert Baillie, in many ways a warm admirer of Hamilton, believed that Strafford was seeking his fall on account of his dealings with the Opposition:

> The Popish-Episcopal faction . . . made the King
> believe that [Hamilton's] power in both Houses was so
> great, as it was easy for him, if he would endeavour it,
> to get Strafford's life saved. They wrought it so, that if
> he denied to deal for Strafford he should offend the
> King; if he [attempted] to deal farther for him, he should

lose the Parliament and us all. Yet it is like the man, in
his great wisdom, will get both the King and
Parliament keeped, and let Strafford go where he
deserves.[29]

Perhaps both Baillie and Strafford magnified Hamilton's part.
On April 24th Strafford wrote him a touching and urgent appeal,
encouraged by his "noble expressions and former friendship".
He asked him to intervene on his behalf in the House of Lords,
where Hamilton sat, of course, under his English title, Earl of
Cambridge:

> All that I shall desire from your lordship is that,
> divested of all public employment, I may be admitted
> to go home to my own private fortune, there to attend
> my own domestic affairs, and education of my children,
> with as little asperity of words or marks of infamy as
> possibly the nobleness and justice of my friends can
> provide for me, with a liberty to follow my own
> occasions as I shall find best for myself. . . .[30]

It was to no avail. Hamilton was neither cruel nor vindictive,
and concerned as he was for his own political safety, he undoubtedly balked at the prospect of Strafford's execution. But he had
no power to influence events at this juncture, and neither did the
King. A Bill of Attainder was hastily drawn up by Pym and his
friends: the Commons passed it by a large majority on April 20th
1641 and the Lords by a small one on May 8th. Henceforward
events moved swiftly towards their dismal culmination: on May
10th the King, who three weeks earlier had assured Strafford that
although he could never again employ him as a public servant he
would not suffer in life, honour or fortune, gave his consent to
the Act of Attainder, and two days later, with indecent haste, the
greatest minister was beheaded on Tower Hill.[31]

CHAPTER XI

THE INCIDENT

The terrible end of Strafford preyed on Hamilton's mind; he was naturally anxious to avoid a like fate himself, and began to search for any means which would preserve him. He could not rely indefinitely on the King's protection: in the long term, Charles might prove powerless to help him. "Put not your trust in princes", Strafford had said, "in them is no salvation." Hamilton was coming to believe that this was true, for with Strafford gone the widespread hatred of him increased anew, and Edward Hyde, the member for Saltash, who seldom bothered to conceal his low opinion of the marquis, was one of those who whipped up feeling against him. He proposed to the Commons "that there might be a day appointed on which upon due reflections upon those who had been most notorious in doing mischief to the public, we might most probably find who they were who trod still in the same paths, and might name them accordingly, and that for his part, if a day were appointed for that discovery, he would be ready to name one, who, by all the marks we could judge by, and by his former course of life, might very reasonably be believed to be an evil counsellor". But the Commons were "exceedingly apprehensive (as they had cause) that he meant the Marquis of Hamilton, who, for the reasons aforesaid, was very dear to them".[1]

So now Hamilton cultivated, more assiduously than before, the friendship of the Earl of Argyll, and they spent a great deal of time in each other's company. Argyll's stake in the friendship was the fact that in time Hamilton might prove useful to him because of his contacts with the Puritans in England. At the beginning of June 1641 there was proof, if any was needed, of Montrose's attitude towards Hamilton. Colonel Walter Stewart, Montrose's messenger, was waylaid and searched, and cryptically coded correspondence from his master to Traquair and Lennox was found on him. "Matters cannot go right till that serpent M, that lies in his bosom, be cut off", ran one letter.[2] At first Stewart maintained that the serpent alluded to Laud, though on closer interrogation he admitted to Hope that it signified Hamilton, as did the "Elephant" in another letter. He declared that "thereby was meant the Marquis of Hamilton, and all others who would oppose the King, and not rest satisfied when religion and liberty should be granted", and Lord Napier claimed that "the Elephant was my Lord Hamilton who was the serpent in the bosom, and that he had strange ambitious designs".[3] The whole of the message, a series of brief instructions, was translated by Stewart as follows:

> How necessary it is the King come down before
> Parliament. To desire that the offices of Estate be kept
> up, till it be seen who deserves them best. That the
> offices of Estate be not bestowed by the advice of the
> Marquis of Hamilton, for fear he crush the King. To
> assure the Duke [Lennox] and Traquair that, except
> they take the Earl of Montrose by the hand, they will
> be kept down, both at home and abroad. To assure the
> King, the Duke, and Traquair, that my Lord Montrose
> will stand by him through all difficulties, religion and
> liberty being granted. That if the Duke or Traquair
> write, it must be in so general a way as no man can
> gather anything by it, and to write to both parties. . . .[4]

For corresponding with the King Montrose was imprisoned on June 11th by order of the Committee of Estates, and on August 23rd 1641 the royal cause was dealt another blow by the sudden death at Richmond of the moderate Rothes. Since the Treaty of Ripon, indeed, Charles had been in an unenviable position. His faithful followers, Finch and Windebank, were in exile overseas; Laud was in the Tower; Parliament was gaining control of the navy, and the army was weakened by the "army plot", a myth fabricated by Pym and exploited by him to kindle popular distrust of the monarchy. Hamilton, making the King's secret warrant his excuse for conduct often so questionable that it seemed like treachery, had so far managed to keep out of serious trouble by his courting of the Commons and the lords of the Country Party [the Opposition peers], although some were still insisting that he and the Earl of Bristol be removed from about the King.[5] "Marquis Hamilton is (for aught I can understand) in great esteem both in the House of Commons and with the Lords of the Upper House", observed Secretary Nicholas with more than a touch of sarcasm. "He is doubtless a wise and able man, and exceeding gracious and powerful with the King."[6] Similarly, his painstaking cultivation of Rothes, Loudoun and Argyll had ensured that the Scots no longer considered him an incendiary.

It would be over cynical, however, to interpret Hamilton's conduct in this respect solely in terms of self-interest. He was astute enough to realise that sooner or later Charles would have to make his peace with his opponents in both kingdoms, and by courting Rothes and Argyll he had opened up the possibility of an understanding between them and the King. Charles's problem was how to pursue a policy in Scotland acceptable to both Argyll and Montrose. It was to Scotland that he began to look more and more, and on August 10th he set out for Edinburgh accompanied by Hamilton and Lennox, who had just been created Duke of Richmond, hoping to break the alliance between the Covenanters and the Puritans which had existed since Newburn. In doing so Charles hoped to retain as much power as possible in Scotland, and this, of course, entailed his successful manipulation of existent factions there.

He arrived in Scotland on August 12th and two days later made a formal entry into Edinburgh accompanied by Hamilton, Lennox and his nephew, Prince Charles Louis, the Elector Palatine. On August 17th he proceeded from Holyrood to the Parliament House, with Hamilton bearing the sceptre before him and Argyll the crown. Parliament, which had been sitting since July 13th, had voted that all its members be required to sign the Covenant, with the result that Hamilton, Lennox, Lanark, Morton, Roxburgh, Kinnoul, Annandale and Carnwath, who had not done so, were forced to wait outside the Chamber.[7] Finding himself thereby deprived of virtually all his chief supporters, Charles had no choice but to request these noblemen to sign. All but Lennox, who refused, did so on the following day, and Lennox, much against his will, followed their example a little later. It was afterwards claimed in Hamilton's defence that although he had signed he had not sworn.[8]

Charles appeared to bend over backwards to please all but the most inflexible Covenanters. Alexander Henderson was appointed to wait on him during his stay in Scotland, and he listened patiently to the sermons of ministers denouncing the bishops and pouring abuse on Episcopacy.[9] He threw a great feast in the Parliament House, and cordially received the Earl of Argyll and other leading Covenanters. Yet despite all these niceties difficult tasks lay ahead, not least the distribution of offices. Not surprisingly, Charles was anxious that his allies in the Royalist and Cumbernauld parties should not be left out, but he knew that Argyll's faction would have to be honoured, and men in Hamilton's sphere of influence would also have their claims. He was further hampered by the fact that whoever he chose could not be appointed without the consent of Parliament. Although Hamilton's men, Lanark and Orbiston, retained their respective positions as Secretary of State and Justice Clerk, and the royalist Roxburgh continued as Lord Privy Seal, the ambiguous Hope was still secure in his post of Lord Advocate, and the Covenanters coveted the three key offices of Chancellor, Treasurer and Clerk Register.

Argyll wanted the Chancellorship, which he had sought in 1635, only to see it go to Archbishop Spottiswoode; Loudoun had his sights set on the Treasurership, which Traquair now held, and Archibald Johnstone of Warriston hoped to become Clerk Register, whose incumbent, Sir John Hay, was then confined in Edinburgh Castle. But Charles, knowing what a dangerous fanatic Warriston was, gave the post to Sir Alexander Gibson of Durie, a protégé of Lennox and William Murray. He did, however, allow himself to be swept along by the general tide of opinion sympathetic to Loudoun's claims on the Treasurership. He had at first offered the post to Argyll on condition that he would accept his father-in-law, the Royalist Morton, as Chancellor, but Argyll refused.[10] In great anger, Argyll put forward four objections to Morton's candidature. He was too old, he insisted, and high office would shelter him unjustly from his creditors; he was a rebel, often "at the horn", and he had deserted Scotland in her greatest need. Morton vehemently denied that he had ever wronged Argyll, still less his country, and he promised to make good his debts. He could scarcely believe his son-in-law's ingratitude: "the Earl of Argyll I educated for twenty years, and esteemed it an honour", he said. "It was myself and my friends who moved King James to pass from a process of forfeiture actually raised against the Earl of Argyll's father and his family." He went on to tell the House of many other acts of kindness he had performed in his interests: "and these, I publicly protest to God, are the worst offices I have ever done to the Earl of Argyll."[11]

Unmoved, Argyll decided to press home relentlessly the subject of Morton's debts, and claimed that he had paid off the old man's creditors. Charles, for once recognising a lost cause, accepted Morton's offer to step down, and, still determined not to nominate Argyll, he proposed Lord Almond, a moderate Covenanter who had once served under Leslie and had since allied himself with the Montrose faction by signing the Cumbernauld Bond. On these grounds, Almond was as undesirable to Hamilton and Argyll as to the extreme Covenanters, and on October 10th he too withdrew his name.

Meanwhile the Scottish Royalists and the nobles of the Cumbernauld Bond were furious, and some of them spoke impetuously of direct action to restore the prestige and authority of the Crown, which the struggle over offices had gravely damaged. They were supported by officers from Leslie's army, bitter because they had not received their full pay.[12] Their wrath was directed particularly at Hamilton, the King's "bosom friend", as Endymion Porter put it,[13] whom they saw in open collusion with Argyll. "It had gone hard with the marquis if he had not fallen in with Argyll, who will bring him off", wrote the Earl of Wemyss, "for believe it, the people here are much incensed against him, but Argyll and he are sworn to one another, and so think to carry all business."[14]

The King, critical of the way in which Hamilton had abused the terms of his secret warrant, remarked to Lanark that the marquis had been "very active in his own preservation",[15] and on September 29th Hamilton was accused of being a traitor to his King and country by Lord Henry Ker, a son of the Earl of Roxburgh. Then in his early twenties, Ker was later to die of alcoholism, and it was after a heavy drinking bout that he sent Hamilton a written challenge by way of Lord Crawford. Crawford, a soldier of fortune who had recently returned to his bankrupt estates, had his own reasons for hating Hamilton, who had secretly persuaded Charles to promise Lindsay Crawford's earldom.[16] Hamilton received him courteously, and then hastened to the King. On bended knee he begged Charles to forgive Ker for Roxburgh's sake, but Parliament censured the young nobleman for his behaviour and expressed confidence in Hamilton as "a loyal subject of his majesty and faithful patriot to his country".[17]

Ker was ordered to apologise to the marquis, which he did, but he came to Edinburgh accompanied by several hundred of his father's armed retainers. It was the first time a Royalist nobleman had adopted the Covenanting practice of travelling with armed men and it heightened the tense atmosphere of Edinburgh. Two weeks later the muddled plot known to history as the Incident burst upon the city.[18]

It appears that William Murray, that tireless tramper of backstairs, had had a series of private talks in Edinburgh with Colonel John Cochrane, a professional soldier whose regiment was stationed at Musselburgh. Murray had told him that there would never be a peaceful solution to the troubles in Scotland so long as Hamilton and Argyll continued to have "the greatest power in the kingdom", and had hinted that if Cochrane would help put the two noblemen out of the way he would incur the King's gratitude. Excited, Cochrane went down to Musselburgh on Friday, October 8th, where, much the worse for drink, he told his officers that if they would stand by him he would make their fortunes. His lieutenant-colonel, Robert Home, whom he drew privately aside, told him flatly that he wanted to hear no more, but Cochrane, undiscouraged, returned to Edinburgh, and that night he joined Crawford, Lord Home, Ogilvy and Kirkcudbright. Over wine they plotted the downfall of Hamilton and Argyll: "I would have the traitors' throats cut!" Crawford allegedly declared.

On Monday morning, October 11th, Colonel John Hurry and Captain William Stewart were walking together in Edinburgh when Colonel Alexander Stewart sent his servant with an invitation for them to join him for a drink. Both followed the man to Stewart's house, but Hurry, who was due to dine with Crawford at eleven, declined Stewart's invitation and resumed his walk. Shortly afterwards he was rejoined by Captain Stewart, greatly agitated, who, swearing him to secrecy, acquainted him with the details of a remarkable plot to kidnap Hamilton, Argyll and Lanark.

It seems that the three noblemen were to be summoned suddenly to the King's bedroom at Holyrood that very night, ostensibly to join Charles and Murray in urgent discussions concerning Parliament, and there they would be seized by Lord Almond with two or three hundred men, who would enter from the garden, bundle them into a coach, and carry them off to a ship waiting in

PLATE VI

JOHN LESLIE, EARL OF ROTHES

by George Jamesone

Reproduced by permission of The Fine Art Society Ltd.

PLATE VII

JOHN CAMPBELL, EARL OF LOUDOUN
an Engraving after Jamesone
Reproduced by permission of the National Galleries of Scotland

JOHN STEWART, EARL OF TRAQUAIR
artist unknown
Reproduced by permission of Mr. P. Maxwell Stuart

Leith Roads. If they resisted they were to be stabbed to death. Then Home and Roxburgh would bring their armed tenantry into Edinburgh to make the city safe for royalism.

Instead of keeping silent, Hurry hastened to General Leslie and told him all he had learned from Stewart. Then both of them found Hamilton and Argyll and informed them of the plot. Argyll urged him to keep his dinner appointment with Crawford in the hope of learning more, but all that Crawford did was to draw Hurry aside after the meal and ask him to come unobtrusively the next day, bringing with him "three or four good fellows" he could trust, and he would make him his fortune.[19]

That afternoon Hamilton joined the King as he strolled in the grounds of Holyrood House, enjoying an unseasonable spell of fine weather. It was his turn to wait on Charles in his bedroom that night, but he begged to be excused, "in a philosophical and parabolical way, as he sometimes had used", claiming that his enemies had poisoned the Queen's mind against him, and that his life was in imminent danger. He implored the King to let him withdraw from Court that night. Annoyed by his unsatisfactory explanation of his fears, Charles refused. But Hamilton ignored the King's refusal, and later that day he and Argyll, accompanied by William Stewart and Hurry, repaired to Lord Lindsay's house for supper, and urgently requested the unsuspecting Lanark to join them.

At first the usually pliable young man refused, for he was in the midst of company he did not wish to leave, and it was only on the fifth summons that, perplexed and irritated, he obeyed them. Once there, it was not difficult to convince him that the lives of all of them were in peril, for he was not yet accustomed to doubting his brother's judgment, and he was particularly impressed by the vows of Stewart and Hurry to "make good their depositions with the hazard of the last drop of their blood". He was not, he confided to a friend, "so much troubled with the hazard of losing a life . . . as with the prejudice I saw this would bring to his majesty's affairs, and the peace and quiet of this poor kingdom".[20] And so, towards midnight, the three noblemen took horse and rode northwards out of Edinburgh to Kinneil, Chatelherault's old house overlooking the Firth of Forth from the high ground near Bo'ness, where the dowager marchioness now lived. There they lay low until the following morning, when Argyll, with Hamilton's connivance, sent for Patrick Maule, the old laird of Panmure, acquainting him with the plot and desiring him to relate the details to Charles. Hamilton had already despatched the King a letter explaining his sudden flight:

> I did the last night show your majesty that the malice
> of my enemies was great, which might necessitate an
> uncertainty of my happiness in the present attending
> on your majesty. The particulars were not then so
> justified, as I could so far build on them as to acquaint
> your majesty therewith. But since upon further enquiry
> I have found them such, as made me forbear returning
> to Court last night, and that I did refrain the place for
> such a cause as the preservation of life, or that which is
> as dear to me, my liberty, is a misfortune beyond any I
> ever knew, for where should I find protection but from
> your sacred self and in your Court, unto your justice
> and favour I still have refuge, humbly beseeching your
> majesty so far to consider my faithful service, and those
> loyal thoughts that shall remain in me till death, as I
> may by your favour and justice, be put in that condition,
> that my enemies may be deterred from longer snarling
> at me, and I permitted in peace and quiet to perform
> that service which I in a high degree owe your majesty
> and wherein [I] never shall be wanting. . . .[21]

But this time Charles would not be seduced by honeyed words. Instead, he appeared that same day before the Parliament and related Hamilton's "philosophical and parabolical" conversation on the lawns at Holyrood prior to his flight. Then, reaching in his pocket for Hamilton's letter, he commanded the Clerk to read it to the House. With tears in his eyes, the King explained that Hamilton's letter distressed him, for if he had ever believed the various reports of his treachery he would have imprisoned him long before this.[22]

Charles was understandably hurt and outraged by Hamilton's claim that he was in danger of his life in the King's very presence. "Neither did he think that he could have found (if any such thing had been) a surer sanctuary than his bedchamber."[23] This was, of course, a reference to that memorable occasion a decade before, when the marquis had found shelter in the royal bedroom at the

time of the Ochiltree allegations. "But since", the King continued
before a hushed House, "he had made such a noise and business,
it surely behoved to be for one of two reasons, either fear, which
he thought could not be inherent to many Scots, much less to
him, or else a great distrust of him [Charles]."[24] Thoroughly
incensed, Charles forbade Hamilton to attend Parliament until
the affair could be investigated, for the marquis had "basely
slandered" him. His whole ire was directed at his favourite, who
had "debauched" the other two. Charles said he hardly knew
Argyll and had no idea what should make him flee, and as for
Lanark, he considered him a "very good young man", and he
had nothing against him.[25]

So perplexed was Lanark at the whole affair that he wrote to
Charles "begging him to believe that I had not a heart capable
of a disloyal thought to him, and that if I believed my brother
had any, he should not be troubled with thinking how to punish
him, for I had both a heart and a hand able to do it".[26] He had
been duped by Hamilton into believing that there really was a
plot to kill all of them, and in his own ardent loyalty to the Crown
he was even prepared to assassinate his own brother.

But things were not going exactly as Hamilton had planned. A
section of the moderate Scots lords had combined against him,
and he had not anticipated Charles' stern anger. The King's
asperity alarmed him, for as always he was not prepared to lose
his sovereign's favour—"without which no joy could possess his
heart"—although there was every reason in the present circumstances why he should. On October 22nd he wrote to Charles
again. "I must confess I cannot express the real sorrow I have for
the cloud of your majesty's displeasure which now hangs over me,
occasioned by misfortune and the subtlety of my enemies", he
began. He repeated the reasons for his flight, but appealed to
Charles to let his "goodness . . . pardon what your majesty con-
ceiveth hath been done amiss. . . ."[27]

The marquis was by this time panic-stricken, for the very next
day he wrote another letter in similar vein. "It is an exceeding
great grief unto me that your majesty's affairs suffer so great
delays through the interruption of this unhappy business which
occasioned my removal from Court upon the grounds I have by
my former letters humbly represented to your majesty", he
gushed.[28] He also professed his devotion to the Crown in a letter

to his brother-in-law, Feilding, who inclined towards the Parliament himself. "As a disloyal thought never entered in my heart, so nothing his majesty can do to me will make me other than his faithful servant, and that I shall ever prefer before what may concern myself."[29] As it was, the Incident, mostly myth, based on the drunken boasts of soldiers possessing a great hatred of Hamilton, who exploited the situation for his own profit, completely ruined the King's chances of building up support in Scotland and returning to England to rally his friends there. Had the "plot" existed, and Hamilton and Argyll been murdered, it might even have destroyed royal authority in the northern kingdom, and possibly also in England. It is obvious that in England men were asking themselves whether a plot did in fact exist and whether the King was indeed implicated, for when rumours of the Incident reached Secretary Nicholas, he wrote in alarm to Charles that since the Privy Council believed it to be "a plot of the Papists there and of some lords and others here", they had ordered the Lord Mayor of London to double the guards in the City and environs: "it is thought that this business will this day in Parliament be declared to be a greater plot against the kingdoms and parliaments of England and Scotland than hath been discovered at all."[30]

But although it discredited Charles, the Incident did nothing to elevate in the eyes of the Royalists the reputations of the two noblemen principally concerned. As Endymion Porter, who had ties by marriage with Hamilton yet had little love for him, put it:

> Where we those quiet hopes we left behind
> Find altered now, and of another kind.
> That Highlander, whose conscience and whose eyes
> Play handy dandy with deceit and lies,
> Hath by extempore prayers raised one side
> A traitorous tumult to support his pride,
> And Hamilton and he are joined, and gone
> To hatch a daring mischief to unthrone
> Our gracious King. A pox upon them all
> That would have monarchy go less or fall.[31]

What support Charles had managed to build up in Scotland over the past three months rapidly evaporated, and to the majority of the Scottish people the three fugitives were heroes. On November 1st Parliament voted to recall them, expressing approval for the steps they had hitherto taken, and so exonerating them from the odium surrounding their flight. Parliament's move was thus most insulting to Charles, and many noblemen attached to his cause protested against it in vain. "Sure their late danger was the means to increase their favour with the Parliament, so whatever ruling they had before it was then multiplied", commented the astute Baillie. "The marquis did not much meddle, but the leading men of the barons and burghs did daily consult with Argyll."[32]

On Saturday November 6th Hamilton and Argyll made a triumphant return to the Parliament House, where they were accorded the respect due to two who seemed to have narrowly escaped martyrdom. It was their finest hour, and Hamilton made the most of it. "It is well known unto your majesty", he began, turning towards the small stiff figure on the throne, "what devilish machinations of late have been plotted, not only against myself, but likewise against many more pious and religious members of this honourable House, and God knows what succeeding danger may now be in agitation." The Incident, he claimed, ranked with the Armada of 1588 and the Gunpowder Treason of 1605 as one of "the manifold plots of the Papists against our Protestant religion".

In view of the "manifold perils" engulfing Scotland, not to mention the recent uprising in Ireland, "that mother of dissension and nurse of rebels", he insisted that Charles would be well advised to "return unto your flourishing paradise, England". The King's presence there would be most welcome to the Queen, and was necessary in view of the attempts of Phillips, a Catholic priest,* to convert the Prince of Wales. "I speak not this", Hamilton continued in his most unctuous manner, "as if we were weary of the employment of your blessed person", but Charles would never be so secure in "this kingdom as in your own". Hamilton's choice of phrase here was remarkable—and unfortunate. Scotland was as much the King's "own" as England was, and the listener might have questioned the meaning of the marquis's words. Was it merely a slip of the tongue, or was it a sinister indication of how Hamilton really regarded Scotland? Were he and Argyll planning to make it their own? His inference that Charles' safety in Scotland

* Father Phillips, a Scot, was the Queen's confessor.

could not be guaranteed—"whether your majesty can be more secure here, or in England, I leave that to your own judgment"— was almost a threat. It was insolent and almost treasonable.

Hamilton went on to urge Charles to "ratify the form of religion in this kingdom" before his departure, and with unnecessary flamboyance he concluded by assuring him that all his prayers "external, internal and eternal" would be for his long life and happy reign.[33] He was so proud of his oratory that he had this speech printed and distributed in pamphlet form. Secretary Nicholas did not think much of it. In a letter to Charles he wrote that "your majesty may see what artifice is here used by his friends to insinuate into the people a good opinion of his lordship's piety and fidelity".[34]

Hamilton was now doing his best to ingratiate himself with the King once more, but Charles was cool and Henrietta definitely hostile, furiously denying her husband's knowledge of any plot and denouncing the marquis' "disloyalty and ambition".[35] Others were equally suspicious of him, and the Venetian ambassador, taking stock of Hamilton's wealth and connections in the northern kingdom, concluded that "he will not lack the means to harass the King considerably and put himself in such a position that he can wait for time to give some favourable opening for the realisation of these machinations, which it is believed he has been secretly nursing in his heart for a long while".[36] Yet again, however, Charles' heart ruled his head and by the end of November Hamilton had been restored to favour. The spell was broken, but the breach was yet to be.

Since the King could not be prevailed upon to make Argyll Treasurer, the post was given to a commission of five; Almond, Argyll himself and his clansman Loudoun, Hamilton's young cousin Glencairn and his brother-in-law Lindsay. For the moment, all parties, except the ultra-Royalists, would be happy. It was clear that Charles had conceded too much, and had lost face. To the dismay of the remaining Episcopalian loyalists in Scotland he had, incredibly, confirmed Hope as Lord Advocate and had given his enemies, Balmerino, Cassillis and Maitland, places on a Privy Council of which already half the members were Covenanting sympathisers. And although the moderate Sir Alexander Gibson of Durie was given the Clerk-Treasurership, which Warriston had coveted, the latter was awarded a knighthood, and a place on the Court of Session, which entitled him to be styled "Lord Warriston". Worse, Argyll was created a marquis and Leslie, who had undertaken—falsely, as subsequent events were soon to show—never again to take up arms against the King, was made Earl of Leven, with the promise of a gift of 100,000 merks from the English Parliament for the "brotherly assistance" he had afforded them. As he left for London, Charles was optimistic about the future conduct of his Scottish opponents, whom he believed had been pacified; but his true friends each side of the Border, looking beyond the illusory compromise, knew that his policy in the northern kingdom represented appeasement without honour.

CHAPTER XII

DELUSIONS OF NEUTRALITY

The Incident seemed to have cemented the growing friendship between Hamilton and Argyll, and a marriage was arranged between their eldest children, nine-year-old Lady Anne and twelve-year-old Lord Lorne. Lady Anne's dowry was set at 100,000 merks, and she was to be guaranteed an annual income of 15,000 merks. If either Hamilton or Argyll should later break the contract, the offending party should pay the other a forfeit of 30,000 merks.[1] Argyll was fully aware of the potential advantages to the Campbells of such a match, for neither Hamilton nor Lanark had sons, and providing Hamilton remained a widower and his brother without male heirs, the whole of the Hamilton inheritance would one day become Lorne's.

Whilst these nuptial arrangements, which ultimately proved abortive, were taking place, Hamilton continued to enjoy the King's intimacy, yet his position as leading adviser was shaken. Although Charles consulted him on the selection of officers for the Irish campaign, this was of trivial importance in comparison to the other issues at hand, and possibly more significant was the fact that he was no longer on the committee dealing with foreign affairs, to which he had been appointed in the autumn of 1639.[2] It was widely believed at the time that he was the contact at Court who informed Pym that Charles intended to arrest him, Hampden, Holles, Haslerigg and Strode—the celebrated "five members"— although the culprit was almost certainly Pym's friend, Lady Carlisle, faithless confidante of the Queen. "Hamilton (to his eternal infamy)", asserted a scurrilous pamphleteer,

> sent private notice to those members of the King's resolution, advising them to absent from the House; which he did on purpose to preserve them, that they might be at liberty to raise tumults and drive away his majesty. This was the devilish Hamiltonian strategem to cause an irreparable breach between him and the Houses.[3]

Immediately the King realised that the members concerned were not in the Chamber, when he went to arrest them on January 4th 1642, he proceeded to the City, where the five fugitives were believed to be hiding, and Hamilton was one of the four noblemen who accompanied him in his coach.[4]

That same month, acting on the King's instructions, Hamilton offered the staunchly Puritan City the eight cannon and stockade of ammunition stored at Vauxhall; this was a bid to allay the suspicions of the Parliamentary party, for Charles could not risk a trial of strength yet. In February Hamilton appears to have been in consultation with the King about the controversial Militia Bill, which Pym and his friends were demanding, and which would have required Charles to transfer to Parliament his power to control the armed forces. On this point, as on so many others, the marquis may have been advocating compromise: "it was Hamilton who advised the King to grant the Estates of England triennial Parliaments and the militia."[5]

Charles's outright rejection of the bill added to the growing resentment among the gentry; when the Earl of Pembroke asked him to reconsider, and to give Parliament control of the militia at least for a time, he replied: "not for an hour!"[6] He had planned that Henrietta Maria should go to the Low Countries to seek financial and military assistance, and he himself would proceed to York, intending, when the opportune occasion presented itself, to march on his hostile capital and his enemies at Westminster. He was confident—no doubt with encouragement from a perplexed Hamilton—that the Scots would help him in such an enterprise, and he had already written to the Scottish Privy Council requesting aid; unable to count on any side yet, he made friendly overtures to Argyll and Loudoun, and also to Montrose. He also courted the Irish Earl of Ormonde. It was getting on for spring now, but war clouds were darkening the horizon. In March Charles left restless and rebellious London and made a leisurely progress northwards.

Hamilton did not join him. In the middle of the month he came down with a chronic infection, and was confined to bed at Whitehall. Persisting over a period of weeks, the illness sapped his strength and depressed his spirits. He was not quite thirty-six, the age his father had been when he died, and the feverish symptoms might have reminded him all too strongly of Mary's condition in the months preceding her death. He feared that he might not recover, and, wallowing deep in self-pity, roused himself from the discomfort of his sick-bed to write to William Murray in a vain bid to counter the rumours then flying around Royalist circles in London, which claimed that his illness was feigned to prevent him joining Charles when he had greatest need of his support, and accused him of encouraging Parliament to press on with its resistance to royal authority. "It is no new thing to find myself traduced to his majesty, but I should wonder very much if he gave credit to a report grounded upon such improbabilities", he told Murray. "I hope he will not now think me so mad, or so great a knave, as to do that which might bring him any inconvenience." Yet he saw that he would have to live with slander: "I see my enemies' malice will have no end . . . and when they want other grounds, sickness is enough for them to take advantage of; but if they had been in the condition that I have been in these three weeks, they would have been more charitable. . . ."[7]

Though Lanark was with Charles in the north, his loyalty, too, was under suspicion. "I have very great reason to fear Lanark", Henrietta Maria warned her husband. "In God's name beware of him."[8] In Scotland, meanwhile, the Earl of Morton was busily engaged in trying to form a royalist faction, and to this end he worked for rapprochement between his son-in-law, Argyll, and Traquair, with the ultimate hope that Charles could be persuaded to come to Scotland. It was a policy which had Hamilton's whole-hearted support, as he made clear in a letter to Argyll.[9] Thanks to Hamilton's influence, Argyll lent his support to Morton, and the plan for Charles to visit Scotland got under way. But it failed, partly because of the opposition of the Queen, and also because of steadily growing hostility in Edinburgh and the Lowlands to royal policy.[10]

On April 23rd the King tried to enter Hull, but the governor, Sir John Hotham, who, ambitious for his family's position in the East Riding, had promised to hold the town for the Parliament, refused to open the gates, and Charles withdrew to York. There he was visited by Loudoun, acting as Argyll's representative, who hoped to mediate between King and Parliament. He was sent back to Scotland with instructions to summon the Privy Council in order that it might formally approve the royal policy, but this proved impossible owing to the implacable hostility of the Kirk.

By the middle of May Hamilton had recovered from his illness, and on Thursday, the 19th, he left London for York. There he undertook to pay for the support of sixty horse in the royal army, but he explained to Charles that he would be useless in his service if he remained in England, where his influence had become negligible, and the King accordingly allowed him to move on to Scotland, where he promised to do all in his power to thwart the King's enemies. "To persuade you to serve me, I suppose I have less need than time", Charles told him, "therefore, in a word, this is a time to show what you are." [11]

Hamilton's arrival in Scotland early in July mystified his countrymen, for as Baillie put it, when he had left "first the Parliament, and then the King, we thought he had come to us with some instructions from one or both, but it seems he had nothing from either, but to eschew drowning, had choosed to leave both for a time, since both could not be keeped, and to both his obligations were exceedingly great".[12] He now spent much of his time in the company of Argyll, dining with him often, and the King's friends each side of the Border watched in a kind of alarmed fascination to see what turn this curious friendship would take, and in mid-July the newly-betrothed Lady Anne set out from London for Scotland, presumably to meet her intended groom.[13]

Hamilton's maternal grandmother had been a Campbell of Glenorchy, and Argyll's ties with that branch of his clan were strong. This may have introduced a personal element into a friendship based primarily on political considerations. The two noblemen wished to maintain the *status quo* in Scotland because it served their own interests, and they hoped that their combined power would enable them to prevent either the Royalist faction or the Kirk party from forcing the nation to take sides in the struggle in England which on August 27th broke out into civil war. The Kirk and its adherents posed the greater threat, for the Royalist leaders in Scotland were as yet ineffective: Huntly was feeble and Montrose mistrusted.

On July 27th the General Assembly of the Kirk convened at St. Andrews for its annual meeting, with the Earl of Dunfermline as the new Royal Commissioner. Charles had requested Hamilton, Argyll and some other nobles to attend the meeting to support Dunfermline, a man slightly younger than Hamilton and an erstwhile, repentant Covenanter; but Hamilton stayed away altogether and Argyll, who attended, made it clear that he did so only as a ruling elder of the Kirk.[14] Since the Assembly was in the grip of Calvinist extremists who sought to impose Presbyterianism on England, Hamilton knew that his appearance would prove futile, and he told his friends quite frankly that he could be of no service to the King.[15]

He thought, in his half-hearted way, that Scotland could only be made to embrace the King's cause if the Queen, then in Holland trying to pawn the Crown Jewels, could be persuaded to come there to mediate between her husband and Parliament. He reasoned that if the Scots invited her to their soil they would be bound by honour to protect her. "I can be of no great use to his majesty anywhere", he wrote, "yet I conceive more here than at York, for albeit I may possibly be able to prevent evil, if I can do no good."[16]

Owing to financial embarrassment—what he called "the miserable condition of my fortune"—Hamilton now excused himself from his undertaking to pay for the sixty horse which he had promised the King at York. Cynical observers, however, noticed that his impoverishment did not prevent him from living all this time in princely grandeur at Holyrood.[17] Seeing his role very much as that of mediator and would-be conciliator, he advised the King that the time had come to call a meeting of the Conservators of the Peace, who had been created by the Scottish Parliament in 1641 to ensure that the terms of the Treaty of Ripon were carried out. The nobles had little influence among the Conservators, who were strongly sympathetic towards the Kirk.[18] Nevertheless, on August 26th Charles gave the order for them to meet on September 22nd, and Hamilton had to shelve some plans he had been making to go to Holland to confer with the Queen, and to extend to her in person an invitation to come to Scotland.[19]

He had, meanwhile, had talks with Argyll at the latter's seat in Inverary, and then at his own house at Hamilton with Loudoun. All three noblemen were apprehensive of the kind of demands the English Parliament were making on the King, and believed that he would have to give way on the issue of religious conformity; otherwise, as Murray warned Lanark, "the two kingdoms will shut upon him, in despite of what his best servants can do".[20] "His majesty", replied Lanark from the King's camp at Nottingham,

hath left no means of accommodation unassayed, for he
hath even descended to make the first offer of a new
treaty, so careful is he of his subjects' lives, that for
their safeties he is even prodigal of his own honour, and
certainly he hath not a subject that hath honour, but
will be sensible of the extremities he is now reduced
to. . . . I hope he will never look on unconcerned where
he is so deeply engaged.[21]

Shortly after this, Charles despatched Lanark to Edinburgh
with a message for the Conservators:

As it ought to be the continual study of all good and
pious princes to preserve their people, so certainly it is
the duty of all loyal and faithful subjects to maintain
the greatness and just authority of their princes, so
that without this reciprocal endeavour there can be no
happiness for the prince nor security for the people.
We are sure our late actions in Scotland will to all
posterity be an acceptable witness of our care in
preserving the liberty of those our subjects, and our
desire to settle perfect peace in that our kingdom.[22]

The Conservators strongly approved of Hamilton's proposal to
go to Holland and invite the Queen back to Scotland, and he had
no trouble persuading most of the leading Covenanters, including
Argyll, Loudoun, Warriston and Henderson, to draw up a formal
invitation guaranteeing her personal security and freedom of
religious worship. They were determined to participate with her
in negotiating a peace between the King and his Parliaments, and
they well knew that if the peace proposals were rejected by the
Parliaments, they would be obliged to support Charles. "This
was carried with great address and managed so prudently", says
Burnet, "that wise men called it the masterpiece of the marquis'
life."[23] But it was not such an achievement to persuade Argyll
and the rest to agree to the invitation, since they, like the English
Parliamentary leaders, would welcome any scheme that prevented
the Queen from fund-raising for her husband. Yet the thought of
such staunch Presbyterians pledging their protection to a Catholic
Queen seemed suspiciously bizarre, and to Hamilton's chagrin
Charles rejected the scheme.

Understandably enough, Hamilton felt rather insulted that

Charles did not trust his assurances of the Queen's safety, although it was well known that he and Henrietta disliked one another, and she had been especially hostile to him since the Incident. He might also have seen his chances of a dukedom vanishing, for Charles had hinted of such a reward: "besides what you have, deserve the mark of favour I intend you."[24] It particularly irked Hamilton that his rival, Lennox, had been created Duke of Richmond in August 1641, that Argyll had been raised to the marquisate and lesser men such as Leven had been recently ennobled. His thoughts turned now to the Duchy of Châtelherault, which had been conferred by Henri II of France on the second Earl of Arran in 1547 with remainder to his heirs; it was not to revert to the Crown of France on his death, as is sometimes supposed. The Duchy had been seized in 1559 by the Parlement de Poitiers, after Henri's death, but this did not destroy Arran's claims to it, and in the following year it was firmly stated that the Scottish "seigneurs, particulièrement le duc de Châtelherault, rentreraient en possession et jouissance de toutes les terres, possessions, heritages, estats, et offices dont ils jouissaient en France avant le sixième mars 1588. . . ."[25] As far as the Hamilton family was concerned, however, the tenure of the Duchy ceased in 1559, yet the pension of 12,000 livres which was included in the original grant was continued to the heirs of the first holder, although it had not been paid for some years. In December 1642 Lord Lothian undertook a mission to France, to petition for the renewal of this pension: this was agreed to, although the first of the 12,000 livres does not appear to have been paid until 1648. Inevitably, it was put about by some that Hamilton was in the pay of Richelieu, and working for the interests of France.[26]

After the Battle of Edgehill on October 23rd 1642, Parliament made a direct appeal to the Scots for aid, blaming Charles for his supposed favours to Catholics and the Spanish faction, and accusing him of planning to use foreign mercenaries against his own subjects. But Lindsay, on his way from London to Edinburgh with a letter to that effect, stopped off at the royal headquarters at Oxford and showed the King the Parliamentary request. Charles sent him on his way with another letter, protesting against the "horrible scandals" attributed to him, and when Lindsay arrived in Edinburgh with the two messages Hamilton insisted in the Privy Council that the King's alone be published, and was

supported in this by Lanark, Southesk and Lindsay himself. Lord
Balcarres alone wanted to publish only Parliament's letter;
Lauderdale and Hamilton's cousin Glencairn advocated the publication of both, while Argyll, Loudoun and Balmerino wanted to
suppress both. But Hamilton won the day, for after much wrangling
the Council agreed by a narrow majority to publish the King's
letter, and had the temerity to inform John Pickering, the English
Parliament's agent in Edinburgh, that it would raise no objection
if he published the Parliamentary one at his own expense.[27]

"I see you are as good as your word", wrote a relieved Charles,[28]
but for Hamilton it proved a hollow victory. The issue at stake
was not so much the publication of a letter as the rejection of the
request for direct aid from Scotland to the English rebels, and
Hamilton's triumph proved "the trumpet that wakened us all out
of our deep sleep".[29] For unfortunately Hamilton had miscalcu-
lated the effects of the royal letter, if indeed he gave thought to
them at all. It alienated those who had been hitherto apathetic,
and there were now increased calls for cooperation with the
English Parliament, and for a combined effort to remove Charles
from the orbit of his malignant and Popish counsellors.

"I have set my rest upon the justice of my cause", Charles told
Hamilton with characteristic stubbornness, "being resolved that
no extremity or misfortune shall make me yield; for I will either
be a glorious King or a patient martyr."[30] He was more optimistic
than the marquis about the future of his fortunes. Inevitably, now,
a rift developed between Hamilton and Argyll, and by mutual
agreement plans for the marriage of their children were quietly
dropped. Pickering believed that Hamilton should be prosecuted
as an incendiary between the two kingdoms, and said so to
Argyll: "I told him further that I thought the Parliament would
take it very ill that the Marquis of Hamilton, a peer of the Kingdom of England and one of the Conservators of Peace between
the kingdoms, should appear a party against the Parliament who
had deserved so well at his hands. . . ."[31] The astute English agent
realised that Hamilton had used the English Parliament as it had
earlier used him.

Hamilton now cultivated Traquair, and together they helped
the Earl of Home draw up a document, known as the Cross
Petition, to be offered to the Privy Council as an alternative to
the Covenanting petitions then coming in, which demanded that

Parliament's letter be published. This petition, urging restraint in the present troubled state of affairs, was signed by many noblemen, but by not a single minister, although churchmen were solicited far and wide. The Standing Committee of the General Assembly attacked it, and pulpits thundered with denunciations of it, since it would impose on Scotland a "detestable neutrality".[32]

In the face of such opposition Hamilton was fast losing his grip on events. He pleaded that other business prevented him from attending a crucial meeting of the Privy Council, and spent the afternoon playing tennis. Deprived of his moderate counsels, and dominated by Argyll and Loudoun, the Council decided to send commissioners to Oxford to press the King to agree to the establishment of Presbyterianism in England and to summon a new Scottish Parliament, and called on him to remove all Catholics from about his person and to disband his popish army.[33] To cap all, the Standing Committee of the General Assembly brought forth a petition of its own, calling for uniformity of religion in the two kingdoms, and the pursuit of every means possible to convert the Queen. This petition, when presented to the Conservators of the Peace, received the strongest condemnation from Hamilton, who demanded a copy of it, something the Covenanters immediately opposed since he was no longer the King's Commissioner, and held no more power than any of the other Conservators, at least not formally.[34] But although Hamilton was denigrated on all sides, the Covenanting extremists were not yet strong enough to drag Scotland into war.

On February 1st Loudoun left Edinburgh for Oxford, carrying with him a petition of the Conservators of the Peace requesting a Convention of the Estates. Hamilton, with Traquair's connivance, then embarked on an elaborate scheme against Loudoun, designed to rob him of his right to certain annuities which the Scottish Parliament had granted to the King who, in September 1641, had sold them to Loudoun. On February 16th Hamilton and Traquair sent Charles a petition requesting him to abandon these annuities: they knew, of course, that such a move would hurt not him but Loudoun. This petition was signed by many noblemen as well as several of Hamilton's tenants, though Argyll used his influence to prevent widespread subscription to it, and berated those members of the Privy Council who had put their names to it.[35]

PLATE VIII

ALEXANDER HENDERSON
attributed to Van Dyck
Reproduced by permission of The National Galleries of Scotland.

ANNE, DOWAGER MARCHIONESS OF HAMILTON
by George Jamesone
Reproduced by permission of His Grace The Duke of Hamilton
and Brandon and the National Galleries of Scotland.

PLATE IX

GEORGE GORDON, MARQUIS OF HUNTLY
attributed to Van Dyck

Reproduced by permission of His Grace The Duke of
Buccleuch and the National Galleries of Scotland.

Argyll need not have worried, for Charles decided to do no more than keep Loudoun in fear of having the annuities taken away, a very unsatisfactory solution to Hamilton. When the earl arrived at Oxford Charles informed him that he saw no reason to call a Convention of the Estates. But, as a sop to his northern subjects, he wrote that he "commends the zeal of the petitioners for the advancement of the true religion, against heresy, popery, sects, innovations, and profanity, and always shall use his best and uttermost endeavours for advancing the one and the utter suppressing the rest". He added that he

> hath formerly expressed himself (and still continues) willing that the debates of religion may be entered into by a synod of learned and godly divines, to be regularly chosen, according to the laws and customs of this kingdom; to which end his majesty will be very willing that some learned divines of the Kirk of Scotland may be likewise sent to be present, and offer their reasons and opinions.[37]

Thwarted in his bid to summon a Convention, Loudoun later consulted with Sir Thomas Hope, who assured him that in an emergency the Estates could be convened without the King's permission, but only for voting finances, not for legislating.

Now that Argyll was no longer pledged with him to keep Scotland neutral, Hamilton tried to swim against the tide, maintaining, despite everything, that he could prevent his country's intervention on the Parliamentary side. Charles, deluded, chose to believe him. Both were counting on a swift Royalist victory, and so was the Queen.

CHAPTER XIII

'SUSPECTED OF ALL, LOVED OF NONE'

Henrietta Maria arrived at Bridlington Bay on February 22nd 1643, having raised for her husband's cause Dutch loans totalling some £180,000, as well as several shiploads of armaments. In addition, a number of distinguished soldiers who had made their names in the German Wars had pledged themselves to the King's service, and as the Queen stepped ashore her hopes of a Royalist victory were high. A few days after landing she moved on to York, where she set up her little Court in style under the management of the Earl of Newcastle, at Sir Arthur Ingram's big house close by the Minster.[1] In those delightful surroundings she was joined almost immediately by the long-ignored Montrose, accompanied by Aboyne and Lord Ogilvie, who described the true extent of the danger posed by the Coven-anters, and reiterated his belief that the only way to prevent what he considered to be an inevitable Scottish invasion on behalf of the English Parliament would be to strike at them before they had time to mobilise. The seeds of an effective Royalist party were firmly planted in Scotland, Montrose assured the Queen, and would sprout and flourish on the first sign of encouragement from the King. Scotland longed to throw off the yoke of Argyll.[2]

Henrietta probably sympathised with the earnest advice of this attractive young man, particularly as he proposed to cooperate with Irish Catholics in pursuit of the King's cause, a scheme dear to her own heart.[3] But his counsel was soon silenced by that of Hamilton, who arrived at York on March 5th after a two-day journey from Edinburgh, intent on counteracting Montrose's advice. He was accompanied by William Murray, and by Traquair, who lent the benefit of his "asiatic eloquence" to Hamilton's own very considerable persuasiveness. The marquis admitted that Scottish intervention on the side of Parliament was possible, but he felt confident that he could keep his countrymen neutral for the rest of the year, and they would be unlikely to invade until the spring of 1644 at the earliest. He repudiated Montrose's advice, insisting that it would be not only a dishonourable breach of the Treaty of Ripon but incredibly foolish to risk a rupture by striking the first blow. The pro-Covenanting Scottish army in Ireland, consisting of some 100,000 crack troops, could hardly be expected to sit idly by in the face of such an attack. Large sections of Scotland were still devoted to the Covenant, and the Royalists were in no position to take the initiative. They commanded no strategic bases in the country, they could not count on active support from the notoriously faint-hearted Huntly, and any troops they might be able to raise in the Highlands could not be relied on not to rush home with their plunder after the first flush of victory, in the traditional fashion of Highland forces.[4]

Supported by Traquair and Murray, he persuaded Henrietta to communicate his advice to Charles, and whilst the royal answer was awaited both he and Montrose amused themselves at the Queen's Court. One day, as he wandered among the statues in Ingram's beautiful Italian garden, Hamilton's reverie was interrupted by the growling of a dog-fight. Unreasonably irritated, he ran his sword through the nearest dog, which belonged to Newcastle's son, killing it instantly. Montrose composed a sarcastic little verse to commemorate the occasion:

> Here lies a dog, whose qualities did plead
> Such fatal end from a renowned blade,
> And blame him not, though he succumbed now,
> For Hercules could not combat against two;
> For whilst he on his foe revenge did take
> He manfully was killed behind his back.
> Then say, to eternise the cur that's gone,
> He fleshed the maiden sword of Hamilton.[5]

These are not Montrose's most felicitous lines, but they do illustrate his total contempt not only for Hamilton's advice to the Queen, but for his character as a soldier and a man.

The King, however, ignored Montrose's advice and chose to accept Hamilton's, relying on his assurances that he could keep Scotland neutral for the rest of 1643. On March 12th he wrote to Henrietta that he considered it a fit time to make Hamilton a duke, something the marquis had sought for a long time. "I am now confident that Hamilton is right for my service", Charles added.[6] On April 12th he was given his dukedom, but news of it was kept secret until the autumn.[7] Baillie, however, heard rumours of it, and of something else: "the report goes, which to me is a fable, of Hamilton's advancement to a duchy, and marriage with one of the Queen of Bohemia's daughters."[8]

The King's acceptance of his advice was a great relief for Hamilton, since if Montrose's proposals had been followed he would have been forced to commit himself to one side or the other in what could only entail a civil war in Scotland: the one thing he dreaded above all, for his wealth and power might suffer a fatal blow. But he was not trusted, for as Sir Robert Poyntz observed:

> If the Marquis of Hamilton keep what he hath promised
> to the Queen, all will be well. But the wiser sort suspect
> him, and e'er long by the consequences it will appear.
> There be more than pregnant reasons to suspect him
> and fear the worst, as some inform. For Montrose was
> the only man to be the head and leader of the King's
> party, and, being of an high spirit cannot away with
> contempts and affronts.[9]

As things now stood, Hamilton was counting on intrigue to keep Scotland out of the war, and he described the current state of the country in a letter to Charles written at Peebles, south of Edinburgh, on April 21st. He advised his majesty to send Loudoun and the other Scottish commissioners back home, since their continuing presence in Oxford had given rise to rumours that they were not only prisoners in the garrison but in danger of their lives. They should be sent in time to attend the Scottish Parliament on May 4th. If necessary, he added, the King's friends in Scotland would "engage our fortunes" for the supply of a Royalist army, and "many of us will do it to the last penny", none more readily than himself, "the humblest, most faithful and most obedient of all your majesty's servants".[10]

Accordingly, Loudoun and all the commissioners except Lindsay, who went to London to negotiate between the English and Scottish Parliaments, returned to Scotland, and Charles, acting on Hamilton's advice, sent all the Scottish noblemen then at Oxford back to Scotland, including Lanark, Morton, Kinnoul, Annandale and Carnwath. "I hope the King's faithful servants will be so much the more firm to his service, that the wickedness of others appears, and will by their care and diligence prevent the malice of others", Henrietta wrote to Hamilton in May.[11] It was widely rumoured that Scotland was to be ruled much as Ireland was, with Hamilton Lord Lieutenant, Callandar his general, William Baillie in command of the foot, and Montrose in charge of the horse. But it was said that Montrose "absolutely refused to join in any service with Hamilton, whom he vowed had been, and ever would be, untrustworthy".[12]

On May 10th the Scottish Privy Council, at Argyll's instigation, met with the Conservators of Peace and the newly returned commissioners to discuss the condition of the pro-Covenanting Scottish army in Ireland, and on the following day it was proposed that the Estates be convened to consider it. Hamilton, alarmed, unsuccessfully requested that the motion be shelved until Lanark had arrived from England, and on May 12th he protested that the Estates could not be called without the King's permission. Yet despite powerful support from Callander, Hope, Southesk, Morton, Dunfermline and his cousin, Glencairn, he was decisively defeated.[13] Lanark arrived several days later, bringing with him a list of instructions from Charles to the seven nobles in whom he placed his greatest trust—the Hamilton brothers, Glencairn, Morton, Roxburgh, Kinnoul and Southesk. The King's main concerns were that they attempt to prevent the Kirk stirring up the Scottish masses and prevent the Scottish army in Ireland from returning.[14]

When Charles learned that a Convention of Estates* had been called without his consent, he immediately despatched a letter to his friends in Scotland instructing them to ensure that no such meeting should take place.[15] "You and others of our Council there", he told Lanark, in a letter praising his brother's service, "know well how injurious the calling of a Convention of Estates without our consent is to our honour and dignity royal."[16] Hamilton, however, ignored the King's instructions when he

* At this time a Convention of Estates was generally appointed by the monarch to reinforce the power of the Privy Council in executive matters. It did not necessarily contain the full membership of a Parliament, but Conventions widely publicised by proclamations, especially those appointed in the reign of Charles I, tended to meet in particularly large numbers, and the Convention of 1643–1644 was in fact composed of the same membership as a Parliament.

tried to persuade Montrose to attend the Convention and lend
him support, and he later justified his behaviour on the grounds
that the instructions had been sent not to him but to the Privy
Council.[17] On June 1st the Council approved the King's declaration for publication, but Loudoun objected to a clause in their
official reply to Charles, in which they undertook to "prevent all
jealousies which may arise upon any groundless report of levying
of arms or maintaining of forces within this kingdom without
special warrant from your majesty and Estates of Parliament".[18]

Hamilton, ensconced in the princely grandeur of Holyrood
House, became dejected yet again, seeing the imminent ruin of
the royal cause in Scotland. "Think not", he explained in a letter
to Jermyn, now Earl of St. Albans,

> that I am discouraged, for never was man more
> resolute to oppose all that shall endeavour the disservice
> of the King than I am, and there are considerable men
> in this country of the same kind. But I ever feared
> our want of power, and never more than now;
> resolution we want not, but means how to put that in
> execution.[19]

And to Henrietta Maria he wrote in equally despondent terms,
blaming the King's opponents in both England and Scotland for
making political capital out of a "papist" scare, and maintaining
that their popular support was such that "I cannot but apprehend
great disservice to his majesty from [Scotland] if the differences
betwixt him and his people of England be not quickly decided
either by treaty or force".[20] The alleged danger from "papists"
was the capture of Lord Antrim on the west coast of Scotland
with letters in his pockets describing a plan—which the Queen had
encouraged—whereby he was to rouse the clans against Argyll.[21]

Meanwhile June 22nd, the date fixed for the Convention of
Estates, was growing near, and Hamilton, through the mediation
of Callander, intensified his efforts to persuade Montrose to
attend the meeting and help him oppose any proposal that Scotland intervene on behalf of the English Parliament. Montrose
intimated that he was willing to do so if Hamilton, in his turn,
would promise that if their joint opposition failed he would take
up arms alongside him in a civil war against the Covenanters. But
the marquis—or duke, as he technically was—made it clear that

he was not prepared to jeopardise his position in this way. "I will protest", he told Montrose, "but I will not fight".[22] Any lingering sympathy that Montrose might have harboured for Hamilton thus evaporated, and he came to detest the man he had at first distrusted and then despised. Four lines from his most famous poem could almost have been written with Hamilton in mind:

> He either fears his fate too much,
>   Or his deserts are small,
> That dares not put it to the touch,
>   To gain or lose it all.[23]

Montrose and his friends refused to attend the Convention and withdrew to their own homes. In a state of delusion now bordering on the imbecile, Hamilton was still hopeful that he could keep Scotland out of the war. "Though the state of affairs here be otherwise than I could wish", he wrote to the Queen on June 10th, in a letter intended for her husband's eyes, "yet I was never so hopeful as at this present that no forces will come from hence this summer into England to disturb his majesty's affairs". It is worth noting that he stressed the summer. He warned her that preparations should go ahead in anticipation of an emergency. "Yet no means ought to be neglected in preparing to oppose them (lest they should do otherwise) nor shall I fail to do the same (whatever malice may whisper to the contrary) with all the power I have, and as freely venture both life and fortune in that as any living shall."[24]

At the Convention on June 22nd Hamilton—"suspected of all, loved of none"[25]—was virtually useless. Lanark delivered a letter from Charles dated June 10th, in which he reluctantly gave his consent to their meeting and permitted them to consider the requirements of the army in Ireland and to discuss matters of domestic concern, but they were not to involve themselves in English affairs.[26] The opening debate in the Convention, initiated by Loudoun, lasted four days. After challenging, in vain, the right of the gathering to consider itself a Convention of Estates, Hamilton announced that he refused to abide by any measures passed in violation of the King's commands. But his protest was not vehement enough for many Royalists, who suspected that he was, in fact, conspiring with those he professed to oppose. It seems likely that he intended his protest to be sufficiently mild to preserve what good relations he still maintained with Argyll.[27] On June 26th he and Lanark withdrew from the Convention, which sat for another two months (and then prorogued itself until January 3rd 1644) and continued its enactments with impunity, in cooperation with the General Assembly of the Kirk, which met in Edinburgh with Hope, of all people, acting as the King's Commissioner.[28]

Unfortunately for the King's party, commissioners from the English Parliament, led by Sir Henry Vane the Younger, a hard-headed fanatic, arrived in Edinburgh for negotiations with the General Assembly; and on September 25th, in London, members of both Houses of Parliament, with the Scottish commissioners, signed the Solemn League and Covenant, by which the Scots undertook to assist the Parliamentary party, while seeking at the same time to impose Presbyterianism on England and Ireland.[29] It issued a powerful warning to Hamilton, no less than to Montrose, though it did not name them:

> We shall also with all faithfulness endeavour the
> discovery of all such as have been or shall be
> incendiaries, malignants or evil instruments, by
> hindering the reformation of religion, dividing the King
> from his people, or one of the kingdoms from another,
> or making any factions or parties amongst the people,
> contrary to this league and covenant, that they may be
> brought to public trial, and receive condign punishment
> as the degree of their offences shall require or deserve,
> or the supreme judicatories of both kingdoms
> respectively, or others having power from them for that
> effect, shall judge convenient.[30]

On October 22nd the Committee of Estates, which carried on the Convention's policies during its adjournment, ordered the document "to be sworn and subscribed by all the subjects, upon the pain of being punished as enemies to religion, his majesty's honour and the peace of the kingdoms, and to have their goods and rents confiscated, and they not to enjoy any benefit or office within the kingdom, and to be cited to the next Parliament as enemies to religion, King and kingdoms, and to receive what further punishment his majesty and Parliament should inflict upon them".[31] Such was the result of the great Hamiltonian stratagem: it had failed miserably.

Early in September the Scottish army began to mobilise under the generalship of Lord Leven, who two years previously had assured the King that he would never again take up arms against him. Argyll privately subscribed £12,000 towards the expenses of the army, and Lanark, in his capacity as Secretary of State for Scotland, was accused of applying the royal signet to the proclamation ordering the mobilisation of all able-bodied males between the ages of sixteen and sixty, which was "given under our signet at Edinburgh the 18th of August".[32] The only explanation for so treasonable an action is that Lanark, like Hamilton, believed the Scots army would be mobilised anyway, and he, again like his brother, was in no mood totally to alienate himself from the Covenanters, at least not yet. In August Hamilton had made a feeble effort to delay the Covenanters' plans, by appealing to the Marquis of Newcastle for armaments and urging him to seize Berwick. Newcastle, however, ignored this, protesting that he was in no position to provide arms, though in reality he might have feared that his taking of Berwick would give the Scots an excuse to invade.[33] Meanwhile the Queen, who had joined her husband at Oxford, was doing her best to keep Hamilton loyal. "This is a mark of the confidence he [the King] hath in you", she wrote, referring to Hamilton's dukedom, which was shortly to pass the patent seals, "which I am assured you will make the world see, was founded on very good reason."[34]

In September Hamilton summoned a meeting of about fourteen Royalist noblemen, in which they resolved to oppose any attempt to raise armies in accordance with the Solemn League and Covenant.[35] By this time, however, the King, who had been joined at Oxford by Montrose and other staunch Scottish Royalists, was beginning to despair of Hamilton's effectiveness and beginning seriously to doubt his professions of loyalty. "I find there hath been a great mistaking of that mark of favour which I thought fit to bestow upon you", he remarked in one letter, but in another he wrote more kindly, as if to assure himself that he was immune to Montrose's disparaging comments: "no ill offices have had the power to lessen my confidence in you, or my estimation of you."[36]

In October Hamilton succeeded Patrick Lindsay, Archbishop of

Glasgow, as Chancellor of Glasgow University: the appointment, by which he became the first lay chancellor in the university's history, was indicative of the cordial relations he managed to maintain with his countrymen. The University of Glasgow "is founded by the House of Hamilton, you are one of its plants, the most of your friends have [had] their breeding there", Baillie, its Covenanting Provost, had reminded him the previous year, when begging financial aid.[37] At the end of the same month the Countess of Roxburgh's funeral at Kelso afforded him and other Royalists an opportunity to congregate; 1,000 horse converged on the funeral, two hundred of them his. However, discord broke out between those present, and they parted without reaching a decision on future policy, but not before Traquair had pointedly asked Hamilton whether he had assured the King that Scotland would keep out of the war. He replied that he had only guaranteed her neutrality during the past summer.[38] When Traquair left for Oxford on October 24th he took with him a letter from the duke in which he made a similar statement, explaining that he had been powerless to prevent the Solemn League and Covenant, and how he was still ready to "venture life and fortune" in the King's service.[39]

But by now Scotland was becoming intolerable for Royalists. At the end of October all the lords of the Privy Council received letters from the Committee of Estates commanding them to sign the Solemn League and Covenant by November 2nd. So many refused that the deadline was extended to November 14th, and still some held out. Hamilton did his utmost to prevent his vassals and tenants from signing it, promising them financial rewards if they obeyed him. But his promises were of no avail against the formidable influence of the Kirk throughout his lands. And now a book appeared entitled *The Mystery of Iniquity*, which accused the King of planning to introduce Catholicism into the three kingdoms from the very beginning of his reign. It further alleged that he had commissioned the war against Ireland under the Scottish Great Seal in October 1641 when it was in Hamilton's custody.[40] These wild charges, exploited by the Covenanting leaders, greatly damaged the King's cause, and false rumours that Prince Rupert had crossed the Border with 20,000 men further alienated the Scots from Royalism.[41]

On November 17th the Committee of Estates issued a decree

against Hamilton, Lanark, Morton, Roxburgh and Kinnoul for not having "sworn and subscribed" to the Solemn League and Covenant, declaring "them and every one of them to be enemies to religion, our honour, and peace of our kingdom, and that their goods and rents do belong to the public, and that they shall not enjoy any benefit, place or office within this our kingdom".[42] They were to be arrested, and killed if they resisted. As an added gesture, the Kirk excommunicated the Hamilton brothers: to such negligent religionists as they, it was but an anti-climax.

The duke had already taken steps to prevent the seizure of his property by entrusting it to Lindsay, but with a price of £500 on his head as the principal Royalist in Scotland both he and Lanark fled into England, taking with them an escort of twelve horsemen and a large quantity of money. It was rumoured that on their way south Lanark had an audience with Sir John Marlay, governor of Newcastle, and offered to betray the town to Leven.[43]

A shock awaited the brothers, for Charles had lent his ear to eight charges which Montrose had drawn up against Hamilton. These charges expounded a common and familiar theme: that he had worked to undermine royal authority in Scotland while ostensibly endeavouring to uphold it. He was accused of deliberately attempting, since 1638, "both by words and actions, to beget in his majesty's subjects both a hate against the government and a contempt of his majesty's own sacred person", suggesting "that they were now but a province unto England, and had lost their liberty, and that Scotland was now under a Pharaoh that knew not Joseph"; at the same time, it was claimed that he "most seditiously endeavoured to exasperate" the King against the Scots "by invectives against them" even before they signed the National Covenant, of encouraging Charles to make war on them, "affirming that his majesty would never be King of Scotland unless he conquered it, which he likewise then averred would be a work only of three months' time", while simultaneously "encouraging them most treacherously to withstand his majesty,* and take from him his power and his rights" and telling the Scots that "if they awed him, he was such a coward they might have of him what they would, but if they gave him his will he would prove a verier tyrant than even Nero". He was accused of urging and encouraging

* Perhaps this referred to the "kindly Scotsman" episode. See below, page 71.

his friends and relatives in Scotland to abandon their hitherto loyal stand and embrace the Covenant, and he was charged with betraying Charles whilst serving as admiral in the first Bishops' War by double-dealing and conspiring with the enemy. The theme common to these charges is neatly exemplified in the fifth—that he was continually "incensing, in an underhand way, the people against the King". Only the eighth charge struck a completely fresh note, though not an original one: "that he hath endeavoured to set on foot a title to the crown of Scotland, having treated with foreign princes touching his claim thereunto, and desired their aid and assistance to his right, protecting and maintaining such as wrote treatises in his behalf and claim to the crown." Overwhelming evidence showed, insisted Montrose, that Hamilton "is of the party with them that have raised this rebellion in Scotland".[44] And this time Charles felt bound to listen. He was by now finally convinced that, however flimsy the allegations against his favourite, he would have to arrest him if he was to come to any agreement with Montrose. Hamilton's imprisonment was the price he would have to pay for Montrose's continued support.

When Hamilton and Lanark arrived at Oxford on December 16th, they came expecting to be treated as heroes who had sought exile rather than choose the easy way of betraying their King by signing the Solemn League and Covenant. Instead, they had a discourteous reception. In a bid to heighten their disgrace, armed men were waiting at the city gates to seize them as soon as they appeared, but they arrived on horseback a little before schedule, and got through, for the sentries expected them to be in the coach behind. Realising their mistake almost immediately, the sentries chased after Hamilton, intending to apprehend Lanark later. He was arrested and confined to his lodgings; guards with muskets barred his exit; only three servants were permitted to be with him; Charles refused to see him, and no one was allowed to confer with him alone. The breach had come, and the Scottish Court giant and jester, Muckle John, had to be restrained from going in to tell him that he was an even bigger fool than he himself was, for coming to Oxford.[45]

Part Three

CAPTAIN LUCKLESS
January 1644 – March 1649

That was him that lost his head at London—folk said it
wasna a very gude ane, but it was aye a sair loss to him,
puir gentleman.

SIR WALTER SCOTT

CHAPTER XIV

"ALL SCOTS HEARTS MUST PITY HIM"

At first Hamilton had reason to believe that his stay in prison would be a short one. When, on the evening of his arrest, Sir Edward Nicholas called to advise him of the gravity of the accusations against him, he intimated that he might expect from Charles all reasonable favour and a fair hearing, and William Murray hastened to assure him that the King had expressed confidence that he could clear himself of all the charges.[1] But as time wore on, he had cause for alarm. His petitions, first for a hearing and then for a trial, were rejected on the grounds that as long as the war lasted this was hardly possible. With justifiable indignation, he replied that it was unfair to postpone his trial indefinitely in this way, for no one could say when the war might be over. "Many here think him a gone man", wrote Baillie, who had heard rumours of his assassination, "not so much for the fury of his accusers as the desperate malice of the Queen against him, and her fears, if he were freed, of his power with the King."[2]

His request that he might remain at Oxford or nearby, pending the feasibility of a trial, was ignored, and Charles refused to consider his claim to the benefit of a royal proclamation promising absolute pardon to all who came to Oxford before January 20th.[3] Instead, he was taken to Woodstock Castle some miles out of Oxford, and from there to Bristol, on his way to Pendennis Castle in Cornwall, where he arrived at the beginning of January 1644.

From the start, Lanark fared better. The main charge against him had been concurrence with Hamilton, and he had been permitted the freedom of the town, although the Court had been forbidden to him. He and the duke had been allowed to confer, but only in the presence of General Aston, governor of the Oxford garrison. Always bolder and more outspoken than his brother, he had declared bluntly that he would offer an explanation of his conduct to no one but the King. Then, on January 17th, he received word that he was to be sent to Ludlow Castle, on the

Welsh border, and, disguised as a groom, he escaped to Windsor. From there he made his way to London, where he joined his old tutor, Baillie, and the other Scottish Commissioners, and signed the Solemn League and Covenant. He assured Baillie later that he had always been a Covenanter at heart. The Covenanters were jubilant at his change of heart: "God did not only rescue him from the power of his enemies, but from those ways wherein he had walked all too long."[4] The King was furious, and it is said that he had to be restrained from hanging Lanark's page, who had aided his escape. Henrietta Maria apparently became quite emotional when she heard of Lanark's flight. "Abercorn", she allegedly exclaimed, "has lost a dukedom!"[5] A little later both brothers were divested of their offices. Sir Robert Spottiswoode took over the seals of Scotland from Lanark, who was never officially replaced as Secretary of State, and Prince Rupert quietly succeeded Hamilton as Master of the Horse.

Meanwhile, the duke was closely guarded at Pendennis. Built by Henry VIII between 1539 and 1543, the castle which served as his prison stood on a high promontory commanding the western entrance to Falmouth harbour, and was in the charge of Colonel Sir John Arundell of Trerice, an elderly and stalwart Royalist who had been appointed governor in the summer of 1643. At first, Hamilton's situation was not pleasant: he was deprived of money and servants, and was provided with writing equipment only when he wished to petition the King. As soon as Charles became aware of these harsh conditions he ordered them to be relaxed, and sent his erstwhile favourite several kind messages by way of Dr. Alexander Frazer, physician to the Prince of Wales. Still, however, there was no prospect of freedom. "He has in my mind done our nation and cause great wrong", reflected Baillie, "yet, since all his suffering is for the Court's hatred of our cause and nation, I think all Scots hearts must pity him, and pray for him, and make for either a speedy rescue of him, if living, or a severe revenge of him, if dead."[6]

In 1644 the Convention of Estates, under Lanark's influence, made an impassioned protest over Hamilton's arrest, insisting that he should have been brought to Scotland to be tried by his peers. Those responsible for his imprisonment, they said, were enemies to the kingdom, and the whole situation was a grave affront to Scotland.[7] The Estates, then, seemed to have rediscovered the

merits of the man they had outlawed and whom the Kirk had
declared excommunicate. He was, for the time, a focus for all
their indignation at the royal policy. Nevertheless, their protest
fell on deaf ears; Charles was very much in Montrose's orbit.

During his incarceration at Pendennis, Hamilton's depressive
disposition got the better of him. As the weeks turned into months
with no hope of release, dark thoughts crowded into his mind.
He felt bitter towards Lanark for escaping and joining the Covenanters, which he believed had increased the severity of his own
punishment. He vowed never to forgive his brother, and began
to persuade himself that the earl was rejoicing at his plight,
hoping that he would languish and die in prison, so that he might
all the sooner succeed him. He was still healthy and robust, and
his complexion, naturally dark, could not easily assume a captive's
pallor. But the enforced sedentary existence made him flabby, and
aggravated the painful attacks of the stone which had begun to
torment him. He unsuccessfully begged Charles to allow him to
go to France for a lithotomy.[8]

But he managed to ingratiate himself with Colonel Arundell
and his family. They were impressed by his gentle charm and
lack of affectation, and began to feel that he might be suffering
unjustly. The Arundells had connections with Exeter College,
Oxford—the deputy governor of Pendennis, one of the Arundells
of Lanherne, had graduated from there in 1624—and this was a
tie with the prisoner. Though a devoted King's man, the governor
even offered to let him escape, but the duke refused: he did not
want to leave Sir John to the wrath of the King, nor did he wish
to compromise his own honour. Such an escape, he insisted,
would only make him seem guilty of the charges.[9]

With little reading matter outside the Bible, he made a virtue
of necessity and sought solace in the scriptures. He was not
particularly religious, but the beautiful Jacobean language, outdated even then, made a distinct impression on a man always
sensitive to the power of words. He seems to have been influenced
especially by the first chapter of Ecclesiastes, for its message that
"all is vanity" appealed to the once mighty nobleman who now
believed himself broken. Even after his eventual release, his disillusionment with worldly riches persisted, and from then on the
aphorisms with which he loved to intersperse his correspondence
increased. They took the form of melancholy observations on the

emptiness of human ambition. His fatalism intensified, and with it his passivity in the face of adversity.

His contact with the outside world was minimal, and he relied on his servants, who were free to come and go, and on the officers of the garrison, whom he met at meals, for news of the war. From them he learned of the decisive Parliamentary victories at Marston Moor, on July 2nd 1644, and Naseby, on June 14th 1645. By the battle of Marston Moor, in which the Scots under David Leslie (including a detachment raised by Lanark from Hamilton's estates)* played a conspicuous part, the King lost the north of England: York fell a fortnight later, and the Marquis of New-castle, the Royalist commander in the north, fled to the Con-tinent. Naseby, a triumph for Cromwell and the New Model Army, lost the midlands for the King and ruined his cause because his only remaining supporters in Wales and the west were too poor either to furnish effective help or to replace the artillery which had fallen into Cromwell's hands. Particularly damning was the discovery that Charles was negotiating with Irish Catholics and foreigners for aid. His wisest course would have been to flee abroad, but he still pinned his hopes on Montrose.

That nobleman had received his commission as lieutenant-governor of Scotland and lieutenant-general of the royal forces there from Spottiswoode (who had, of course, taken over the Great Seal of the kingdom, though not the actual Secretaryship, from Lanark) on February 1st 1644. Since then he had won some of the most spectacular battles of the war, routing Elcho at Tippermuir on September 1st 1644, and at the end of the same month capturing Perth and Aberdeen, where, to his discredit, he took lives needlessly. In 1645 he soundly defeated the Campbells at Inverlochy, routed General Baillie—a cousin of the eminent Covenanter—at Kilsyth, and captured Glasgow, which he entered on August 18th to a tumultuous welcome, making himself master of Scotland. So that his troops would not wreak havoc on Glasgow he camped some way outside the town, at Hamilton's property, Bothwell Castle, which he pillaged, to the intense rage of its owner. Highland clansmen ensured Montrose's victories, but after each one they dispersed, and he was finally defeated at

---

* The Committee of Estates appointed Lanark colonel of the Lanark-shire levies on April 16th 1644. His force comprised 1,000 foot and 500 horse.

Philiphaugh on September 13th 1645 by David Leslie. The royal cause was lost. Some Lowland Royalists had flocked to Montrose's banner, but most stood sullenly aloof from this man who had brought "Irish and popish rebels" to fight against his own country-men.[10] He was further hampered by the attitude of Huntly, who refused to join forces with one who had fought against him and who was his junior in both age and rank. "He was naturally a gallant man", Burnet says of Huntly, "but the stars had so sub-dued him, that he made a poor figure during the whole course of the wars."[11]

In June 1645, with the Parliamentarians pressing hard on the West Country, the Queen, who gave birth to her last child, Princess Henrietta Anne, two days after Naseby, moved on to Pendennis for safety. "I pray God save poor Hamilton from her malice", wrote Baillie.[12] They did not meet, for after a couple of days Henrietta set sail for France. And then, in February 1646, the Prince of Wales, who was in Cornwall to collect his revenue from the duchy, came to Pendennis to inspect its fortifications. Arundell, who entertained him, had been given strict instructions that on no account was Hamilton to be brought into his presence. Accordingly, to avoid the possibility of a chance encounter, the duke, to his deep indignation, was temporarily transferred from his apartments in the castle to the rougher comfort of one of the soldier's houses.

But soon after this his request to speak with Sir Edward Hyde, who accompanied Prince Charles, was granted. The Chancellor viewed Hamilton with deep distrust; indeed, he probably despised him, and he listened to his professions of innocence with a prejudiced ear. Hamilton began by telling him that since the crushing defeat at Naseby the King's cause in England was ruined, and the only hope for Royalism lay north of the Border. Because of this, he was prepared to put aside feelings of animosity and revenge towards Montrose, and would take up arms alongside him in common cause. If Lanark, who had, of his own accord, resumed the Secretaryship in January 1646 on the controversial execution of Spottiswoode* (who had been taken at Philiphaugh and whose death Lanark had done nothing to prevent) opposed him in this enterprise, he would henceforth regard him as an

* Spottiswoode's "crime" was that he issued Montrose with his commission as the King's lieutenant-general in Scotland.

enemy. He assured Hyde that if the King did agree to his release he would in no way endanger the royal cause, since he would only be out on parole, and if he found that he could be of no use to Charles, he would return voluntarily to Pendennis.

Hyde replied tartly that no one but the King could order his release, and he suggested that if the duke really wanted to serve Charles he should urge Lanark, Montrose's principal opponent in Scotland, and his other friends and dependants in the northern kingdom, to declare for the King, who now felt so demoralised that he seemed about to treat with the Scottish army in England. Hamilton demurred. If he wrote directly to Charles offering his services, he said, the King would think he did so out of a desire for freedom. Besides, his influence in Scotland had diminished since his imprisonment, which many of the uncommitted, no less than the Covenanters, chose to interpret as God's judgment on him for refusing to join them. He was confident, he continued, that if he were released many Scots, out of loyalty to him or through respect for him, would rally to his side, and he would be able to persuade such men that their interests coincided with the King's.

Yet despite Hamilton's apparent earnestness, Hyde was not convinced, and the interview ended. It was resumed the following day, when the duke passionately repeated his case. But the Chancellor dashed his hopes of freedom at once. On the previous day he had listened impatiently yet politely; now he was deliberately brusque. He told Hamilton plainly that since he refused to contact his friends in Scotland, urging them to support the King, his sincerity was in question. Indeed, he said, as if to rub salt into the wound, he had felt all along that Hamilton was guilty of Montrose's charges and that his imprisonment was thereby justified. He told him that if he and Lanark had been unequivocally committed to their royal master they would have nipped the Scots' rebellion in the bud. And Hyde added, with malicious relish, that since Hamilton's imprisonment the Scottish Royalists had prospered more than they ever had when he was amongst them. This being so, he could not in good conscience, and without Montrose's approval, advise the King that he should be set at liberty.[13]

If Hamilton was hurt by the Chancellor's remarks he did not show it. They cannot, after all, have come as too much of a surprise. When he could get a fair hearing, he said, he would be able to clear himself. If only he had been permitted to speak with Charles at Oxford he could have done so, and would have returned immediately to Scotland as the King's representative, with the intention of building up a Royalist party there. He believed his brother to be "an honest man", and although Montrose's successes in Scotland seemed little short of miraculous, he did not regard them as so overwhelming in their results as to preclude help from his quarter.[14] Hyde took his leave, and shortly afterwards made good his promise to present Hamilton's case to Charles. The latter was urged to release him, restore his offices and make use of him, by the French special envoy, Jean de Montereul, a young lawyer sent to England by Cardinal Mazarin to intercede between the King and his rebellious subjects with the purpose of reaching a settlement from which France could reap political capital.[15]

Lord Culpepper also believed that Hamilton might prove useful if released, and he and Dr. Frazer went down to Pendennis to question him. He was in a difficult mood, claiming that his countrymen felt so strongly about his imprisonment that they would never come to terms with Charles or support Montrose until he had been released or brought to a lawful trial. He also appeared to have backed down from his promise to persuade Lanark to embrace Royalism, so that the Privy Council, on Culpepper's advice, resolved not to insist upon his release, "not only upon the former knowledge they had of his disposition and nature, in which they had no confidence, but also that they believed if he were not sincere he would do much mischief, and the more for being in any degree trusted."[16]

The Privy Council's opinion reflected that of many people, for alarm greeted a rumour that he was due to be freed. "It seems to me", observed a correspondent of Lord Digby, "inconsistent with policy to permit so guilty a person [to be] in a possibility of surviving his punishment and redoubling his former villainy, for it is most certain there is none can equally prejudice his majesty if he escape, and the governor is not impossible to be wrought upon, for to my knowledge he savours deeply of the Puritan."[17] Arundell was surely guiltless of the taint of Puritanism, but Hamilton's influence over him had become common knowledge and greatly irritated the King and his friends. In September 1645 Prince Rupert lost Bristol, the worst blow that had befallen the Royalist cause in the west of England, and for which an angry Charles forced him to leave the country. It was now considered advisable to move Hamilton elsewhere, lest he somehow manage to betray Pendennis into enemy hands.

And so, in mid-November, he was transferred to the fortress at St. Michael's Mount, off the coast of Marazion, under the command of Sir Arthur Bassett, another Exeter College man, who was dismayed by the great expense the charge of so distinguished a prisoner entailed, and complained bitterly of it to Hyde. Hamilton himself protested that his stone was so painful he could not possibly ride the fifteen-odd miles from Pendennis to Marazion, and claimed that he would be dead within a year if he did not have an operation; but when he realised that his objections were futile he mounted the horse provided for him and quietly rode off with Bassett. Arundell and his men were sad to see him leave. It had been arranged that if the enemy got too close to the Mount, he would be moved to the Scilly Isles, whose governor, Sir Francis Godolphin, was instructed to prepare for his commital there.[18]

By this time the population of Cornwall, like that of the rest of England, was thoroughly sick of the war, and Bassett could no longer rely on their sending him money and provisions; on March 19th 1646 one hundred men deserted the garrison and on April 1st eighty others were surprised unarmed at Marazion. These events demoralised the garrison and on April 16th Bassett, not prepared to sacrifice his own or his family's interests in defending a lost cause, agreed to surrender. Fairfax, glad to be spared a siege, granted him easy terms: the officers were allowed to proceed to their homes or to the Scillies with their arms. Hamilton was released and immediately took horse for London— a long hard ride which, as Clarendon cynically noted, he passed very well despite the stone.[19]

CHAPTER XV

THIRTY THOUSAND PIECES
OF SILVER

Having spent twenty-seven months in prison, Hamilton's first reaction following his release was one of resentment towards all that had put him there. He resolved to retire from public life and return for ever to his Scottish estates, and so his story might have ended as it had begun, amid the verdant peace of Clydesdale. Lanark was at first amused and then irritated. "I can in no ways [*sic*] approve of your resolution to spend your days in a more private or retired place than you came from . . . you should make use of your freedom and those natural gifts which God hath bestowed upon you for his service", chided the more spirited younger brother.

By this time Lanark, like many others, had experienced misgivings about the conduct of the Covenanters, who had gone far beyond the aims of the National Covenant, which had long since been achieved, and were fanatically determined, in accordance with the Solemn League, to establish Presbyterianism in an England which did not want it. Although he had signed the latter document, Lanark, like his brother, was a moderate in religion and a gradualist in politics, and he hoped that now Hamilton would urge the Covenanting leaders to shelve their plans to implement Presbyterianism south of the Border until such time as the English people were in a more receptive frame of mind, or a compromise settlement with the King had been reached. "The distracted condition of their kingdoms calls for help from every honest heart", he told the duke, "and your particular friends look for countenance from you at this time of their public calamity."[1]

Hamilton's mood of detachment was short-lived, for as Clarendon remarked he "enjoyed his liberty and his pleasure at London, and in his own house at Chelsea as long as he thought fit".[2] It is difficult to say what were the pleasures of a man who, as his servants long afterwards told Bishop Burnet, became something of a reformed character after his release from prison.[3] Whatever they were, one of his first acts was to request his collection of paintings back from Lord Denbigh, to whom they had been entrusted after his arrest, and he applied to the House of Lords for a pass for himself and his younger daughter, Lady Susanna, who had been residing with the Denbighs, to enter Scotland, where Lady Anne had been living for the past four years.[4] He also made plans to lease Chelsea Manor for £20,000, and the Scots Parliament restored to him the property it had confiscated at the end of 1643, when he refused to sign the Solemn League and Covenant.[5]

Meanwhile the King, his position gravely weakened by the serious dissensions within the ranks of his own supporters, the persistent unpopularity of the Queen, and the revelation that in the depths of his desperation he was not averse to calling in help from Irish Catholics and foreigners, resolved to surrender to his own countrymen, whose army lay before Newark. "I shall be received into the Scots army as their natural sovereign", he assured his wife, "with freedom of my conscience and honour, and all my servants and followers are to be there safely and honourably protected."[6] He had to act before the New Model Army completely surrounded Oxford, thwarting his escape. And so, on April 27th 1646, in the early hours, he slipped out of the city accompanied by a servant, Jack Ashburnham, and his chaplain, Dr. Michael Hudson. On May 5th he gave himself up to the Scots, who set off for Newcastle four days later, taking Charles with them. There, they were at a safer distance from the English to debate what they should do with their prize.

Several possibilities were open to them. They could, or course, have set him at liberty to go abroad, but he could have fled to the Continent on his own, and they were very conscious of the fact that he had now surrendered his person and liberty to them: their own "native-born sovereign" had given himself up to his Scottish subjects. If they arranged to have him safely conveyed to France, they ran the risk that he would make terms with the English Parliament disadvantageous to Scotland. "Two aphorisms I think you will not controvert", wrote Sir Robert Moray to Hamilton later. "One is that the most zealous of those that meddle in state matters in London looks at something more intentively than religion; the other, that no Englishman will ever in his heart hold it a necessary condition of the peace of England that Scotland must be satisfied with it, far less that it must be of the Scots' framing."[7] Such considerations weighed heavily with the Scots,

and they were later to hand Charles over to the English Parliament, rationalising their decision in terms of the interest of
both kingdoms. Charles was a pawn in their hands: they could
force him to impose Presbyterianism on England and Ireland, and
his presence greatly assisted their bargaining power to get the
£400,000 owed them by the English Parliament in return for their
military assistance.* Indeed, their true nature and intentions soon
became clear to their wretched prisoner, for no sooner had he
surrendered than they badgered him to sign the Solemn League
and Covenant. They also informed him that they expected Presbyterianism to be established in England as soon as possible. But
Montereul, who in the ensuing months assiduously cultivated
Argyll and Hamilton, pressed for better terms, and managed—or
so it seemed—to persuade them to change their minds. Although
they refused to commit themselves in print, they promised to
"secure the King in his person and honour" and undertook not
to press him to do anything "contrary to his conscience". Further,
they pledged that if the English Parliament refused the King's
request to restore him "to his rights and prerogatives, they should
declare for the King, and take all the King's friends into their
protection".⁸ Even Argyll appeared reasonable. "We are to look
that we persecute not piety and peaceable men", he declared in a
speech at Westminster on June 25th, before the Committees of
both Houses, by which he meant those whose consciences absolutely forbade them to sign the Solemn League and Covenant, so
long as they offered no active resistance to its aims.⁹

Having received a pass to enter Scotland, Hamilton arrived at
Newcastle on July 17th, a fine summer's day, to pay his respects
to the King he had not seen for so long. The moment he bent to
kiss the royal hand, his enemies insisted later with childish
malice, the sun went in and "there began a terrible thunder, with
lightning and rain, which continued extraordinary all the night".¹⁰
Whatever effect his presence had on the elements, it did cause
some strain and embarrassment, for both he and Charles faltered
and blushed, were awkward and tongue-tied after their long
separation, and Hamilton, not yet confident of his master's
favour, lost his aplomb and tried to slink back into the crowd.

* The Scots had originally demanded a total of £600,000 and the
House of Commons had offered £100,000. £400,000 was a compromise
sum.

But Charles prevented him, expressed something of the old affection, and a long earnest conversation followed. The Oxford accusations were mentioned, regretted and forgotten. Painfully aware of his popular image as principal architect of the King's misfortunes, Hamilton explained that he doubted whether he would be entirely accepted as a Royalist leader and told Charles that he sought a tranquil life far removed from politics, even a voluntary exile beyond the seas. But Charles insisted that he abandon such ideas, for he needed his support more now than at any other time.[11] Though no longer infatuated, the King had entered once more the fatal orbit of the most disastrous adviser a monarch ever had.

Paramount in Charles's thoughts was the fate not only of himself and his kingdom, but of Montrose. Since he had recalled the marquis's commission as lieutenant-general, his future military actions were, strictly speaking, treasonable, and were liable to be dealt with as such. Remembering, as he always did, the death of Strafford, Charles determined that Montrose should not fall victim to popular fury. Though he himself was powerless to save him, he asked Hamilton to do his best by Montrose. The duke agreed readily enough, but transferred the immediate responsibility for Montrose's safety to Colonel William Lockhart, who was serving under Lieutenant-General Middleton. The latter had helped defeat Montrose at Philiphaugh, and now he played the chief part in negotiating his submission.

Montrose's future was not so important to Hamilton as that the King should save his throne, and now the arch-apostle of compromise implored his royal master to meet his captors' demands, especially in the field of religion, which, of course, had never been of overriding importance in Hamilton's scheme of things. But for once his advice was dictated not by his own vague prejudices or self-interest, but by harsh political necessity. The English Parliament, Presbyterian in its sympathies, had joined the Scots in demanding that Charles sign the Solemn League and Covenant, and Hamilton felt that only by an alliance with Presbyterian Scotland and the Presbyterian City of London could Charles hope to maintain his throne. The first basis for a deal would therefore be for him to make a pretence of espousing Presbyterianism by signing the Solemn League and Covenant and abolishing Episcopacy.[12]

However, Hamilton underestimated the King's deep commitment to Anglicanism. He himself had signed the Solemn League and Covenant on his arrival in London after his release, and was to sign it again in August. His Reformer forefathers notwithstanding, his action had been motivated purely by political considerations, and he advised Charles that if he did the same "God would not lay it to his charge since his inducements to it were so strong and unavoidable".[13] Loudoun, too, urged the King to modify his stance: "if you lose England by your wilfulness", he warned, "you will not be permitted to come and reign in Scotland."[14] But Charles, who was, of course, bound by his Coronation oaths to uphold the Episcopal form of religion in his kingdoms, was bent on becoming the "patient martyr" he had referred to in a letter to Hamilton years earlier; for he protested that his conscience was more precious to him than the crown and even than the peace of his kingdoms: "he would willingly ruin the hazard of all his crowns below rather than endanger that above."[15] Still hoping for Irish aid, he stalled for time; he despatched Argyll, Loudoun and Dunfermline to London to try to work out the basis of a new compromise, and he sent Hamilton to Edinburgh in a bid to persuade the Estates to agree to his accepting the Covenant not entirely but in part.[16] He was in no hurry to restore Hamilton to absolute favour, and was considering giving the Earl of Southampton the Mastership of the Horse, vacant since Prince Rupert's disgrace after the fall of Bristol on September 10th, "not more for goodwill to him as out of fear that Hamilton might return into a capacity of recosening me".[17] Yet he bore the duke sufficient affection to make him Hereditary Keeper of Holyrood House on August 10th, just after his return to Scotland.

In Edinburgh Hamilton did his best for Charles before the Committee of Estates, arguing that the King's refusal to sign the Solemn League and Covenant proved his integrity, and that he would be all the more likely to concede their other demands, since it would have been easy for him to accept all the proposals, only to break all his promises at a later date. If the Scots deserted Charles now, he went on, and withdrew their army from England leaving Charles to the mercy of the English sectaries, they would court universal opprobium, and they should not recall their army until a definite peace was established. But he failed to persuade the Kirk leaders who at this time controlled the Estates: they refused to countenance any action on Charles's behalf until he had complied with their demands and signed the Solemn League and Covenant, and instead they sent Hamilton, Cassillis and Crawford-Lindsay* back to Newcastle early in September.[18]

The three men found Charles adamant. "I do assure you that nothing but the preservation of that which is dearer to me than my life could have hindered me from giving you full satisfaction", he told them, and yet, "if it be so clear as you believe, that Episcopacy is unlawful, I doubt not but God will so enlighten mine eyes that I shall soon perceive it, and then I promise you to concur with you fully in matters of religion."[19] He was encouraged in his obduracy by reports from the Earl of Lauderdale, permanent Scots Commissioner in London, which indicated growing hostility to the Presbyterian party, for he calculated that if this increased the Scots would be forced to take his part against the Independents, irrespective of whether he signed the Solemn League and Covenant. Aside from an affection that he felt despite himself, he had little faith in Hamilton, whose optimism had proved so groundless in the past. "There is no compliment but threatening, which is the only phrase used to me now", he wrote to Henrietta, "albeit Duke Hamilton brags that he hath hindered much. . . ."[20]

Charles's obstinacy annoyed Hamilton, who had always known which side to choose when his interest conflicted with his conscience, and once more he was tempted to retire from the brutal realities of political life. Again Lanark taunted him. Was he a monk? Was he such a craven defeatist that he simply gave up when faced with adversity? Again Charles implored him not to desert his cause. But that curious congenital Hamilton melancholy held him in its grip, and he made up his mind to go into exile in Holland: "so he left the King, and carried home with him a heart so fraughted with melancholy that all that could be done was not able to raise him out of it, and neither the tears of his dying mother, nor the entreaties of his friends, nor the constant persecution of Lanark were able to divert him from his resolution, for having overcome Charles's dislike of it, which was stronger than all other things with him, he was proof against everything else."[21]

Whilst in this frame of mind, he received a letter from the Queen. Henrietta, then at St. Germains, and frantic with despair,

* Lord Lindsay received the Earldom of Crawford in 1644.

was prepared at this stage to put her trust in the man she had come to dislike so intensely, in anyone, indeed, whose efforts would put her husband back in possession of his kingdom. Both she and Jean de Belliévre, the experienced diplomat whom Mazarin had sent to Scotland in support of Montereul, urged Charles to sign the Solemn League and Covenant: to Henrietta, he, as a non-Catholic, was already a heretic, and she could not understand his refusal to compromise his conscience. She begged Hamilton to stand by him and give him the benefit of his advice.[22]

Four days later, on September 26th, Charles, alarmed at Hamilton's intention to leave the country, wrote him a cynical little letter showing that in the midst of his turmoil he was fully alert to the dangers around him:

> Those at London think to get me into their hands, by
> telling our countrymen that they do not intend to make
> me a prisoner. Oh no—by no means!—but only to give
> me an honourable guard, forsooth, to attend me
> continually for the security of my person. Wherefore
> I must tell you . . . that I will not be left in England
> when this army retires and these garrisons are rendered
> (without a visible violent force upon my person) unless
> clearly, and according to the old way of understanding,
> I may remain a clear man, and that no attendant be
> forced upon me under any pretence whatsoever.[23]

Upon receipt of this letter Hamilton's hard attitude began to soften as, given his vacillating nature, it was bound to; he became more amenable to the views of those urging him not to abandon public life, and he had second thoughts about going abroad. In particular, the argument of Sir Robert Moray, who wrote from Newcastle on the King's instructions to remind him how men would say that he intended the ruination of the royal cause, made a deep impression on him, for, understandably, he was by this time painfully sensitive to accusations of treason or disloyalty. Their frequency was never to make him immune from hurt and anxiety.[24] Now, in the quiet of Kinneil House, where his mother lay in her last illness, he changed his mind. Gradually emerging from the stranglehold of depression, he penned Charles a long-winded and characteristically unctuous letter on October 6th: "the thoughts I formerly had of leaving, as it were, the world . . .

shall be changed into a resolution of being most miserable in your dominions if it shall not please God to deliver you out of those difficulties your majesty is in. . . ." He pledged his loyalty and devotion, and hoped that "God in his mercy will so direct your majesty, as by timeously granting the now necessary and most pressing demands of your kingdoms", which would prevent the "great evils" threatening the monarchy.[25]

There can be little doubt that Hamilton had, as he professed, the King's interest at heart, and to one less principled than Charles his advice, based as it was on compromise and expediency, but also on a sound appreciation of the realities of Scottish politics, might have appeared acceptable. But the King remained stubborn, and his repeated refusals to make a deal with his opponents puzzled and exasperated Hamilton, whose new-found enthusiasm for the royal cause began, once more, to wane. Why Charles could not sign the Solemn League and Covenant, as his Scots captors, in collusion with the Presbyterian-inclined English Parliament, had ceaselessly demanded, was totally beyond his comprehension. He could not understand, either, why Charles refused to relinquish control of the armed forces for twenty years, a step which— according to the expedient Hamiltonian morality—could always be revoked later, on the grounds that he had been coerced into it: surely any compromise was permissible when a kingdom was at stake. But all the King would agree to was the establishment of Presbyterianism in England for a period of three years, a plainly unsatisfactory solution for those who sought his assent to nothing less than the nineteen points contained in the "heads of the proposals". It was becoming increasingly evident—to Hamilton no less than the King—that his rejection of the proposals meant probable deposition and possibly death, though few at this stage allowed themselves to dwell upon the latter. The Scots were the King's last hope, and Loudoun had already told the English Parliament that they "would not do so base an act as to render up their prince's person, who was come to them for safety in so great a danger; and that this act could not consist with their duty and allegiance, or Covenant, or with the honour of their army, it being contrary to law and common practice of all nations, in case even of private men".[26]

Nevertheless, for the sake of English gold—the £400,000 owed to them by the English for their "brotherly assistance" in the war—the Scots were indeed prepared to deliver up their sovereign into the hands of men who would almost certainly depose him, and perhaps even put him to death. In June they had agreed with the English Parliament that the King must sign the Solemn League and Covenant and give up control of the armed forces, and now that he had refused they lost sympathy for him and his position. Lanark was one of the few still prepared to seek a solution favourable to Charles. "Whatever other men's carriage be", he assured him, "I am resolved to die rather than concur with them."[27] Elsewhere, echoing his brother, he pleaded with Charles to forsake his conscience for the future of his throne, but could not prevail upon him: "pity your hopeful children and posterity, pity your subjects, and suffer us not to ruin ourselves", he wrote. "All possible means have been used in a parliamentary way, which is the only means left to prevent the extreme resolutions that are now taken, but all is to no purpose; our best friends forsake us upon every motion, which may infer the least latitude about the Covenant and religion", he continued, adding, "I take God to witness, I write this with a sadder heart than I would receive a sentence of death against myself."[28]

Whereas Lanark expressed his opposition to the King's imminent betrayal in terms of unequivocal rage, Hamilton became merely morose and withdrawn. Both brothers, however, protested vehemently against the proposal to surrender Charles into the hands of the English. Such a move, a betrayal of the King's trust in presenting himself to them, would be also a betrayal of fifteen centuries of Scottish monarchy and would damage Scotland's reputation in the eyes of the world. "What a strain it would be to the whole reformed religion! and what danger might be apprehended both to the King's person and to Scotland from the party now prevalent in England."[29] The Committee of Estates rejected these appeals to emotion, and voted that Charles be given up to his enemies. "As God shall have mercy on my soul at the great day", cried Lanark, "I would choose rather to have my head struck off at the Mercat Cross of Edinburgh than give my consent to this vote."[30]

On January 30th 1647—two years to the day, as it happened, before his execution—the King was delivered into the hands of the English Parliament and the Scots withdrew from Newcastle in return for an immediate payment of £200,000, and a further

£200,000 in return for their military services, to be paid in instal-
ments—£50,000 of it in three months' time, another £50,000 in
six months and £100,000 within the next two years. When Charles
received news of their decision he continued quietly with a game
of chess: "the King", Sir Robert Moray reported to Hamilton,
"hath heard of the particular appointment of the payment of the
£200,000 and the march of our army with his wonted unmoved-
ness."[31]

Out of this prize money, the Committee of Estates voted Argyll
and Hamilton £30,000 each and Warriston £3,000. Argyll
received his share in compensation for the losses he had suffered
during the Civil War, in particular for the raids upon his lands in
Kintyre and the Isle of Bute in 1644 by Antrim's kinsman, the
Royalist Alasdair MacDonald, and his forces, who were in league
with Montrose. Warriston was awarded his sum in gratitude for
his efforts on behalf of Church and State, during the course of
which he had "expended himself and his fortune".[32] Hamilton's
£30,000 was given in respect of his losses, and especially for the
damage Montrose had inflicted upon Bothwell Castle and the
surrounding Hamilton properties when he and his Highlanders
camped there in 1644. Hamilton was heavily in debt, the King
owed him £15,000, and he accepted his money without hesitation. But this Judas-like betrayal preyed on his mind and he
became anxious and ill.

He was not the only one. In February Charles was taken to
Holmby, a spacious Elizabethan country house in Northamptonshire, where, although technically a captive, he was treated with
courtesy and respect. Surrounded by a small group of trusted
servants, he felt reasonably content and comfortable, with no
deeply-grounded apprehensions, and as the weeks passed he began
to entertain renewed hopes for the securing of his throne. But then
a quarrel broke out between the Independents in the Army and
the Presbyterian majority in Parliament. Anxious to be rid of the
menace of the Independents, Parliament ordered the Army to
disband; it refused, and determined to seize the person of the
King. With the moderate Fairfax temporarily removed from the
scene through illness, the Army moved into Cromwell's control;
on June 4th Cornet Joyce, acting on his orders, adbucted Charles
from Holmby and escorted him to Newmarket. The King was
now at the mercy of the New Model Army.

CHAPTER XVI

THE ENGAGEMENT

Three parties were now emerging in Scotland. The first, led by Argyll and the Kirk, consisting of most of the ministers and some of the nobles from the west, notably Hamilton's brother-in-law, Crawford-Lindsay, and relative by marriage, Lord Eglinton, would consider no proposals for the King's rescue, unless he first sign the Solemn League and Covenant, and agree to the establishment of Presbyterianism in England, and would recognise its legitimacy in Scotland. The second, the "King's Party", which had outspokenly championed Charles and aimed at attracting all former Royalists to its ranks, had the support of many noblemen, principally Traquair and Callander, but its power in the nation was limited. The makings of a third party lay in the support beginning to crystallise around Hamilton. To many Royalists he was still the most hopeful means of rallying effective support for Charles, for although he had received £30,000 for his part in handing over the King, the blame for that action was firmly fixed on Argyll and his associates.

The surrender of the King at Newcastle was "the most unpopular and ungracious act" ever performed by the kingdom of Scotland, explains Clarendon, and the deep feelings of guilt and revulsion which immediately gripped the Scots helped the Royalist revival under Hamilton, whereby "the honour of the nation might in some degree be repaired or redeemed".[1] For to others, as to Hamilton, the giving up of the King was a grave mistake, because the power of the army in England was increasing at the expense of the Parliament, and the chances of ever establishing Presbyterianism were slim. Joyce's seizure of Charles had enraged moderate public opinion, and in the back of Hamilton's mind there arose a terrible fear for the ultimate fate of the King. In June Charles had refused to accept the "heads of proposals" made by the army. These were that Parliament control the militia, navy and officers of state for ten years; that religious toleration be extended to all except Catholics; that Parliamentary seats be fairly redistributed and no Parliament should sit longer than two years. Only five Royalists were exempted from pardon. But the King held out for better terms, hoping to play one faction off against another, and he was still relying on the Scots.

Hamilton was now bent on Charles's rescue, and believed that an army would have to be formed for the purpose; but unlike the "King's Party", who advocated an immediate recourse to arms, he stressed that such a move could not be rushed. His natural caution made him determined not to move ahead of public opinion, and his aim now was to defeat Argyll at the polls. At first, enemies of both noblemen tried to induce Lennox to come to Scotland and form a party capable of resisting both of theirs. But he would not, and little by little Hamilton won over most of the nobles and gentry of Scotland. They were alarmed by the growth of religious fanaticism in Scotland, which had set in motion forces which were rapidly moving beyond their control, and they were jealous of the great power of the Kirk, which had first counterbalanced and then supplanted their own influence in the land.

During this time, when the duke was drawing away so markedly from his erstwhile ally, Argyll, he still maintained an ostensibly cordial relationship with him. So often did they dine together, so amicable was their behaviour towards each other, that many observers began to consider that their differences were feigned.[2] And yet, in reality, they had embarked upon a struggle for power in Scotland which each was resolved to play à outrance. The uneasy alliance was over.

In his bid for supremacy Argyll, at once possessed of a more dangerous cunning and shrewder mind than his equally secretive rival, tried to win Cromwell over to his side by the hypocritical claim that he believed England and Scotland should become united by politics and religion just as they were one island. It was an empty attempt, since Argyll well knew that in both Parliament and the army were members of sects which could not hope to be reconciled with the Presbyterians. When Montereul requested that Scottish Royalists captured by David Leslie at Dunaverty in May 1647 be released, Argyll, anxious to get his hands on his brother-in-law Huntly's estates, offered him instead some Gordons under Huntly's third son, Lord Lewis Gordon.

The news of Charles's abduction had not only enraged Hamilton and the Royalists: it greatly alarmed the Scottish Parliament, which watched panic-stricken whilst leading Presbyterians withdrew from the English Parliament, leaving the army in complete control of that kingdom. The Scots feared for their own religion, and feared still more that Charles might, in some way, reach an agreement with the army, which would be far more likely to respect his conscience in matters of religion than the Covenanters and English Presbyterians would be prepared to do.

Both Hamilton and Argyll were anxious that the Prince of Wales, a lanky, dark, sallow boy of eighteen, should come to Scotland; Hamilton because he believed that the young man's presence would serve as a rallying-point for the Scottish Royalists, Argyll because he wished the prince to sign the Solemn League and Covenant, thereby lending prestige and influence to the Kirk Party. Time and time again Hamilton and his agents wrote to the Queen at St. Germains, imploring her to send her son over to him. But Henrietta had grave doubts about ever trusting the Scots again, especially Hamilton.

The latter now believed that David Leslie's forces, which had stamped out the last vestiges of Royalist activism in the Highlands, should be disbanded, so that he might raise new forces which would be more sympathetic to his own policies. But Argyll, supported by the Kirk, wished to retain Leslie's army because it was staunchly pro-Covenant, and he argued that it was necessary in view of the Scots' undertaking to defend the King's person, now in such grave danger from the Independents. In "a fine speech" Hamilton declared that he urged the disbandment "only as a thing that he believed to be useful to his King, to his country, and to his religion, which he would maintain in spite of the devil".[3] The controversy raged throughout September, and Argyll succeeded in referring the matter to a committee whose members he had summoned from among his minions in the remotest parts of the nation, and who voted against disbandment until the situation in England appeared less threatening. To lessen the strain on Scotland's economy and forego the need for increased taxation, they even browbeat many army officers into accepting that it would be a patriotic gesture to dispense with a third of their pay. "The Marquis of Argyll", wrote Montereul, "is not satisfied with having the people preached to by the clergy that it is betraying their religion and their country to consent to the disbanding of an army which they will require for the defence of the one and the other, and those of his faction publish loudly that the Duke of Hamilton pretends to raise a new one which will be a greater burden and less useful to the kingdom than the present, whereas the duke on the contrary says that the Marquis of Argyll wishes to have the present army maintained for his own interests and in order to ruin the country."[4]

By the end of August 1647 both Hamilton and Argyll had withdrawn to their own estates, and from the Lanarkshire countryside the former watched with resigned despair as the battle seemed to be turning in his opponent's favour. He felt that never at any time was he to carry out his new resolution of building—however belatedly—effective support for the royal cause in Scotland. Then, on September 16th, the old marchioness died. She had been ill since the beginning of the year, and her death was not a surprise. Her outlook was entirely Presbyterian and Scottish; she had not been completely happy with her elder son, and his newly kindled Royalism cannot have met with her whole-hearted approval, especially as she had considered his imprisonment to have been endured for the sake of the Covenants. The wording of her will was characteristic of her strong nature.[5]

In October the elections gave Hamilton a vast majority in the Parliament which was due to meet in March; the Provost of Edinburgh firmly backed the duke's party, as did over half the burgesses and almost half the lairds—those sections of the populace which had hitherto been Argyll's greatest source of support. This turn of events was due to the reaction which had been setting in among the Scottish people against the Argyll Party's surrender of the King. Once more Hamilton had emerged from the political wilderness.

Meanwhile Charles, fearing an assassination attempt, had escaped from Hampton Court to the Isle of Wight, where he mistakenly believed that Robert Hammond, the Governor of Carisbrooke Castle, would protect him. In September he sent for Traquair and Callander, the Royalist leaders in Scotland whom he felt he could trust, although Montereul disapproved. "They are both party men", wrote the Frenchman to Mazarin, "the first is considered to be with the Marquis of Argyll and the second with the Duke of Hamilton; although all the three parties here act quite together in order to ruin their King, the most moderate of them having conducted themselves with violence enough in opposition to his service during these troubles so as to preclude their expecting rewards from him, were he ever in a position to punish them."⁶ He also noted that Callander "appears closely attached to the Duke of Hamilton" but at the same time "keeps up a very good intercourse with the friends of the Marquis of Argyll".⁷ But Traquair accepted Charles's invitation, went to Carisbrooke, and for the next few months acted as an intermediary between the King and the Scots Commissioners, who arrived in London in October. A secret treaty was being negotiated.

His success at the polls gave Hamilton renewed confidence. He was now actively communicating with Charles, and felt secure enough in his new-found image of loyalty to request Montereul to approach the King of France for the six years' arrears of annuity due to him from the Duchy of Châtelherault. Just before Christmas the Scottish Commissioners, Lanark, Lauderdale (a leading Hamiltonian) and Chancellor Loudoun, who had for the time slipped out of Argyll's orbit though he would shortly enter it again, arrived at Carisbrooke. Their ostensible purpose was to protest against the "heads of the proposals" made by the English Parliament earlier in the summer, but the true reason for their mission was to conclude the treaty which Hamilton and Traquair had been working on throughout the autumn. It was signed by Charles and the three noblemen on December 26th, and represented the triumph of expediency as well as the personal ascendancy of Hamilton. The King consented to the establishment of Presbyterianism in England for a trial period of three years, although his personal form of worship, like that of the Royal Household, could remain unaffected. He also agreed that Scotland should share in the trading rights which England enjoyed—something the Scots had been urging for years and had now perceived it opportune to demand. In return they hoped that a "free and full Parliament" would be held in England, and they promised to help Charles go to London in "honour, safety and freedom". They vowed that if the Parliament would not agree to the general demobilisation of the army and a personal treaty with Charles "wherein they shall assert the right which belongs to the Crown in the power of the militia, the Great Seal, bestowing of honours and offices of trust, choice of privy councillors, the right of the King's negative voice in Parliament, and that the Queen's majesty, the Prince, and the rest of the royal issue, ought to remain where his majesty shall think fit" they would send an army into England "for preservation and establishment of religion, for defence of his majesty's person and authority, and restoring him to his government, to the just rights of the crown and his full revenues, for defence of the privileges of Parliament and liberties of the subject, for making a firm union between the kingdoms under his majesty and his posterity and settling a lasting peace".[8]*

The Engagement was the high-water mark of Hamilton's career: it represented months of undercover negotiation and was his only real political success. Although it was to end in disaster because of his mismanagement, the principles underlying it were sound, for as Professor Gordon Donaldson has pointed out, it:

> showed some sense of realism, and it anticipated the
> settlement which was in the end to be made in 1690 and
> 1707. Scotland was to be presbyterian, but the Scots
> acknowledged (though as yet very grudgingly) that the
> people of England might have some say in the choice
> of a constitution for their own church.[9]

Bishop Burnet, many years later, claimed that Lauderdale told him that Charles had secretly promised Hamilton that if the Scots would engage on his behalf he would consent to the incorporation of Northumberland, Cumberland and Westmorland into Scotland, but dared not publish his intention for fear of English hostility. According to this story, Newcastle was to be the "seat of the government", and the Prince of Wales would hold his Court permanently in Scotland, the King would visit his northern kingdom once every three years, and every third place in the King's Household was to be filled by a Scot.[10]

At last the tide seemed to have turned for Hamilton, and not only politically, for the line of succession in his family seemed to have been secured by the birth, just before the Treaty of Carisbrooke, of Lanark's only son, James, Lord Polmont. But the capture of Huntly, and his imprisonment in Edinburgh Castle, seriously embarrassed the Hamiltonians, who did nothing to procure his release for fear of offending Argyll, who was thirsting for his blood. Knowing that to publish the terms of the Treaty of Carisbrooke would be to arouse the bitter opposition of Argyll and

* See Appendix One.

the clergy, Hamilton determined that it should be kept secret until he was sure he had the country with him. But Charles, hoping that the Campbell chief would concur, since he believed his concessions would satisfy even the most rigid Covenanters, and realised that such support would mean that Scotland was united behind the Engagement and bring more pressure to bear on the English Parliament than the Hamiltonian Royalists alone could do, wrote to Argyll seeking his goodwill:

> Howsoever, heretofore, you and I have differed in
> judgment, I believe now the present state of affairs are
> such as will make you heartily embrace my cause. . . .
> I have given such satisfaction to the Scots commissioners
> that, with confidence, I desire your concurrence in what
> hath been between them and me, knowing your zeal to
> your country, and your many professions to me. . . .[11]

But far from lending his support to the Treaty of Carisbrooke Argyll opposed it, and disclosed its terms to the Kirk, which proclaimed that no army was required to punish the Independents, since God had no need of men. In February, Birch, Marshall and Ashurst, commissioners from the English Parliament, were sent to Edinburgh to lodge formal protest against the Engagement, and were warmly received by Argyll. On February 25th the terms of the Engagement were made public by Loudoun and Lauderdale, who arrived hotfoot on the heels of the English commissioners. The Kirk, in a frenzy of confused indignation, for it scarcely knew whom it loathed the most, Engagers or Independents, demanded that nothing be agreed upon without its consent, a claim ludicrous to Hamilton, who remembered how the Kirk had once preached against the bishops' claim to participate in secular affairs, and to Lanark, who disapproved strongly of clergy meddling in politics. The Kirkmen were quick to denounce the Engagement and to vilify its chief authors from their pulpits. One minister predicted that Hamilton would bring the curse of God not only upon himself, but upon all his posterity, if he threw in his lot with the Royalists.[12]

The King's friends in England were delighted at the turn of events in Scotland, at the ascendancy of a Royalist party under the aegis of so prestigious a leader. Now that Hamilton appeared to have summoned within him a more resolute spirit, the desperate cavaliers were prepared to forget the rumours of his treachery in the past, and some of them believed his attitude was more extreme than he professed it to be. "Whatever you hear of the Duke of Hamilton declaring", one of them insisted, "be confident that he is for Episcopacy, and will in time make their kinsmen [the Scots] know it."[13] Unfortunately, many right-wing Presbyterians who might have joined him chose to believe this too, and remained aloof from his cause. Nevertheless, the Engagers were in the majority, and when the new Scots Parliament assembled on March 18th the strength of the Hamiltonians was demonstrated in full.

Out of a total of fifty noblemen, less than ten were on Argyll's side, for the Engagement was essentially an aristrocratic enterprise, and Hamilton commanded the most able orators. The Kirk, pitted against this formidable opposition, issued a Declaration against the Engagement, which it ordered to be read from the nation's pulpits, and Argyll, unwilling to rely solely on the support of the clergy, sent the Earl of Lothian on a secret mission to England with the aim of negotiating a treaty with Cromwell and the Independents. In this he was thwarted, for Cromwell could not be persuaded that his party had anything to gain from such a treaty, and convinced that he could gain more by fear and intimidation he moved his troops menacingly close to the Border.

Whilst Lothian unsuccessfully wrangled with Cromwell, relations between Argyll and his clerical allies were becoming increasingly strained. In March the Kirk had found it necessary to rebuke him publicly for arranging to fight a duel with Crawford-Lindsay on the Sabbath, and he was embarrassed by the new oath which it presented to the Estates for ratification and requested to be included in the Coronation Oath, by which the Scottish nation was to swear to do nothing for the King until he had signed the Solemn League and Covenant, to suppress all sects both sides of the Border, and to make no alliance with any former Royalist. Argyll knew that such outrageous demands alienated moderate opinion from his camp and played into the hands of Hamilton. Therefore he embarked on a desperate attempt to prevent Hamilton raising an effective army with which to fulfil his pledges to Charles. But although several second-rank officers supported Argyll, he failed to persuade high-ranking officers like Middleton to eschew the Engagement policy.

On April 11th 1648, still angling for an understanding with Cromwell, Argyll and Warriston, with a handful of ardent supporters, voted in Parliament against the motion that Charles be brought to London in, as the Treaty of Carisbrooke put it, "honour, freedom and safety", that the English be forced to disband their army of Independents, and that religion in England be established according to the Solemn League. Later that month, amidst many amendment proposals by Argyll, the Articles of the Engagement were passed by the Committee of Estates, and early in May a proclamation was issued calling the country to arms.

All this time Hamilton and his allies in Scotland had been in close contact with English sympathisers, who advised them minutely on the state of the country. Two women were active as intermediaries: Hamilton's old friend, the Countess of Devonshire, pro-Stuart mother of staunchly Royalist sons, who advanced £2,000 for the cause, and the fascinating Countess of Carlisle, whose brother, Northumberland, had been a Parliamentarian from the outbreak of the war. Now middle-aged and pleasingly plump, the still beautiful Lucy Carlisle had been the confidante of Strafford, Pym and Holland, and possibly the mistress of all three. She was later imprisoned by Cromwell for passing information from Lord Holland, who was plotting an uprising in London, to Hamilton, and she pawned her pearl necklace for £15,000 in order to supply Holland's officers with provisions.[14] Many veteran Royalists were armed with commissions from the Prince of Wales, notably Lord Byron as Commander-in-Chief of Cheshire, Lancashire, Shropshire and North Wales, and Sir Marmaduke Langdale, a Catholic Yorkshireman, as commander in the north. Time and again these English friends of the Engagers urged Hamilton to a swift invasion. "I dare say if ye intend to settle affairs here", one of them wrote to Lanark in March, "ye shall never do it so well as at the head of an army in England, with swords in your hands".[15]

At the end of April, in the face of bitter opposition from Argyll and the clergy, the officers of the Engagement army were appointed. Hamilton was proclaimed Commander-in-Chief, a decision from which Argyll and six others dissented. In view of his past performance on the battlefield, the choice was ill-advised, and probably the duke himself was very reluctant to assume the high command. Yet Montrose, the most obvious choice, was out of the running: Hamilton would not work with him, and he remained in France in self-imposed exile. "They made choice", scoffed Patrick Gordon, a hostile Royalist commentator,

> of the greatest man of the kingdom, and thought to be
> the wisest man, the most profound man, the greatest
> statesman and deepest politician, not only of the three
> kingdoms, but of all Christendom: in this only he was
> defective, that he had never practised the airt militarie.
> He was fitter for a Cabinet council [than] for a council
> of war; he could have been president in the gravest
> Senate that ever sat in the Vatican. . . .[16]

He badly needed a strong second-in-command, but David Leslie, who had played such a distinguished part at Marston Moor, and defeated Montrose at Philiphaugh, refused to connect himself with the Engagement owing to pressure from the Kirk, and the choice fell instead on the Earl of Callander, formerly Lord Almond, who while a brave man with experience of the Continental wars, was too much a martinet, and almost from the beginning of the enterprise he was at loggerheads with Hamilton. William Baillie, who long ago had been a volunteer under Gustavus Adolphus, and since then had served the Covenanters ably, was made Lieutenant-General of the Foot. John Middleton, a gallant man of thirty, who had seen service in both the Covenanting and Parliamentary armies, became Major-General of the Horse.

On May 1st Hamilton, Lanark, Callander, Lauderdale, Crawford-Lindsay and Roxburgh sent the King an invitation for the Prince of Wales to come to Scotland: "We have presumed, from the encouragements we have received from your majesty, to hope the prince's highness will countenance our endeavours for his father's rescue with his presence amongst us, which would certainly give an extraordinary vigour and life to all our motions."[17] They also issued a similar invitation to the prince himself. Then, on May 17th, they passed Charles some news which must have cheered him: "the Duke of Hamilton is to command in chief, who joys to meet with so happy an occasion to vindicate his loyalty." Neither the duke nor the King had forgotten the recriminations of the past. "He will be found active in his trust, and seconded by the most gallant and eminent persons of the kingdom."[18] This favourable view, however, was not common to all: old suspicions died hard. "I am clearly of [the] opinion that Hamilton is not now acting [in] your King's interest, but his own, and pursuing the old designs of his family," ran a letter of intelligence that spring.[19]

Hamilton and Lanark managed to raise £22,000 sterling for the Engagement, but they had difficulties recruiting, especially in the Glasgow area. Such was Argyll's "bitterness and violence" against him that Hamilton voiced strong fears that, if he did not have 20,000 men in arms by the end of May, the foundations of his policy would crumble, and he would lose his head.[20] From virtually every pulpit in the land ministers railed against the "unlawful Engagement" which had undertaken to help an uncovenanted King, and even Hamilton's own tenants were loath to join their master on his march into England, and six hundred men from his estates at Avendale and Lesmahago actually rose against him.[21] Still, the leading gentlemen of his name were staunch Engagers, and he persuaded an illegitimately-descended kinsman, the Reverend James Hamilton, to come along as chaplain to the army. Hamilton's view of the Engagement was expressed in the will he drew up at Holyrood House on June 12th 1648: "this expedition, which I conceive tends to glory, as well as the restoring of the King and happiness of the kingdoms."[22] Argyll and the Kirk had caused widespread mistrust of the Engagement by inferring that its principal architects had no intention of abiding by the article in the Treaty of Carisbrooke whereby Presbyterianism was to be established in England for three years, and although many right-wing Presbyterians in both kingdoms, alarmed by the growing power of the Independents and fearful of the anarchical inclinations of the Levellers, joined Hamilton and the Royalists, most Presbyterians preferred the safety of neutrality. Although Cassillis and Eglinton remained bitterly aloof from the Engagement, the Scottish aristocracy was overwhelmingly on Hamilton's side. As Cromwell was to remark later, "the greatest part, by far, of the nobility of Scotland are with Duke Hamilton".[23]

It was agreed that about 1,200 horse and 2,100 foot from the Scottish Army in Ulster, which had been sent to Ireland in 1642 to suppress the rebellion there, should join the main body of Hamilton's army; they were commanded by Sir George Munro, another veteran of the German wars, who held the rank of major-general. Meanwhile Argyll, seeking by any means to disrupt the Engagement, tried to insist that Hamilton's chief English allies,

Sir Marmaduke Langdale and Sir Philip Musgrave, be made to sign the Solemn League and Covenant.[24]

In England the Royalist plots which had been fomenting since the end of 1647 were coming to fruition, and Lanark in particular was in constant communication with their instigators. "I doubt not but upon the first entrance of your army in England the greatest part of Lancashire, Cheshire and North Wales will declare for the King, and that the principal places of strength in those counties will be secured for his service", Lord Byron assured him.[25] From Sir Philip Musgrave he learned that "most of the prime gentry of the north of England, besides many from other parts of principal quality now with us, are resolutely bent to hazard their lives in this present action".[26] The Prince of Wales was anxious to join Hamilton at the head of the army, and was planning to sail to Berwick. Owing to the exertions of Lord Willoughby, even East Anglia, a Puritan stronghold since the turn of the century, was manifesting encouraging signs of crypto-Royalist activity. Most officers of the first Civil War had earned parole by their pledges not to take up arms again as adversaries of the Parliament, and many, like old Sir Jacob Astley, stood on their honour and would not break their word; yet all over the country not only the most uncompromising Royalists, but moderate Presbyterians and Parliamentarians, hostile to the army leaders, were thinking in terms of saving the monarchy. Everything depended upon the Scots. "All men", wrote a contact in London to Lanark early in the year, "are here about at the gaze, looking northward for a better settling to their expectations."[27]

Then suddenly, in March, a rising broke out in South Wales, when the Presbyterian governor of Pembroke Castle, Colonel John Poyer, saturated with the Scriptures and with spirits, refused to obey orders to relinquish his command and declared for the King. A month later, Major-General Laugharne, the Parliamentary commander in the area, followed his example, and before long other castles in South Wales—Tenby, Carmarthen and Chepstow—were in Royalist hands. Musgrave seized Carlisle and Langdale Berwick; a party of disguised Cavaliers from Newark captured Pontefract, and Scarborough Castle declared for the King. Royalist insurrections broke out in Northamptonshire, in Cornwall, and, more seriously, in Kent. Part of the fleet lying in the Downs mutinied, put itself under the command of Prince

Charles, controlled the Cinque Ports, and menaced the mouth of the Thames. The Earl of Norwich led five hundred cavaliers in a vain attempt to win over the citizens of London; falling back upon Essex he was joined by Lord Capel and took refuge in the fortifications of Colchester. The Earl of Holland and the young Duke of Buckingham led a rising in Surrey.

It was time for the Engagers to strike, and the English rebels looked forward to "the march of your army, till which all our little plots and tumults are insignificant", as they informed Lanark. "Till the Scottish army be in England, or all people's minds possessed with the fear of it, it is not possible to raise any considerable sum of money in the City for your assistance, and if it should be obtained it will be so small and unworthy of your acceptance that it would hinder your more just demands of a greater sum, and confirm the common opinion your enemies have of your necessities."[28]

But it was not so easy for Hamilton to march at once. Before him lay the sober realities of national politics. The Kirk, not content with the great numbers who, through its influence, had declined to join the Engagement, had turned its attention to alienating those already under arms, and the levying of further recruits was severely impeded. Ammunition and oatmeal were in short supply. Hamilton was now Colonel of Edinburgh, and the city's Provost was virtually his puppet; he sent forty men to occupy the Castle, and had a printing press installed for the express purpose of feeding the populace with news of his army's progress. But he did not enjoy the complete affection of Edinburgh's citizenry. On May 31st, as he rode down the Cannongate with between three and four hundred horsemen, he was insulted by a group of women who shouted obscenities at him, and the following day, as he walked to the Parliament House, accompanied by some eight or nine hundred supporters, a Mrs. Kelty, leaning out of a window of her house, expressed her opposition to the Engagement by hurling three stones at him. But they missed him, and with typical clemency he refused to prosecute her.[29]

Argyll, to whom Hamilton had, incredibly, given a colonel's commission, had used it in the south-west of Scotland to levy troops hostile to the Engagement, and he assembled these men, along with a force of 2,000 foot and five hundred horse raised from the peasantry by some fanatical Ayrshire gentlemen, at Mauchline

Moor, near Stirling, inviting Lambert, whose army was lying near the Border, to join them. But on June 12th Middleton and a band of Engagers fell upon them; the gentry who led them surrendered, but the rest of the insurgents put up a stubborn fight, in the course of which Middleton was wounded. The day was saved only by the arrival of Callander and the cavalry. This uprising, although suppressed, did not augur well for the Engagement. As Professor Donaldson has observed, "Scotland was a country divided as it had hardly been since Pinkie, a hundred years before".[30]

Lanark, who had been very sick in the spring of 1648, an illness undoubtedly aggravated by the death of his only son, baby James, in March, had constantly urged his brother to secure his position by imprisoning Argyll. "While we are tearing ourselves in pieces through factions and self-interests . . . our King is forgot", he complained.[31] He feared that once Hamilton and the army were over the Border the Campbell chief would stab him in the back; but the duke, conscious of the power of the Campbells, failed to heed Lanark's advice. It is probable that he thought that such a move would embroil Scotland in civil war, for he freely admitted that although he and his party were supreme in the Scots Parliament, Argyll and his adherents enjoyed formidable support in the country at large. Nor did he attempt to procure Huntly's release, and so the marquis languished on in the discomfiture of Edinburgh Castle, an easy prey to the designs of his brother-in-law, Argyll. In November 1647 his principal followers, Gordon of Newton and Patrick Leith of Harthill, had been executed by Argyll's order, despite the former's special pardon from the King, and the Gordon resistance was broken. It must be to Hamilton's eternal discredit that, owing to unnecessary timidity and caution, he did nothing to aid or encourage those who would have made common cause with him in the service of the King.

At the beginning of July, Middleton, Callander, and Sir James Turner, a distinguished professional soldier to whom Hamilton had entrusted the difficult task of raising recruits in the Glasgow area, rode over to Hamilton Palace for a consultation with their commander-in-chief. All were upset by Langdale's premature march into Lancashire with the 3,000 horse he had levied, for this had afforded Parliament "a just pretext" to send Lambert hotfoot after him with a considerable force, and had frightened

Langdale so much that he had been forced to seek shelter at
Carlisle, where he faced certain defeat unless the Scots arrived in
time to relieve him. The dilemma the Engagers now faced was
well expressed by Turner:

> To march to his relief were to leave the half of our forces
> in Scotland unlevied, and an enemy behind our hand,
> ourselves in very bad condition, without money, meal,
> artillery or ammunition; to suffer him to perish was
> against honour, conscience, and the reason both of state
> and war. It would have given our enemies an occasion
> to insult; would have brought the duke's honour
> (rudely enough dealt with by some before) to an
> everlasting loss, and would have given such just
> apprehensions of jealousies to the Royalists in England,
> that never one of them would have joined with us, or
> owned us.[32]

It was decided to postpone further discussion until Hamilton,
Callander and Middleton had consulted the Estates. Colonel
William Lockhart was despatched to Annan to command some
cavalry brigades and Turner was sent to Dumfries to assume
command of some half dozen infantry regiments which were on
their way there. Lockhart was presently joined by Hamilton,
Callander and Middleton, who brought along many regiments,
none of which were filled to capacity, and later Turner arrived
with his infantry and a little ammunition, and a great supply of
oatmeal which had been ordered from Edinburgh and elsewhere.
The Engagement forces were poised to march.

As soon as Lambert, lying outside Carlisle, learned of the
presence of the Scottish army so close to the Border, he lifted the
siege, thus enabling Langdale to exercise his men and find fresh
grass for his horses, and he drew his army close together in
preparation for Hamilton's invasion. On July 6th the Scottish
commander, from his camp at Annan, sent his trumpeter to
Lambert at Castle Sowerby, with a courteous yet unreasonable
message, requesting the Parliamentary general not to resist his
army's progress. "I expect, therefore", he wrote, "you will not
oppose this pious, loyal and necessary undertaking, but rather
join with me in the prosecution of those ends."[33] Perhaps not
wishing to appear too grand before the young Yorkshireman, the

duke signed himself "your humble servant, J. Hamilton". It was a touching gesture, but it was a sign of weakness.

Two days later, in a long despatch, Lambert stated the Parliament's case. "I conceive their [the Committee of Estates'] resolutions are wholly grounded upon mistakes; desiring you also to consider whether not contrary to the [Solemn League and] Covenant.[34]

Clearly, the time had come to march. And at last, on July 8th, the day of Lambert's reply, Hamilton's troops crossed the Border, preceded by his guard of horsemen wearing rich liveries, flying his standard of white taffeta bearing a crown in the centre, and underneath the proud motto, "Date Caesari". They arrived at Carlisle that same day.

CHAPTER XVII

FOR RELIGION, CROWN AND KINGDOM

The magnificent equipage of Hamilton's advance guard belied the raw nature of his army. None of his regiments was up to strength; indeed, many barely exceeded half their establishment. Although the cavalry was well mounted, the bulk of the infantry was untrained and undisciplined, and it was estimated that one man in five was ignorant of the fundamentals of weaponry, knowing how to handle neither pike nor musket. Oatmeal, in short supply, was strictly rationed, and the great numbers of pressed men proved troublesome on the long march southwards. From the outset Hamilton found it difficult to maintain order. That seasoned veteran, Sir James Turner, considered him "too sparing of taking lives", with the result that the men took advantage of his clemency and terrorised the English countryfolk through whose neighbourhoods they passed.[1] There were stories of murder and violence, rape and robbery, of women stripped to their "hair laces" and of children kidnapped and ransomed back to their terrified parents at extortionate sums. Herds of sheep and cattle were let loose by the marauding troops, homes were ransacked and kitchens plundered bare. So many Scottish women were believed to accompany the soldiers that fears were entertained that Hamilton had promised his men the right of settlement in the invaded areas. "Scarce in the whole time of these wars", lamented a contemporary historian, "did any army exercise greater cruelty towards the poor inhabitants of England."[2]

Because of the lack of horses to carry what little artillery there was, wagons and horses belonging to English countrymen were seized, and their outraged owners forced to drive them. But this arrangement was hardly satisfactory, for if not closely watched the reluctant drivers would naturally make off for their homes, taking horses, wagons and artillery with them, and Hamilton often had to linger in the rear of his army, awaiting the arrival of fresh vehicles and horses, and then escorting them with his life-guards to prevent thefts and defections.

From the very start, the army's progress was hindered by the frequent squalls and storms which had already made that summer the worst in living memory, not only in England but elsewhere in Europe. The relentless beating of those heavy rains caused rivers to burst their banks and streams to swell; wooden bridges were swept away and roads became deep mud tracks. For cavalry and infantry alike the journey proved a hideous experience: horses' hooves slipped on the soggy grass and stuck in the mire, boots became saturated and clothes soaked through, and powder was only with great difficulty kept dry. Several times during that nightmarish campaign the order to march had to be postponed, for Hamilton preferred that his men remain in the comparative shelter of a town rather than risk death from exposure by camping overnight in a rain-soaked field.

His arrival at Carlisle was greeted by the firing of cannon and the pealing of bells, and he remained there for six days, receiving the garrison from Sir Philip Musgrave, and also Langdale's three thousand foot and several hundred horse, which had been raised in the northern counties. Leaving Carlisle on July 14th, Hamilton moved on to Penrith, where his cavalry vainly tried to engage Lambert's in battle. Three days later he attacked Lambert in Appleby, but after a few days' fierce skirmishing the Parliament men safely retreated, and Hamilton quartered at Kirkby Thore, between Penrith and Appleby, where he remained until the end of the month, and issued a tough but ineffectual warning to any soldier who damaged civilian life or property.[3] Here he was joined, at last, by the regiments which were still being raised in Scotland when he left. They disappointed the optimistic commander, for they were far below their expected strength: fears of reprisals from the Kirk had worked their worst.

In the meantime Lambert's men, surrounding the area around Barnard Castle, were keeping a wary watch on the Pennines from the High Pass over Stainmore, in the belief that Hamilton would try to push his way through in a bid to relieve Pontefract. But at the same time they were prepared to strike at his flank should he decide to advance through Lancashire. They were exhilarated by the surrender of Pembroke Castle on July 11th, and the knowledge that Cromwell was hastening to join them. Cromwell, marching up from South Wales via Gloucester, picked up reinforcements in the Midlands, shoes from Northampton and hose from Coventry

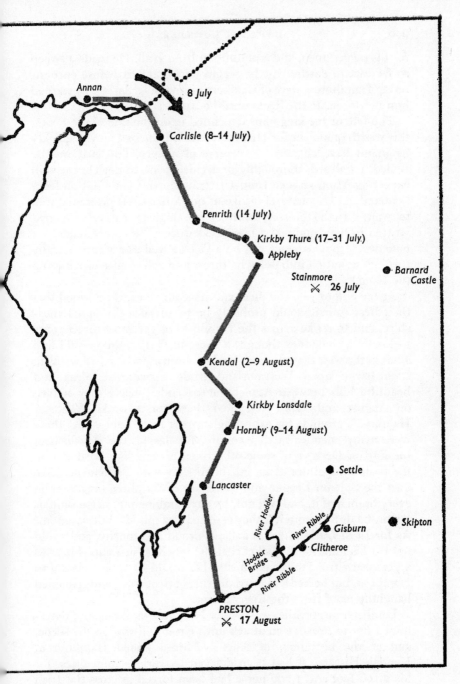

Fig. 1. The Preston campaign: Hamilton's advance.

for his ragged men, and ammunition from Hull. He made a sweep so far east to ensure that he would join Lambert before encountering Hamilton. Aware of Lambert's impetuous daring, he warned him not to tackle the Scots until he had arrived.

The fate of the kingdoms depended upon the fate of the Scots: this was the moment for Hamilton to act. If he had moved quickly he might have changed the course of history, but as it was he stalled, paralysed, thoroughly undecided what to do. He was still expecting Munro's men from Ulster, and extra ammunition from Scotland, and his natural dislike of quick decisions prompted him to wait. "In all crosses, even of the highest nature", he had written to his daughters a few weeks earlier, "the only remedy is patience."[4] But patience can be a vice as well as a virtue, and by turning hesitation into delay he threw away all chance of restoring the King.

At the end of July the duke and his council of war decided that their best course would probably be to advance through Lancashire, and to strike across the Pennines for the most direct route to London, since they thought it more likely that they would find allies in the west than the east. And so the army which had wreaked such havoc upon Westmorland trudged over the bleak and beautiful hills between Appleby and Kendal, where they arrived on August 2nd. They remained there for a week. Whatever Hamilton's grounds for expecting support from Lancashire, there were many enemies in that county, for despite the Royalism of the Earl of Derby and some other men of rank like Lord Byron, the basic sympathies of its inhabitants lay with Parliament. "We own the Solemn League and Covenant of the three kingdoms in every branch of it, and will not, by any combination, persuasion or terror, be drawn from it", they asserted in a muddled declaration.[5] As for Lord Derby, he was gallant, proud and touchy, and could not rid his mind of the belief that the rebellion in Lancashire was a personal affront to his authority. He would have been useful to Hamilton, but he had a bigoted distrust of Scotsmen, and remained haughtily aloof from the Engagement.

Lambert, meanwhile, was wisely lying low in Yorkshire, determined not to provoke an attack until Cromwell was on the scene, and at the beginning of August Munro joined Hamilton at Kendal. His arrival had been delayed by various difficulties, for his 2,100 foot and 1,200 horse had been forced to cross the Irish

Sea at night, in small vessels, for to their dismay they discovered that they were being dogged by two Parliamentary warships. Knowing the mood of Lancashire better than Hamilton did, they had not dared land there as originally planned, and had disembarked instead on the coast of Galloway. As they marched southwards through Dumfriesshire to join Hamilton they were insulted from the pulpits, and the Scottish countryfolk, faithful to—or perhaps, more accurately, afraid of—Argyll and the ministers, refused to billet them. And now further trouble threatened. The first of many bitter squabbles broke out in Hamilton's camp, for Munro would not take orders from Callander, who in turn saw no reason why Munro should be given a separate command. To avoid a showdown Hamilton sent the Ulstermen to Kirkby Lonsdale along with two regiments, one under Musgrave and the other under Sir Thomas Tyldesley, to wait for the ammunition which was still expected from Scotland. It was an unfortunate waste of some of the best troops in his army, but it was a compromise, that fact of political life that Hamilton understood so well.

Still, however, he remained optimistic. No less than Cromwell he believed that Heaven was on his side. "God increase the distraction of London", he wrote to Langdale, now based at Settle, and trying to persuade the Governor of Skipton to betray the Castle into his hands, "and send you Skipton, and preserve our friends in Colchester."[6] On August 9th the Scottish army moved out of Kendal and marched on to Hornby in Lancashire, where they remained for five days. The people of Lancashire were thoroughly alarmed, and on Hamilton's arrival at Hornby several clergymen from the northern part of the county fled into Lancaster. In a letter to them dated August 10th the duke declared that the object of his coming was "for settling Presbyterian government according to the Covenant, liberating and re-establishing his majesty, and for other ends conducing to the good and peace of the kingdom" and assured them that no harm would befall them or their families.[7] But the ministers would not be convinced, and replied that it was "incredible to us how we should have safety and freedom with your army, knowing our old enemies of religion and the King's peace are with your excellency".[8]

By this time Cromwell, strengthened by the ammunition

rushed to him from Hull, had left Pontefract Castle to be besieged by the Midland reinforcements he had recently acquired, and had himself moved on with the more experienced siege troops to meet Lambert. He caught up with him on August 12th between Leeds and Knaresborough. Together they had no more than 9,000 men compared with a combined 21,000 of the English Royalist and Scottish forces, but they were, in the words of Captain Hodgson, one of their number, "a fine, smart army, and fit for action".[9] They were, moreover, led by a brilliant strategist, of whose proximity Langdale and Hamilton were unaware.

In the Scottish camp at Hornby another council of war was called, and it was hotly debated whether they should continue their march through Lancashire or whether they should turn into Yorkshire. For once Callander was silent, sullen and uncommunicative, apparently having no strong opinion. Middleton and Turner favoured Yorkshire, holding that the heathland there would afford better conditions for the cavalry and pikemen. They feared that the enclosures of Lancashire would benefit the more experienced musketeers of the enemy, who would be able to hide behind the hedges and pick off the raw Scottish troops as they marched. But Hamilton, supported by Baillie, was adamantly in favour of the Lancashire route. He had set his heart on capturing Manchester and was counting on support from the Royalists of the area, especially those then in arms under Lord Byron in North Wales. "I have indeed heard him say that he thought Manchester his own, if he came near it", wrote Turner. "Whatever the matter was, I never saw him tenacious in anything during the time of his command but in that."[10]

Hamilton's view prevailed, but if he was seriously banking on support from the undeclared northern Royalists he should have done his utmost to bring Lambert to battle during those wasted weeks in July, when he had him so greatly outnumbered. A victory would have rallied—if anything could—the Royalist gentry who had not flocked to his standard, and would have given him a tremendous numerical advantage over Cromwell, when he eventually arrived. As matters stood now, the decision to pass through Lancashire was a lucky one for the Scots, for if they had advanced by way of Skipton they would have stumbled into Cromwell's path. On August 14th they set out for Preston, along the banks of the River Lune.

On August 13th Cromwell quartered at Otley and arrived at
Skipton the following night. No strategy had yet been worked out
in his mind, beyond the resolution to destroy the enemy as soon
as possible. Naturally, he dreaded the consequences of Hamilton's
joining with the Royalist insurgents in North Wales and the
Midlands. He need not have worried. The long line of the Scottish
invasion was straggling badly, for Hamilton had been completely
won over by Middleton and Callander, who were loath to compete
for the limited quarters and meagre provisions with the infantry
brigades, and insisted on marching far in advance of the rest of
the army. Unaware that Cromwell was so near, Hamilton was in
a fool's paradise. He believed his flank fairly well secure, since
Langdale was moving down Ribblesdale from Settle, and a brigade
of Callander's cavalry was manoeuvring near Clitheroe. In fact,
Cromwell's son, Henry, a captain in Harrison's regiment, led a
party of horse out of Skipton and chased Langdale's forward
patrols out of Gargrave.[11]

Cromwell reached Gisburn, in the Ribble valley, on August
15th, when his scouts brought him news of Hamilton's march to
Preston. That same day Lancaster Castle was surrendered into
the duke's hands, and he stayed that night at Aston Hall, home of
Colonel Wainman, three miles outside Lancaster. The next day
Cromwell set out across the hills towards Clitheroe, and although
his advance guard captured Colonel Tempest and a Royalist
cavalry patrol near there, and wrecked the quarters of another
group of the enemy's men, so poor was the quality of the latters'
intelligence that Hamilton and Langdale were still blissfully
unaware that their great adversary was upon them. Cromwell
was three miles past Clitheroe, at the bridge crossing the Hodder
just above its junction with the Ribble at Great Mitton, when he
paused to hold a council of war. He had to decide whether to
cross the Ribble to Whalley and intercept Hamilton's advance
towards the Midlands, or whether to take the north bank of the
river to Preston. His main aim was to make Hamilton fight, and
since he believed—on the basis of a false rumour—that the duke
would stand his ground at Preston in order to wait for Munro, he
chose the first course, hoping to fall upon the Scots and annihilate
them. He knew that if he placed himself across Hamilton's path
south of the Ribble the duke would be driven back upon his
allies, still able to make mischief in Scotland and the north. He

resolved, therefore, to cut off Hamilton's line of retreat. Thus, "upon deliberate advice we chose rather to put ourselves between their army and Scotland".[12]

That night Cromwell and his army lay in the park of Stonyhurst Hall, nine miles from Preston and only three miles away from Langdale's quarters on Ribbleton Moor near Longridge. Now, and only now, did Langdale learn the alarming truth. Immediately he realised that it was Cromwell who was encamped so near, he informed Hamilton and asked Callander's nephew, Lord Livingstone, to tell his uncle, who had returned from the cavalry quarters at Wigan, to pass the news on to Middleton. But both Hamilton and Callander thought that Langdale must be mistaken, and no action was taken on his information.[14]

The following morning, August 17th, Langdale rode over to Preston Moor where he found Hamilton and Callander with most of the Scottish infantry drawn up in preparation for marching south across the Ribble. The Yorkshireman was fast becoming disillusioned with these difficult allies of his. Again he insisted that it was Cromwell himself who was only three miles away, and again they scoffed at him. They were for marching to Wigan, and to his deep disgust made no attempt to recall Middleton and the cavalry from their quarters some sixteen miles further south. Yet just half an hour after this unsatisfactory meeting, two hundred of the Parliamentary horse under Major Smithson fell upon Langdale on Ribbleton Moor, forcing him to skirmish until another four hundred men under Major Pownall and Captain Hodgson arrived to press home the attack, who then drove the Royalists back towards Preston across the treacherous waterlogged ground.

The conditions underfoot made ordinary cavalry tactics impossible, but at about four in the afternoon Cromwell, with the main body of his horse and foot, decided to launch a full-scale if rather improvised attack. He sent Harrison's regiment and one of his own to press their way down the lane into the town, and despatched two more regiments of horse to the right and the rest to the left to explore any weakness in Langdale's flanks. But he was relying mainly on his infantry regiments, who forced the English Royalists back hedge after hedge, yet not without a bitter struggle. Outnumbered more than two to one, Langdale's men resolved to sell their lives dearly, and put up a ferocious fight—"a very sharp dispute" Cromwell called it[15]—lasting up to four hours, although their general himself believed that it was closer to six. "As the Scots acknowledge, they never saw any foot fight better than mine did", he wrote later.[16]

While his English allies were thus being cut to pieces, Hamilton did nothing, for instead of believing that Cromwell had attacked, he insisted that Langdale's adversaries were only Colonel Ashton, an ardent Presbyterian, with his 3,000 Lancashire levies, who had risen to oppose the army of the Engagement on the grounds that it had set out from Scotland without the permission of the General Assembly. But Langdale, angry and exasperated now, soon rid Hamilton of this notion. He informed the duke's messenger, Sir Lewis Dyves, that they must assume that the entire Parliamentary army—"all the power they could make"—lay alongside them, since it was unlikely that a small force would dare to press so close to such a considerable army as they, the Scots and English Royalists, had. He urgently requested Hamilton's assistance, and asked for more powder and ammunition to replace his losses.[17] And this time Hamilton was convinced: it was not Colonel Ashton, it was the Ironside himself.

CHAPTER XVIII

PRESTON

When Hamilton, waking as if from a stupor, became convinced at last that his allies were bearing the full brunt of Cromwell's attack it was too late to save them. We can probably discount what he is alleged to have said at first: "Let them alone, the English dogs are but killing one another." [1] But Langdale never forgave him for his lack of support, and complained bitterly of his "treachery and cowardice". He afterwards asserted that if the Scots had sent him an extra 1,000 foot he would have carried the day. [2] As it was, the help Hamilton sent Langdale was too little and too late, consisting of only 700 infantrymen and a few barrels of gunpowder.

The duke's immediate plan was to draw his men up in battle formation where they stood, on Preston Moor. But the only cavalry he had was his own troop of life-guards, for the other regiments which had accompanied the infantry were still lagging far behind—in some cases as much as fifty miles, a lamentable reflection on Hamilton's generalship. Now, just after noon, he sent Sir James Turner at full speed after Middleton to bring the horse back from Wigan, some sixteen miles farther south, and Callander chased hot-foot after Baillie, to prevent the foot from crossing the Ribble.

Callander, however, was simmering with rage, and when he caught up with Baillie's infantry, drawn up just north of the bridge, his temper flared. Instead of ordering Baillie to return, he swung around and sped back to Hamilton on Preston Moor. There, with typical arrogance, he berated his commander, protesting that it made better sense for the infantry to cross to the south bank, where they could join forces with Middleton's cavalry, who, having received Turner's instructions, would be returning from Wigan. But if, as Hamilton intended, the infantry fought on Preston Moor, they would surely be cut to pieces by Cromwell in the absence of the cavalry which had not yet caught up with them.

Callander's arguments appealed to Hamilton, whose weaker nature habitually quailed before the overbearing manner of his

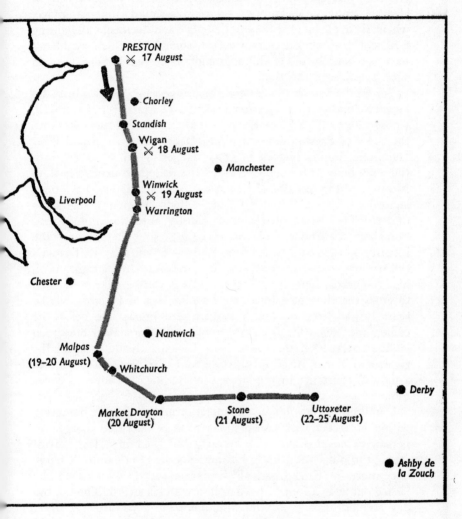

PRESTON
╳ 17 August

● Chorley

● Standish

Wigan
╳ 18 August

● Manchester

● Liverpool

Winwick
╳ 19 August

● Warrington

Chester ●

● Nantwich

Malpas
(19–20 August)

● Whitchurch

● Derby

Market Drayton
(20 August)

Stone
(21 August)

Uttoxeter
(22–25 August)

● Ashby de
la Zouch

Fig. 2. The Preston campaign: Hamilton's retreat.

second-in-command, to the complete bewilderment of Turner and the other officers. And admittedly, from the point of view of abstract strategy, Callander's advice was sound. But his advice, when taken, meant abandoning Langdale and his men, still fighting ferociously, to almost certain defeat, something which might not have sat happily on Hamilton's conscience had he not been in such a desperate situation.

For Baillie had hardly crossed the bridge when the two brigades he left behind to defend it came under fierce attack from Cromwell, whose vanguard under Harrison had already forced their way into the town of Preston along a muddy lane, "very deep and ill".[3] Hamilton, finding himself in grave danger of being cut off from the main body of his army, ordered the rearguard cavalry back to Munro and the security of Lancaster, but what should have been an orderly retreat became a frantic flight as enemy regiments under Pride, Read, Bright and Ashton bore down on them. Somehow Callander had managed to rejoin Baillie and the infantry on the south bank of the Ribble—a "miracle" in Turner's estimation—and at all costs Hamilton meant to do the same. With his life-guards, Langdale, Turner and a few other officers he tried to cross the river at a ford about a mile east of Preston, but he scarcely had time to find it swollen and impassable before he came under heavy fire from two troops of Parliamentary horsemen on the outskirts of the town. Now Langdale made to swim the river, and Turner tried to organise some fleeing musketeers into a show of resistance by imploring them to line the hedges to cover him.

Hamilton was bewildered. Desperation and panic were mounting within him. Yet with conspicuous courage he twice charged in person to cover Langdale's retreat, and then in a last valiant attempt to put some fight in his men he called to them to "Charge once more for King Charles!" Seeing one trooper hold back, he lashed out as in a frenzy, beating him with his sword. Though the day seemed already lost he would not die a coward. "Truly", says Turner, "he showed here as much valour as any man could be capable of."[4]

The third charge drove the enemy sufficiently far away to allow the duke and his stranded comrades to swim in safety to the south bank and join Baillie, whose men were positioned among easily held enclosures on a hillock just south of the Darwen. The advantage, however, lay with the Ironsides, who had taken the Scots quite by surprise, and had captured so many prisoners that their opponents were already demoralised. "There came no bands of foot to fight that day but did it with incredible valour and resolution", reported Cromwell proudly to Speaker Lenthall. "And indeed", he added, "I must needs say, God was as much seen in the valour of the officers and soldiers . . . as in any action that hath been performed, the enemy making, though he was still worsted, very stiff and sturdy resistance."[5]

Dusk had descended now, and the two brigades which Baillie had left to guard the Ribble bridge were in a desperate situation, for they found themselves attacked by several bands of Parliamentary foot, notably Fairfax's regiment, who were backed up by a troop of horsemen, and who were firing from behind the hedges of a steep slope near Preston which they commanded. Callander, perhaps not very wisely, sent 600 of his musketeers to reinforce them, but as they traversed the open land from the Darwen to the Ribble they were repelled by a sharp volley of musket fire, and one of the bullets smashed the arm of Colonel Claud Hamilton, one of the duke's relatives.

The Scots, however, put up a furious resistance lasting two hours, but they were eventually beaten from the bridge by pikemen under Colonels Pride and Dean, and shortly afterwards they were driven from their defence of the Darwen bridge as well. They would have sought shelter upon the little hill south of the Darwen, but as they began to climb it the enemy doggedly pursued them, and they retreated until they had fallen back upon Baillie and the main body of their comrades drawn up near Walton Hall.

Amid all this confusion, the English countryfolk, who had so unwillingly been transporting the Scottish wagons, had quite understandably taken the opportunity to slip off home, taking their horses with them, and Hamilton and his officers watched in horror as the enemy seized the stranded wagons and dragged them off. As they slipped and thudded down the slope one of them overturned, and all Hamilton's plate spilled out before the triumphant gaze of the Ironsides.

It was pitch-dark by now, and a heavy rain was falling. Huddled miserably "within a musket shot" of each other, the two armies settled down to await the dawn, when the fight would begin again in earnest. But Cromwell was taking no chances. The Scots had lost between 4,000 and 5,000 arms, almost as many prisoners, and 1,000 slain, and he was afraid that Hamilton might take advantage of the darkness to sneak off and escape northward across the bridge over the Ribble at Great Mitton. So he ordered seven troops of horse there from Clitheroe.

The Scots did indeed intend to escape, but not the way Cromwell anticipated. For as soon as the Ribble bridge was lost Hamilton had summoned all his officers together on horseback for a council of war. Callander, who though he had no right to, spoke first, was for marching away that night to seek out Middleton's cavalry on the Wigan road. Baillie and Turner protested, pointing out the folly of expecting tired and hungry troops to attempt such a venture on a dark wet night along such muddy tracks and entailing "the inevitable loss of all our ammunition". Though his sympathies seemed to Turner to lie with this view, Hamilton made no attempt to contradict Callander, and ordered a drumless march. The only ammunition his men took with them was what they carried in their flasks, for Hamilton intended—despite the heavy rain—to give instructions for the bulk of the ammunition to be blown up by a long fuse three hours after their departure, for to blow it up immediately would, of course, have notified the enemy of their flight.

Hamilton's troops—numbering some 7,000 or 8,000 foot and 4,000 horse in Cromwell's estimation—stole away unperceived, and were a good three miles out of Preston on the Wigan road before Cromwell discovered their flight. "We were so wearied with the dispute that we did not so well attend the enemy's going off as might have been", he explained.[6]

But the Scots' luck was wearing thin, for the ammunition which they had left behind at Preston fell undamaged into Cromwell's hands, since their general, with incredible stupidity, had neglected to give the order for it to be blown up. Moreover they completely missed Middleton, who was advancing northwards from Wigan through Chorley while their unsupported infantry were making their way south towards Standish by a route further west. When Middleton reached the south bank of the Darwen and, to his great surprise, found Cromwell there but not Hamilton, he realised what had happened and turned back. Picking up the tracks of the infantry he hurried after them but, Cromwell had sent "that worthy gentleman" Colonel Francis Thornhaugh, a close friend of his son-in-law Ireton, with two or three cavalry regiments after Middleton, and he was forced to skirmish the entire way, which prevented him from adequately guarding Hamilton's rear. In one charge Thornhaugh, "pressing too boldly", was run through the body, thigh and head by a Scottish pikeman, but his men continued to press hard on the heels of the Scots, killing and taking scores of prisoners. [7]

Meanwhile Cromwell, with 3,000 foot and 2,500 horse and dragoons, had taken up the chase, after sending the Lancashire levies back to Preston to guard the prisoners and garrison the town against a possible attack by Munro and the Ulster troops, who were still in north Lancashire. By now Hamilton, marching towards Wigan in the face of driving rain, was losing many of his men; for fatigue, hunger and confusion took their toll. Early on the morning of August 18th they drew up in battle array on some high moorland overlooking Standish, where Middleton's cavalry joined them. The location was conveniently dotted with enclosures, but to provoke another encounter with Cromwell was impossible, since the rain had completely destroyed the only powder they carried, and no more could be obtained. "Very dirty and weary", [8] they pressed on to Wigan once more, with Middleton again covering their retreat.

If Cromwell is to be believed the inhabitants of Wigan, "a great and poor town, and very malignant", were plundered by the fleeing Scots "almost to their skins". [9] But Wigan offered the fugitives no sanctuary, and that night they set off again, to stagger on to Warrington. As he was marching the last band of infantry out of Wigan, Sir James Turner learned that one, perhaps more— he did not know for certain amid the garbled and piecemeal panic-stricken reports that kept coming in—of Middleton's regiments had been routed, and he formed up his pikemen shoulder to shoulder in the market square, flooded with the light of a full moon. He instructed the regiments ahead of him to continue their march, and when Middleton's exhausted cavalry stumbled and splashed into the town, he ordered the fast ranks of pikemen to stand aside and let the cavalry through.

But, immediately, pandemonium broke loose, for the pikemen refused and accused him of being in collusion with the enemy, and two of them rushed at him, wounding him slightly in the thigh.

The horsemen balked at his incredible instructions to charge the pikemen, and did so only when he raised the false cry that the enemy had caught up with them. The cavalry dashed forward and the pikemen fled. The less agile were trampled under the horses' hooves, but order was eventually restored by Middleton.

There was no end to the Scots' torment, for when they resumed their tragic retreat the next morning, Cromwell, who had camped close by Wigan, after marching "twelve miles of such ground as I never rode in all my life",[10] followed them again in close pursuit. Half-starved, footsore, weary and demoralised, the Scots made one last and not unheroic stand against their formidable opponent. They took up a position just north of Winwick, in a pass protected by a steep bank, known as Redbank, and this they successfully defended for several hours, charging every move of Cromwell's infantry with their pikes, and once even forcing the enemy to yield ground, although that was quickly recovered. But their brave resistance was broken at last when some local men, embittered by the Scots' plundering, directed the Roundhead officers to where their foot could attack the Scots' flank, and they were pushed back towards the village green near Winwick Church. Those who could escaped to Warrington, where the rest of the army was barricading the bridge, leaving behind 1,000 fallen comrades and a further 2,000 in enemy hands.[11]

Callander, perceiving that further fighting was fruitless, urged Hamilton and the other officers to flee, leaving Baillie to capitulate. Hamilton was now in the same piteous condition as his men, exhausted and ravenous, sodden with sweat, splattered with mud, drenched with rain, dispirited and utterly confused. With that peculiar tendency of his to delegate responsibility, he readily gave in to Callander, in whose presence he seems to have lost all command, and at the council of war which followed he said hardly a word. He had withdrawn into himself, melancholy again, sensing ruin, knowing he was morally weak. For it was now all too clear, even to one who had long sought to delude himself about the quality of his military prowess, that he was no general, nor of the stuff of which commanders are made. Despite a superficial grandness and a deceptive optimism he was neither confident nor assertive; lacking charisma and an authoritative personality he was not a leader of men, and, devoid of decision and foresight, he had no gift for military strategy. Moreover, he was opposed to

PLATE X

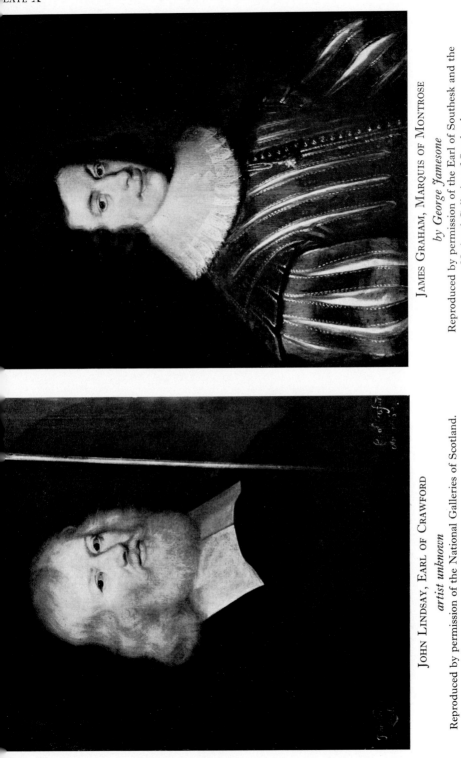

JOHN LINDSAY, EARL OF CRAWFORD
artist unknown
Reproduced by permission of the National Galleries of Scotland.

JAMES GRAHAM, MARQUIS OF MONTROSE
by George Jamesone
Reproduced by permission of the Earl of Southesk and the
National Galleries of Scotland.

PLATE XI

ARCHIBALD CAMPBELL, MARQUIS OF ARGYLL
by David Scougal

Reproduced by permission of the National Galleries of Scotland

MAJOR GENERAL JOHN LAMBERT
after Robert Walker

Reproduced by permission of the National Portrait Gallery, London.

a general of genius whose men, unlike his own, possessed a zealous belief in the righteousness of their cause and would fight to the death to defend it.

When Baillie was told that his fellow officers had ridden off with their troops, leaving him to make terms with the enemy, he was aghast with disbelief, and as soon as his mind grasped the reality of the situation he lost his habitual self-control and begged his men to shoot him in the head, rather than allow him to surrender. Growing calmer at last, perceiving that his subordinates had no stomach for the fight, he reluctantly sent an officer, Major Fleming, to treat with Cromwell. But the Parliamentary general insisted on parleying with Baillie himself, and they met on Warrington bridge. "Considering the strength of the pass, and that I could not go over the River Mersey within ten miles of Warrington with the Army, I gave him these terms", reported Cromwell, "that he should surrender himself and all his officers and soldiers prisoners of war, with all his arms and ammunition and horses to me, I giving quarter for life, and promising civil usage, which accordingly is done." [12]

Hamilton and the cavalry, in the meantime, were riding towards Chester, making for North Wales, still in the ill-founded belief that Lord Byron could help them. "Most of the nobility of Scotland are with the duke", noted Cromwell. "If I had 1,000 horse that could but trot thirty miles, I should not doubt but to give a very good account of them, but truly we are so harassed and haggled out in this business that we are not able to do more than walk an easy pace after them." [13] But before too long the Scots had second thoughts about trying to make for Wales, and, turning south, they spent a wretched night in the damp open fields near Malpas in Shropshire. Here they held yet another council of war, debating whether to head for Pontefract in Yorkshire, or Herefordshire, where they believed that Sir Henry Lingen was still in arms for the King, although in fact his uprising had been quashed several days earlier. Some intelligence of his defeat may have reached them, though, for they decided on the Yorkshire route, intending to return to Scotland by a horse-shoe turn, putting a safe distance between themselves and the enemy.

Next day they marched once more, through Whitchurch and Market Drayton, halting at noontime at Stone in Staffordshire, where Hamilton departed from his accustomed policy of clemency and ordered a trooper who had killed his company's captain to be shot. After resting, they marched again, Middleton as usual covering their rear. But he was set upon by a band of the county militia, who killed his horse under him and took him prisoner.[14] Later that day the Scots reached Uttoxeter, in "most tempestuous, windy and rainy weather" and "in great disorder".[15] "The duke and Callander fell out, and were at very high words at supper, where I was, each blaming the other for the misfortune and miscarriage of our affairs, in which contest I thought the duke had the better of it", recalled Turner, a frank admirer of Hamilton:

> And here I will say that my lord duke's great fault was
> in giving Earl Callander too much of his power all along,
> for I have often heard him bid him do what he pleased,
> promising to be therewith well contented. And therefore
> Callander was doubly to be blamed, first for his bad
> conduct (for that was inexcusable) and next for
> reproaching the duke with that whereof himself was
> guilty.[16]

When the order to march was given the next morning the troops were feeling understandably rebellious, and although they obeyed readily enough, they had not gone very far when it became obvious that officers as well as men were unwilling to march any farther, and they surrounded Hamilton in what amounted almost to a mutiny, telling him to return to Uttoxeter. Shock and strain over the defeat and dread of the consequences, combined with hunger, exhaustion and pain from the stone, made him ill, and he himself was almost too sick to march. Yet he resolved rather to surrender "with sword in hand in an open field, than to be cooped up in a town".[17]

But his men forced him to return to Uttoxeter, where they intended to rest until the following morning, when the disorderly flight would resume. Seeing all hope gone, Langdale and some of his officers rode off. He was later captured in a Nottinghamshire ale-house, but he managed to evade his captors and escaped to Holland. In the midst of this confusion a trumpeter arrived from the governor of Stafford, Colonel Henry Stone, commanding Hamilton to surrender himself and his army, but this he contemptuously refused to do.

Believing that their leaders planned to follow the examples of Traquair* and Langdale and desert them, Hamilton's men placed heavy guards on their officers' lodgings. It was a humiliating position, the more so as it was done in sight of the enemy trumpeter, who could tell his superiors of dissension in the Royalist ranks, and the next morning Sir James Turner called to the guards from a window of the duke's bedroom, upbraiding them for their treatment of their general and advising them to release him, which they did. Callander's nerves were shattered, and brushing aside Hamilton's protest he invited all who would to ride off with him. About half the remaining company did so, and the despicable, swaggering, second-in-command deserted his men, taking many of the best horses with him, and was fortunate enough to reach Holland in safety. Hamilton would have accounted it an irony indeed had he known that in later years his niece Mary, Lanark's daughter, would marry Callander's son.

It had now become evident to the duke and his remaining officers that it was lunacy to think of regaining Scotland. Everywhere the countryfolk were rising against them, impeding their march; they were stalked on Cromwell's orders by Lord Grey of Groby, commander of the Midland Association, by Sir Edward Rodes and Sir Henry Cholmeley with the Yorkshire militia, and the Staffordshire militia numbering some 3,000 men had all but surrounded them. The men would go no farther, and neither would the horses. So on August 25th Hamilton sent three officers, Colonel William Lockhart, Colonel James Foules and Sir James Turner to treat with the governor of Stafford. Their negotiations took place at Chartley Hall, an Elizabethan manor house a few miles to the south-west of Uttoxeter, where Mary Queen of Scots had once been imprisoned—an unhappy omen to the three Scotsmen. Hoever, they found the governor's representatives polite and seemingly prepared to grant fair and honourable terms; but a message from General Lambert, now lying very close to Uttoxeter, interrupted their talks. He explained that they must now treat with him, and he sent three officers, Robert Lilburne (later a regicide and brother of the rabid reformer, John

* Traquair and his son, Lord Linton, had raised a troop of horse for this campaign. With four other noblemen they left the army on its march to Malpas on August 19th. They were captured, and were prisoners in England until 1654.

Lilburne, author of Leveller tracts), Hezekiah Hayns and Edward
Manwaring, to parley with them. It is said that he offered Hamilton
a safe-conduct into Scotland if he would order the surrender of
Berwick and Carlisle. Hamilton, however, refused: in his present
straits he did not think that any commands of his would be
heeded, and he would not, in any case, be an instrument in anything prejudicial to the King's cause.[18]

Whilst the negotiations were in progress there rode up—
unfortunately for Hamilton, as it later turned out—Lord Grey of
Groby, claiming the duke as his prisoner. Lambert was a reasonable man, but Grey was cast in an entirely different mould. Only
twenty-five, eldest son of the first Earl of Stamford, who had been
a Parliamentary commander in the first Civil War, he was, despite
a surface charm, ambitious, ruthless and cruel: his signature
stands, bold and flowing, directly beneath Bradshaw's on the
death warrant of Charles I. Hamilton sent Colonel Gilbert Kerr
to tell him that he was already in treaty with Lambert, who
implored the Scots to sign the articles quickly: he could not consider Hamilton his prisoner until the articles were returned and
ratified by him, but he would not countenance Grey's claim
that he had captured Hamilton since he had no authority from
Parliament.[19]

So the articles were signed* and Hamilton, whose pain from
the stone was so acute by this time that he could hardly stand,
surrendered formally to Lambert. His life and safety and the lives
and safety of his officers had been guaranteed by the second clause
which stated: "that the Duke of Hamilton, with all officers and
soldiers of the said Scottish forces at Uttoxeter, shall have their
lives and safety of their persons assured to them, and shall not be
pillaged or stripped of their wearing clothes, or what they have
about them, or otherwise wronged, beaten, or abused, upon the
delivering up of their arms, or afterwards, and shall have civil
usage during the time of their imprisonment."[20]

Thus ended the political and military career of the Duke of
Hamilton in disgrace and disaster. Perhaps the most poignant
moment for him was when he handed Lambert his sword. It had
been in his family for generations, he explained, and he begged
Lambert to take good care of it. "As we rode from Uttoxeter",

---

* See Appendix Two.

recalled Turner, then on his way to captivity at Hull, "we made
a stand at the duke's window, and he looking out with some kind
words, we took our eternal farewell of him. . . . So we left him to
act the last and worst part of his tragedy."[21]

CHAPTER XIX

"THE POWER OF MERCILESS MEN"

Hamilton was now at the nadir of his fortunes. The calamitous end of the Engagement had sealed both his fate and the King's. It is said that when Charles, on tenterhooks at Carisbrooke, was informed by his gaolers of the defeat, he exclaimed that this news was the worst that ever came into England. To which Robert Hammond retorted that this was hardly so, since if Hamilton had been triumphant he would undoubtedly have seized the thrones of both England and Scotland. Charles, falling silent for a moment, presently replied: "You are mistaken. I could have commanded him back with the motion of my hand."[1] Nevertheless, the belief that Hamilton had undertaken the venture for his own ends was given considerable credence at the time.[2]

In the days immediately following his surrender the duke knew a variety of prisons. From Uttoxeter he was taken to Derby, from there to Leicester, then to Loughborough, and finally to Ashby de la Zouche, where he arrived on August 28th and remained for over three months. While he was there, Colonel Marten and commissioners from Parliament rode over to question him about English Royalist involvement in the Engagement, but met with no cooperation. In December he was transferred to Windsor, where he was strictly guarded. On his second evening there, feeling in need of exercise after supper, he began to stroll in the courtyard. But he had not gone very far when a sergeant stepped out from amongst the sentries and brusquely ordered him back to his chamber. Surprised, hurt and embarrassed, Hamilton obeyed at once. The incident, trifling in itself, was yet another reminder to him of the mutability of human affairs. How ironic, he remarked to his close kinsman, Lord Bargeny, who had led a regiment of foot at Preston, and was imprisoned with him, that he who not long ago had commanded thousands of men was now himself commanded by an ordinary sergeant.[3]

By and large, his men fared badly. Colonel Claud Hamilton

and other wounded Scottish prisoners were well treated by Cromwell, as Hamilton himself later testified: "indeed he was so very
courteous and so very civil as he performed more than he promised,
and I must acknowledge his favour to those poor wounded gentlemen that I left behind, that were by him taken care of, and truly
he did perform more than [I] did capitulate for."[4] Sir George
Munro's regiment, which had taken no part in the fighting,
managed to escape without trouble to Scotland, but the rest of
the Engagement forces were not so lucky. Lord Lanark, anxious
to give Argyll no excuse to call in Cromwell's troops, refused to
let the English Engagers cross the Border, and so Musgrave and
Tyldesley and their men huddled at Carlisle, finally surrendering
at Appleby in October. Many of the Scottish fugitives who
escaped capture were massacred by English peasants in retaliation
for the havoc they had wreaked on the north country. As for the
prisoners, the pressed men were set free, but the volunteers were
sold as indentured servants to the planters of Virginia and the
West Indies. Their fate was seen as poetic justice. "It is a wonderful thing, and God's last judgement", a contemporary newsletter
proclaimed, "that those that sold their King not two years ago
for £200,000 should now be sold for two shillings a piece to be
carried to new Plantations."[5]

Meanwhile, in England, events had taken a terrible turn for
those who had aided and abetted the second Civil War. One by
one the Royalist garrisons surrendered, and the Prince of Wales
returned to Holland. Hamilton's captured colours were paraded
before the defenders of Colchester, who, thoroughly disillusioned,
surrendered on August 27th, the privates being given quarter
but the officers being required to capitulate on terms. Two young
officers of outstanding ability and courage, Sir Charles Lucas and
Sir George Lisle, were selected to be shot in cold blood as examples.
Their executions, ordered by the usually lenient Fairfax, possibly
urged on by the vindictive counsels of Ireton, were a result of the
exasperation felt by the military masters of Parliament against the
remaining Royalist resistance. This bitterness was well expressed
by Cromwell, when he declared that "their fault who have appeared
in this summer's business is certainly double [to] theirs who were
in the first, because it is a repetition of the same offence against
all the witnesses that God has borne, by making and abetting to a
second war."[6] To Cromwell, as to Ireton and other Army leaders,

their victory in the first Civil War was a sign that God sanctioned the Parliament's cause, and since they now regarded themselves as the lawful rulers of England, any further resistance was considered treason.

Not surprisingly, since Hamilton's defeat was ascribed to "the blessing of God upon the Parliament forces", a Day of Universal Thanksgiving was proclaimed for Wednesday, August 23rd, to celebrate this "wonderful great success".[7] In Scotland, especial significance was attached to the fact that August 17th was "St. Covenant's Day", the anniversary of the signing of the Solemn League, and news of the Preston fiasco was greeted by Eglinton's "Whiggamore Raid" on Edinburgh, a rising of the fanatical Presbyterians of the West. The Committees of Estates, so lately under Hamilton's control, fled in alarm to Stirling under Munro's protection. "It is well-known", Cromwell wrote to the Committee from Berwick on September 16th, "how injuriously the Kingdom of England was lately invaded under Duke Hamilton, contrary to the Covenant and to our leagues of amity, and against all the engagements of love and brotherhood between the two nations."[8] The Committee's reply, four days later, showed how intense was the Scottish reaction against Hamilton and his friends:

> Only we must agree with you, that the righteousness of
> our God, who judgeth the Earth, hath evidently
> appeared in defeating that army under the command of
> the Duke of Hamilton, which grievously oppressed all
> such in this kingdom as out of conscience to keep the
> Covenant and treaties betwixt the kingdoms, would not
> join with them in their wicked Engagement against
> England. And surely had they prospered, there was
> just cause to fear, that piety and justice, which they
> so much pretended, should have been exceedingly born
> down and suppressed. Wherefore we do account it a
> special providence, that their designs were disappointed,
> and do look upon it as a mercy accompanied with great
> advantages to both kingdoms.[9]

On September 21st Cromwell and his army entered Scotland and struck up a wary alliance with Argyll, so that, as he wrote to Speaker Lenthall a few weeks later, "the affairs of Scotland are in a thriving posture, as to the interests of honest men" and

Scotland was "like to be a better neighbour to you now than when the great pretenders to Covenant, religion and treaties (I mean Duke Hamilton, the Earls of Lauderdale, Traquair, Southesk and their confederates) had the power in their hands...."[10] The Hamiltonian party was completely discredited. "Until the Lord", thundered the General Assembly in October, "beholding the affliction of his people and taking notice of the pride and blasphemy of the adversary, did scatter that army, and bring upon them so shameful and total an overthrow as will be a witness unto the following generations of his sore displeasure against the breakers of his Covenant and despisers of his word."[11] Not content with voicing their displeasure to Cromwell and the Parliament, the Committee of Estates denounced Hamilton to the King himself, at the same time justifying Cromwell's presence and the "Whiggamore Raid":

> We do seriously profess that since the raising of forces
> under the command of the Duke of Hamilton, this
> kingdom hath laboured under many and great
> distractions, and the sufferings of your majesty's
> faithful subjects have been lamentable and grievous
> beyond expression. We could see no security for
> religion nor good to your majesty nor anything which
> did tend to the peace of these kingdoms in that
> unhappy Engagement against England, wherefore we
> did dissent from and protest against it in particular,
> and were lately necessitated to rise in arms against the
> promoters and abettors thereof, who were likewise
> disturbing the peace of this kingdom, whereby it hath
> pleased God in his good providence to restore this
> kingdom to a better condition.[12]

On January 23rd 1649 the Act of Classes was passed, severely punishing the Engagers and all others who had not adhered to a strict interpretation of the Solemn League and Covenant. Those prominent in Montrose's "horrid rebellion", or in the Engagement, were disqualified for life from holding public office. This included "general officers who led and accompanied the army into England, and all those officers that continued in the Engagement . . . and all those persons who were plotters, chief actors, and prime promoters of the late unlawful Engagement from the

beginning to the end thereof in Parliament, committees or otherwise...."[13] Less influential Engagers, and all who had been
previously censured as Royalists or malignants, were disqualified
for ten years; those who had shown sympathy with the Engagement or failed to protest against it were disqualified for five years,
and for good measure all public persons guilty of immorality
or neglect of family worship were disqualified for one year.
Re-admission was in all cases to be subject to the sanction of the
Kirk, which thus retained control over public appointments.
Lanark, who was in the first category, was succeeded as Secretary
of State by Lothian, and Scotland did not readily forget the
Engagers' crime, which was that they "led a forced multitude to
slaughter or slavery with so great reproach and disgrace to the
nation, and occasioned a powerful army to enter the bowels of
this kingdom, and so laying the land open, and making it liable
to the guilt and misery of an unjust and offensive war, drawing
from God's judgment, and exposing us and our posterity to
invasion from our neighbour kingdom, if God in his providence
had not remedied the same.".[14]

As for Hamilton himself, the provisions at Uttoxeter might
have given him no immediate cause to fear for his life. Yet he
knew his situation was desperate. There is some evidence that at
the very beginning of his captivity he had been taunted, even
insulted. "Coward", "traitor", "treacherous Scot" are the words
that Hugh Peters and others are alleged to have used.[15] But
shortly afterwards, Cromwell's army chaplain became positively
unctuous in his treatment of Hamilton; perhaps he and his
master believed that such behaviour would make him part more
readily with the names of his English associates. The whole
history of these events is obscure. Whether Hamilton offered to
buy his freedom—and subsequently his life—as Nedham and
Walker claim, whether he did in fact give Peters money and even
his "George", as is sometimes suggested, is not clear. According
to Ludlow, Hamilton had surrendered his "George" at Uttoxeter,
and Turner implies that it was removed from him at that time.[16]
On November 13th the House of Lords, finding itself short of
money, agreed to set Hamilton free and banish him on payment
of a fine of £100,000, but exactly one month later, on December
13th, this decision was repealed. The following day, at Hamilton's
request, Cromwell galloped to Windsor, believing that at last

Hamilton was willing to speak. The duke's motivations in asking Cromwell to visit him are shrouded in mystery, and what passed between the two men is not known. Perhaps Hamilton did offer to join interests with Argyll and the Independents, as some held at the time.[17] "Cromwell hath been privately at Windsor with Duke Hamilton", reported the Royalist news-sheet *Mercurius Elencticus* "who (to show himself complete coward) hath discovered all he can, to save himself and ruin others."[18] At the same time Marchamont Nedham's *Mercurius Pragmaticus* informed its readers that "it's thought that cunning coward (for as yet we must not call him traitor) hath told tales", though four days later it reported that "much discourse had passed between Hamilton and Cromwell at Windsor, but in conclusion he protested that he was not invited in by his majesty, nor by any member of Parliament".[19]

Though in January an unknown Parliamentary sympathiser confidently wrote to a friend in France that "our chief evidence (we think) against the King is Duke Hamilton",[20] the duke refused to implicate others and involve them in his downfall. "I under the power of the sword and merciless men, no favour to be expected; oft examined, nothing discovered, being innocent", he wrote to his brother in lemon juice, a crude invisible ink. "Perhaps you will abide the same trial; beware if you do."[21] His servant, Andrew Cole, who was interrogated by Sir Hardress Waller, likewise steadfastly refused to give any information which might implicate the English Engagers, and there is, in fact, some evidence that the top Army leaders were divided as to what should be done with him. Cromwell wanted his trial to precede the King's, in order to give Charles more time to agree to Parliament's proposals, but Ireton, personally bitter as he was against Hamilton on account of the death of his great friend, Thornhaugh, believed that Charles should be brought to justice first.[22]

Meanwhile Ireton's creature, Colonel Pride, had purged Parliament of its moderate members, leaving a rump of between forty-five and fifty who could be relied upon to concur with the Army's decisions. The King was removed from the Isle of Wight to Windsor, where he arrived on December 23rd. Learning that he was due there that evening, Hamilton persuaded his gaolers to allow him a glimpse of the sovereign he had served so disastrously. The castle where, in happier times, he and the King had made merry, feasted and hunted deer, was now their prison, and as Hamilton shivered in the drizzle, waiting for Charles to enter the courtyard, he might have smiled at the bitter irony of it all. Then, suddenly, the King approached, haggard and grey-haired, and Hamilton fell to his knees. "My dear master!" he exclaimed, but further words failed him. The King embraced him: "I have been so indeed to you."* And then the brief exchange was over, for the guards hastened Charles away. His eyes misty with tears, Hamilton stood transfixed, watching the King as he passed from view.[23] Perhaps he sensed they would never meet again. In his own way, he was truly attached to Charles. "I have had the honour since my childhood to be near him, till now of late", he remarked on the morning of his own execution, "and during all that time I observed in him as eminent virtues and as little vice, as in any man I ever knew."[24] The two never met again, for Cromwell and Ireton expressly ordered Colonel Whitchcott, governor of Windsor Castle, that no further intercourse between them was to be permitted.[25] There was nothing left for Charles and Hamilton but to act out the closing scene in their respective tragedies.

On January 30th 1649, as the grey winter twilight deepened into dusk, a hot and breathless horseman galloped into Windsor: it was Andrew Cole, with news of the King's execution a few hours earlier. These tidings were not unexpected, and Hamilton had little time to dwell on them. For as soon as sentence of death had been pronounced on Charles three days before, the resourceful Cole had arranged a plan of escape for his master. Now that the King was dead, Hamilton knew that his own death was imminent.

Cole had been in touch with a Southwark wagonner, Mr. Owen, who had agreed to take Hamilton to Dover. The duke's ultimate destination is not clear; he may have been intending to make for France, where he had property, or, as is most likely, Holland, for young Prince Charles had established his head-quarters in The Hague, and the bustling coastal town had become a mecca for Royalist emigrés. Whatever his intentions, Hamilton bribed his gaoler and, under cover of darkness, walked out of Windsor Castle unchallenged just as the gates were being closed for the night. He was disguised as best he could be, in an unosten-

---

* Charles was playing on Hamilton's choice of adjective, in the sense that he [the King] had cost him dear.

tatious suit such as a merchant might wear, but deep in his pockets he had £120 and a diamond ring, valued at £100, which he probably intended to turn into cash. A little way off, concealed behind some trees, a servant and two horses were waiting for him. Cole was to follow him to London later with money and provisions, but he had warned his master that on no account was he to enter the City before seven the following morning, because of the troops who patrolled the streets.[26]

Hamilton ignored this sound advice. Any good intentions he may have had vanished when he grew restless and entered Southwark in the early hours. At four o'clock he came to what he believed was Mr. Owen's house, and, with a great upsurge of relief, he pounded on the door. But it was not the right house, and his repeated knockings, ignored by those inside, drew attention from a passing band of troopers, hunting for Sir Lewis Dyves, one of Langdale's men, who as luck would have it had also escaped the previous night. They did not ask the duke's identity, but they did enquire as to the nature of his business so early in the morning. He was, he replied as coolly as he could, searching for a carrier who would take him to Dover. The troopers' suspicions might have been allayed had not one of them, more observant than the rest, noticed his accent and asked him if he were a Scot. This he denied, but the man persisted, saying he had fought at Preston and was sure that he had noticed him in the Scottish army. At this point another band of patrolmen rounded the corner; by this time news of Hamilton's escape had been received, warrants were out for his re-arrest, a reward of £500 was offered to those who apprehended him, and thus these men, unlike the others, were on the look-out for him. Directly they saw him one of them, another Preston veteran, declared that it was the Duke of Hamilton himself, for he would recognise him anywhere, despite his disguise.[27]

So he was seized and searched, and the money and diamond found in his pockets. This was later shared, at Parliament's instigation, among the three troopers who had the greatest hand in apprehending him. In the guardhouse he made little further attempt to conceal his identity, for when his captors offered him a pipe he recklessly went to light it with several documents confirming who he was, and before the papers could shrivel into flames the guards snatched and read them. So resigned was he to his fate that when Cole, having traced him to the guardhouse, arrived at length, Hamilton gave a shrug of despair. "It was God's will", he told him simply, "that it should be thus!"[28] He seemed, in fact, to have a death wish, and something of this fatalistic, masochistic quality, this mysterious sense of virtue in failure, can be traced throughout his public career. Indeed, his complex personality, with his ambiguity, his deep-seated anxiety and depression, his defeatism, may afford an interesting psychological scrutiny outside the scope or competence of this study.

On Tuesday, February 6th, a new High Court of Justice was appointed to try him, and also Holland, Norwich, Owen and Capel; and three days later, in the fading grandeur of Westminster Hall, from whose ancient timber beams his captured colours hung mockingly, his ordeal began. Of those assembled there to try him, only John Bradshaw, the Court President, seated on a crimson velvet chair, and one Vincent Potter, had sat in judgment on the King. But the prosecution lawyers, John Cook and Attorney-General Anthony Steele, were among those who had framed the charge against Charles Stuart. Cook was a Puritan visionary who believed he was called to fulfil the Old Testament prophecy "I will bind their kings in chains and their nobles in links of iron", and had distinguished himself by the ferocity of his case against the King. The stage was set for another mock trial.

Standing at the bar, looking towards the west window where his judges sat in rows, grim-faced, the prisoner betrayed no emotion as the Attorney-General unfurled the scroll of parchment and intoned the indictment: "that the Earl of Cambridge, about the 19th of July last, traitorously invaded this nation in a hostile manner, and levied war to assist the King against the Kingdom and People of England, and had committed sundry murders, outrages, rapines, wastes and spoils upon the said people; and particularly about the 20th of August, near Preston, did make war, join battle and fight against the forces of the Parliament, and therein did murder and kill Colonel Thornley [sic] and others."[29]

The duke protested, in vain, that he was known by a more familiar title than that on the charge-sheet. It is possible that the use of his English title disconcerted him, although he should have remembered that the Parliamentarians refused to acknowledge any title bestowed after the outbreak of the war. As a Scottish peer he could not properly be tried in an English court, but they judged him, as Bradshaw curtly explained, not as Duke of Hamilton in Scotland but as Earl of Cambridge in England.[30]

Yet he still had faith in the strength of his defence. As yet no lawyer had been given the court's permission to appear for him, but he had always been an effective speaker and it cannot have been without confidence that he launched into his three-pronged plea. He had invaded England, he told them, by command of the Scottish Parliament, and reluctant as he had been to accept the generalship of the army, he could not refuse it without risk of punishment from his own country. His father had become a naturalised Englishman in April 1624 when Hamilton was seventeen. Now, he claimed, he was still an alien, having been born in Scotland before his father's naturalisation and therefore not liable to trial in England. Here, however, he was not strictly correct, since by the law of *post-natus* enacted in 1603 Scottish children born after the union of the crowns, as he was, were granted citizenship of England, just as by the same law English children became citizens of Scotland. Finally, he insisted, he was a prisoner of war whose life and personal safety were guaranteed by the terms of the articles of capitulation drawn up at Uttoxeter between his commissioners and Lambert's.

Having presented his main arguments, he begged for more time to prepare his defence, asking to be allowed to send to Scotland for witnesses and documentary evidence. The prosecution was visibly annoyed. He had been in custody for the past six months, Bradshaw reminded him sharply; he should have made the necessary arrangements during that time. The court adjourned until the next evening without giving him an answer. Hamilton left the hall with tempered optimism.

On Saturday he made a short appearance and was allowed counsel, and on the following Tuesday his lawyers were appointed. Of the four chosen, one, Dr. Walker, declined to appear for him owing to his employment by Parliament, and was replaced by the eloquent Mr. Heron. Then came Mr. Parsons, young and earnest, then Mr. Chute, confident and well-versed in the letter of the law, and finally the youthful Mr. Hale, afterwards Lord Chief Justice of England, intense and voluble.

Two days later Hamilton's request for more time to prepare his case was denied on the grounds that it would waste too much of the court's time, since there were many prisoners to be tried. The duke took this badly, for he had reminded the court that, seven years earlier, Strafford had been given time to send to Ireland for evidence. During the three weeks that followed he and his lawyers developed the three arguments with which he had opened his defence. He made use of the Biblical passages he had pored over at Pendennis to cite Old Testament examples of clemency towards prisoners of war. "Wouldst thou smite those whom thou hast taken prisoner with thy sword and thy bow?" the prophet Elisha had asked. Such arguments, the desperate man must have reasoned, would be received sympathetically by his Puritan judges. But he also reminded them of more timely examples, of Prince Rupert and Lord Cottington, who, though excepted from pardon and promise of life by act of Parliament, were nevertheless, by the articles of surrender at Oxford, allowed to go into exile overseas. Similarly, the Earl of Bristol and Lord Paulet, who were also excepted from pardon, were in no danger of their lives after the surrender of Exeter.

He was, he repeated, sent by the kingdom of Scotland, whose laws and commands he was bound to obey, having his "birth, honour and fortune there".[31] Had his army been successful, he ventured, it would have been as welcome to the English people as the Scottish entry into England in 1640 had been. It was without precedent that a prisoner of war should be tried for his life. He had been born in Scotland of a Scottish mother who was never naturalised, and they could not prove that he had been born after 1603, which would make him a *post-nati*. His possession of an English earldom could not be held to naturalise him, for naturalisation could occur only by act of Parliament, whereas an earldom was conferred by the King. Indeed, if it had been put to the test, he declared, he would probably have been expelled from sitting in the House of Lords, just as a Scottish member of Parliament, Walter Stewart, had been expelled from the House of Commons.

He had, he averred, become Lord Grey's prisoner only by Lambert's orders and he had made no surrender until the articles were signed and delivered. This claim was substantiated by Andrew Cole, and other witnesses, who testified that Hamilton had bluntly refused to surrender to Grey, and that the treaty of surrender was drawn up and signed, and the duke already Lambert's prisoner, before Grey arrived. The articles agreed upon were explicit in their meaning, and were not subject to interpretation according to the "mental reserves" of the signatories.[32] The first article made it clear that he was a prisoner of war and the second that his life and the lives and safety of his followers were expressly and unreservedly guaranteed. By escaping from Windsor he had not violated the articles, since they bound him only to deliver himself a prisoner, not to remain one.

On the face of it, if justice was to be done, Hamilton's case was unassailable. But in reality his trial was the scene of a power struggle between the extremists in Parliament who believed that he, like the English Engagers, was guilty of treason and must pay with his life, and many officers—among them Hugh Peters—who cared, and cared deeply, that the honour of the Army was in jeopardy, and held that the trial violated a military treaty. The strength of Hamilton's opening plea on the first day of the trial had embarrassed the extremists, who held with Cromwell that he had committed "a more prodigious treason than any that had been perpetrated before, because the former quarrel on their part was that Englishmen might rule over one another, this to vassalise us to a foreign nation".[33] They had assembled a number of prosecution witnesses, bribed and primed to deny that the treaty was binding upon Parliament, as Hamilton had claimed: "it was clear that Lambert, being a general officer, commissioned by Parliament, was empowered to capitulate both by the Parliament and by Cromwell, Grey having no authority from the Parliament, only by Cromwell's letter."[34]

Hamilton's own attempts to bribe Lambert to admit he was his prisoner had failed, for Lambert was afraid to contribute the truth to a court which chose not to hear it. The vindictive and unscrupulous Lord Grey asserted that Hamilton refused two summons to yield to him, and Lilburne maintained that his own meaning of preserving the duke's life (he did not know how the rest meant) was only "to preserve him from the violence of the soldiers and not from the justice of the Parliament".[35] When Hugh Peters jumped to his feet in protest, shouting that if this was so it should have been made clear in the articles, Bradshaw coolly interjected: "you say well for the future, but it is now too late."[36]

Still, Peters could not be silenced. On Monday, February 19th, when Colonel Waite testified that Hamilton had surrendered to Grey and requested protection from the mutineers, he leapt up crying "He lies, he lies!" Peters had been present at Uttoxeter, and knew well that it was to Lambert that Hamilton had surrendered. It was in vain that he and others argued thus; the court had already reached its verdict. On February 26th in an eloquent speech, Steele neatly disposed of Hamilton's defence. Although the duke was a Scot he was not an alien, for he partook of all the privileges an Englishman could enjoy, being a peer of England, possessing land in that country and marrying there. He could reasonably be considered *post-natus* since he had not shown the court convincing evidence to the contrary. The Army had no power to protect him from the justice of Parliament, to which it was subordinate. "No security from the stroke of civil justice belongs to the prisoner by this refuge", Steele icily pronounced, "for as to the military, that is not the contention."[37] The articles merely safeguarded his life during his imprisonment, but his escape from Windsor ended the Army's obligation to abide by them.

On March 6th the judges assembled in their scarlet robes to pronounce their verdict. Thirty-five names appeared on the warrant which declared him "convicted, attainted and condemned of High Treason and other high crimes" and which sentenced him "to be put to death by the severing of his head from his body . . . in New Palace Yard at Westminster upon Friday being the ninth day of this instant month of March between the hours of nine in the morning and six in the afternoon. . . ."[38] The same predictable verdict and fearsome sentence was passed upon Holland, Norwich, Capel and Owen, who stood accused with him.

So the long pretence ended. The only emotion Hamilton had allowed himself during the whole of the proceedings was when Whitchcott, the governor of Windsor, asserted that the duke had given him an undertaking that he would not escape. This provoked a spirited outburst from Hamilton, who declared that so shamefully did this reflect upon his honour that if he were not on trial he should certainly challenge Whitchcott to a duel for the allegation, and he could name no better location for it than Westminster Hall.[39] Now he returned to St. James's, and the pious exhortations of the kindly Royalist divine, Dr. James Sibbald. A Scot from Aberdeen, he had known the duke for a long time, had performed Lanark's marriage ceremony and had been one of those who, over a decade ago, had refused to sign the National Covenant. During the past weeks he had been Hamilton's only comfort.

During the two days following sentence friends of the convicted men—"the grand delinquents"—were busy organising appeals to save them; it is said that Denbigh tried in vain to persuade Parliament to issue *carte blanche* for Hamilton to sign.[40] Cromwell, who would not modify his hatred for the architects of the second Civil War, was bitterly opposed to any appeals being considered by the House, but the Commons voted to debate them. Norwich was saved by the casting vote of the Speaker, and Owen was also reprieved, perhaps because he was a modest Welsh gentleman with no powerful friends to plead for him, although there is in fact some evidence that the Dutch and Spanish ambassadors interceded on his behalf.[41] But Hamilton's petition was rejected without a division. Capel's was also unsuccessful, despite his wife's eloquent pleas for mercy, and Holland's was also rejected, even though his brother, the Parliamentarian Lord Warwick, and Lord Fairfax, brought their influence to bear in a bid to save him.[42]

In vain did seventeen-year-old Lady Anne plead with Argyll to intercede for her father's life. The calculating Campbell chieftain, who had "preached off [Hamilton's] head in Scotland before it was cut off in England",[43] ignored the tears of the distraught girl, telling her that it was hardly fitting for the Scots to approach the English regicides for mercy.

On Thursday, March 8th the Army Council met to debate whether it should mediate with the Parliament for the lives of any of the condemned men. For several, yet, the honour of the Army was the burning issue. "Did Lambert send word to him [Hamilton] that he had no power to give him his life?" Sir Hardress Waller wanted to know. "Would any man give up two thousand horse without some assurance?" But others echoed the fanatical regicide Colonel Goffe, who begged them to consider "the providence of God that hath appeared to us for the bringing of us thus far". Lambert, explained Colonel Whalley, did not intend that Hamilton should be preserved from the power of the civil authority, nor did he have power to do so. "God", declared Major Carter, "never afforded an opportunity for us to do justice till now."[44]

Hugh Peters hoped that Hamilton's execution could be postponed until the Army Council had debated the matter further, and in vain did Lord Denbigh continue to plead with Cromwell for his brother-in-law's life. The iron will of Parliament had triumphed over the conscience of the Army. And so the convicted men, as well as the two reprieved (who were not released until May 7th) prepared for their last night on earth in the room at St. James's which they had shared for the past six weeks. There, in the failing light, Hamilton wrote his last letter to Lanark. His servants were granted permission to sleep in an adjoining room, being determined to be with him until the end. Visits from friends and relatives prevented the prisoners from going to bed until very late, and it was well past midnight before they fell into a shallow slumber.

CHAPTER XX

THE RECKONING

The short night was soon over. Hamilton awoke at half-past three. He was outwardly composed, and called Cole to sit at his bedside, giving him final instructions to be carried to his brother. After he had dressed, and spent some time in prayer, he wrote to "his most dear children", Anne and Susanna:

> It hath pleased God so to dispose of me as I am
> immediately to part with this miserable life for a better,
> so that I cannot take that care of you which I both
> ought and would if it had pleased my gracious Creator
> to have given me longer days. But His will be done,
> and I with alacrity submit to it, desiring you to do so,
> and that above all things you apply your hearts to seek
> Him, to fear, serve and love Him, and then doubt not
> but He will be a loving father to you while you are on
> earth, and thereafter crown you with eternal happiness.
> Time will permit me to say no more; so the Lord bless,
> guide and preserve you . . . I

Thinking of his only surviving sister, the Countess of Crawford-Lindsay, and his illegitimate half-sister, Lady Belhaven and their husbands, he asked that this letter remember him to "my dear sisters, brothers and other friends, for it is all I write". Feeling that he might be prevented from speaking freely upon the scaffold, or that some points might slip his memory, he had prepared a speech, which he delivered to those assembled in the room. It was, he said, "the last testimony of my loyalty to my King, for whom I now die, and of my affection to my country, for the pursuance of whose pious and loyal commands I am now to suffer".[2]

The speeches of dying men are always suspect as a precise indication of their feelings and motives. Yet Hamilton's provides, however superficially, an interesting insight into his secretive soul. Speaking first of his religion, he declared himself "of the true reformed Protestant religion, as it is professed in the Church of Scotland". As for Charles, "among all his subjects there could not be found a better Protestant than himself; and surely also he was free from having any intent to exercise any tyranny or absolute power over his subjects". He attributed the late King's misfortunes more "to the sins of his people than to his own" and declared "for my own part, I do protest never to have swerved from that true allegiance which was due to him". He asserted that he would die "a true and loyal subject" to Charles II: "I hope, though I do not live to see it, that God's justice and goodness will in his own time establish himself on the throne of his father. . . ."

Thinking of Cromwell, Ireton and the rest, Hamilton expressed confidence that "so long as men deeply plunged in guilt and self-interest usurp power and government these kingdoms will fall short of peace or any other permanent happiness". He then spoke of various political activities in the past. Montrose's bitter charges at Oxford in 1643 rankled with him still. "It is well known what calumnies and aspersions have been thrown upon me by men of several parties and interests, not excepting those who would seem to carry much affection to his late majesty, as if I had expressed disservice or disloyalty unto him . . . how malicious and groundless they were, I appeal to God. . . ."

Nine years had passed since the sacrifice of Strafford, yet the memory of it haunted Hamilton as it had tormented Charles:

> Neither did I at all deal with his majesty for his consent
> to the bill of attainder for taking away the life of the
> Earl of Strafford, whose great parts and affection it is
> known I highly valued. Yet some have been pleased to
> attribute to me the cause of that concession, but were
> his majesty now living I am confident he would publicly
> clear me in both these, as he hath been pleased many
> times in private formerly to do.

In similar vein, he repudiated suggestions that he had ever consciously given Charles mischievous advice or used the great seal of Scotland for authorising the war in Ireland. Nor had he betrayed the army under his command or his English associates: "indeed it was so contrary to my conscience, and so derogatory to my honour, that if I had been able, yet should I never have prejudiced any in that nature, though it had been to save me a hundred lives."

He was not vindictive. "I am void", he affirmed, "of all rancour or displeasure against any, though I am within a few hours to die, adjudged by a lawless and arbitrary court . . . and though my death is no less than murder, yet I forgive all, and pray to God to do it, and that my blood be not laid to their charge. . . ." He denied the right of the court to judge him, and reiterated the justice of his defence, yet "I do with all Christian humility submit to the punishment, which for my other personal sins the Lord hath justly brought upon me".[3]

He had not long closed this speech when, at about nine o'clock, Colonel Beecher arrived at St. James's to convey the prisoners to Westminster. As he prepared to leave, Hamilton reflected that Cole's outstanding loyalty to him during the past few weeks merited a special recommendation to Lanark, and he requested pen and ink, so that he could scribble his brother a final hasty note. "There is nothing more certain than that a faithful servant is an humble friend", he wrote of Cole, and more personally to Lanark, "as I have loved you all my life, so do I now at the end of it."[4]

The three condemned noblemen, as well as Norwich and Owen, were carried in sedan chairs through St. James's Park to Sir Robert Cotton's house, a splendid mansion close to Westminster Hall, where the King had lodged during his trial. With their chaplains they were ushered into one room, where they remained for at least an hour. Holland's white satin suit contrasted sharply with the sombre clothes worn by Capel, and the unhealthy gauntness of the one and the towering height of the other emphasised the burly stockiness of Hamilton. The ministers attending them were of some comfort, but stronger stuff was needed to sooth their frayed nerves, and while Capel puffed on his customary pipe Hamilton and Holland thankfully accepted an offer of wine.

Hamilton's reputation for treachery was such that even now Cromwell sent some officers to him, with offers to spare his life if he would reveal the identities of his English collaborators. Still he refused, telling them that if he had as many lives as hairs on his head, he would lay them all down rather than redeem them so dishonourably.[5] Close on the heels of the officers, and probably echoing their request, came the Earl of Denbigh, to take a sorrowful farewell of the brother-in-law with whom he had enjoyed a long friendship. He assured Hamilton that he need not worry about the futures of Anne and Susanna, so soon to be orphaned. He seems also to have hinted that, even at this late hour, he would continue to press Cromwell for clemency.

When they were told by Beecher to get ready for the scaffold, Holland's chaplain said a general prayer for all of them. Toasts were drunk, and after mutual embraces Hamilton, the first to suffer, walked to his doom. Accompanied by Dr. Sibbald and three servants, Cole, Lewis and Sir James Hamilton, he passed through Westminster Hall to the scaffold. As he stepped out into the bright sunshine of that mild March morning, a formidable sight met his eyes. Drawn up in the yard, row upon row, were several regiments of the Parliamentary foot, and many spectators crowded near the scaffold. The judges who, three days earlier, had passed sentence on him and the other peers, were seated at a vantage point, that they might witness the executions they had commanded. Nearby, in a room in the Hall once occupied by the Star Chamber, Cromwell and some of his officers stood watching the scene through "perspective glasses".[6]

Colonel Beecher handed Hamilton over to the Under-Sheriff of Middlesex and a guard of his men. Alderman Sir Thomas Viner, Sheriff of London, to whom the death warrant was made out, had been taken ill the day before, and the Under-Sheriff came in his place, to see the execution carried out. As the little party began to ascend the scaffold, Denbigh approached. Since he had just taken leave of Hamilton at Cotton's house his sudden appearance now made the duke wonder whether he carried news of a reprieve. As a high-ranking Parliamentary officer Denbigh might have gained an eleventh hour stay of execution, and Hamilton could scarcely conceal his agitation. But Denbigh came to say that all hope was gone, and the deputy sheriff assured the prisoner that he had a warrant to execute him.[7]

Upon the scaffold Hamilton was characteristically calm; he behaved with unhurried dignity and studied courtesy to all around him. "His countenance", wrote an onlooker, "was cheerful, and all the time of his being on the scaffold there appeared in him no fear, disorder, change of countenance or discomposure."[8] He was surprised that the crowd was not loud or unruly and seemed to expect some kind of speech from him. Yet he feared that his voice was too low for his words to reach beyond the first rows of spectators. Therefore he did as the King had done, addressing his remarks to the little group on the scaffold. Standing hatless, he turned to the Under-Sheriff and declared that he loved England equally with his own country, and had wished her no harm. "What I did was by command of the country where I was born, whose commands I could not disobey, without running into the same hazard there of that condition that I am now in. . . ."[9]

Noticing that the sun was shining directly into the duke's face, Sibbald interrupted, and suggested he change his position. But Hamilton smilingly refused: "no, sir, it will not burn it. I hope to see a brighter sun than this very speedily." "It pleased God", he resumed, "so to dispose of that army under my command, as it was ruined, and I, as their general . . . stand here now ready to die." Observing that several of those in the crowd standing near enough to hear were taking notes, he broke off to explain that since he had not anticipated making a speech, his remarks were not as coordinated as they would otherwise have been. He hoped they would not publish anything detrimental to his memory. "Terrible aspersions", he reminded them, "have been laid upon myself, truly such, as I thank God, I am free from."[10]

He declared himself a loyal servant of the late King. "What I pretended was for the King, there was nothing less intended than to serve him in it . . . his person I do profess I had reason to love, as he was my King, and as he had been my master." Drawing to a close, he told them "I wish the kingdom's happiness, I wish it peace . . . I wish this blood of mine may be the last that is drawn . . . I freely forgive all . . . I carry no rancour along with me to my grave." He saw no point now in discussing affairs of state, but of his own part he said: "my own inclination hath been to peace from the beginning . . . never was I an ill instrument betwixt the King and his people; I never acted to the prejudice of the parliament; I bore no arms, I meddled not with it; I was not wanting by my prayers to God Almighty for the happiness of the King."[11]

The kindly Sibbald, who was convinced of Hamilton's sincerity, did his best to comfort the duke, who now prepared to die. Having agreed with the executioner on the signal for the axe to fall, Hamilton told the man that he forgave him and that his servants would settle with him afterwards.[12] He then had a private conversation with his servants, asking them to remember him to his mother-in-law, the dowager Lady Denbigh, and to his old friend, Lady Devonshire, who perhaps would no longer doubt his loyalty.

Then, taking Sibbald in his arms, he took a cheerful leave of him; "I bless God for it, I do not fear ... I go with so clear a conscience that I know not the man I have personally injured." Turning to his servants again, he warmly embraced each in turn, and it was noticed that he was particularly affectionate to his secretary, Mr. Lewis. "You have been very faithful to me", he told them, "and the Lord bless you." [13]

Throwing off his cloak and doublet, he arranged his long hair under a white satin cap, leaving his neck uncovered. He knelt at the block with Sibbald, who prayed aloud for several minutes. When the minister arose Hamilton placed his head in preparation for the axe. He had been ordered to lie facing towards the High Court of Justice, a sign of his submission to its verdict. As at the King's execution the block was low, forcing him to assume an almost prone position. After a short inaudible prayer, he stretched out his right hand, the signal for the executioner to strike. His head fell at one blow. Unlike that of Charles, it was not displayed to the onlookers, but was immediately wrapped by two of his servants in a strip of crimson taffeta. His remains were then taken to Sir John Hamilton's house in the Mews.* A few days later they were shipped to Scotland, and, in accordance with his wishes, quietly interred—"without pomp or ceremony"—in the ancestral vault at Hamilton on May 1st.[14]

"So the glory of the world passeth away", noted the Earl of Leicester in his diary, "and those that think themselves great, happy and safe, are set in slippery places, suddenly perish and come to a fearful end." [15]

*   *   *

When Lanark, eventually fleeing Scotland after the passing of the Act of Classes had made his position there intolerable, arrived at the Court of the young King in Holland and learned of his brother's death, he was overcome with grief. Brooding alone in his rooms for several days, he would be comforted by none of those who called to offer their sympathy.[16] Much as he repented of his own defection to the Covenanters in 1643 and regretted having been led by Hamilton down paths which called his own

* Near the site of Trafalgar Square.

loyalty seriously into question, he knew full well that the duke
had been far more generous to him than was usual on the part of
an elder brother. For to Hamilton's "extraordinary kindness" he
owed almost everything he had in the world.[17] Now he held in
his hand his brother's last letter to him, a poignant document
revealing the sincerity and depth of Hamilton's feelings for the
younger man:

> I know you will do undesired (as far as is in your
> power) what I now briefly mention. First, that you will
> be a father to my poor children, and that they be not
> forced to marry against their wills. The debts I owe
> are great, and some friends are bound for them, but the
> estate I leave you is such as will satisfy what I owe and
> free my cautioners from ruin. You are just, and I doubt
> not of your performing this. . . . Dote not upon the
> world; all is but vanity and vexation of spirit: grieve
> not for what is befallen me, for it is by the appointment
> of Him that rules in earth and heaven.[18]

Henrietta Maria, who had never really cared for Hamilton, or
trusted him, and, it seems, liked Lanark little better, nevertheless
sent her condolences from Paris on April 22nd: "though my own
inexpressible loss hath made me incapable of feeling else that can
befall me in this world, yet it hath not made me insensible of your
brother's death, both on his own account and on yours."[19]

In his will Hamilton commended his two daughters to the care
of Lanark. "As there hath always been an infinite love betwixt
us", he had written, "so I am confident he will express his to
them."[20] And the new duke did not fail his brother in his expectations. Writing from Holland to the broken-hearted Lady Anne
three months after her father's death, he expressed the hope that
she was:

> settled in Hamilton, where you have, as is most just,
> the same power your father had, and I beseech you to
> dispose as absolutely upon everything that is there. All
> I have interest in, so long as they will acknowledge me,
> will obey you. . . .[21]

Lanark found that he had fallen heir not only to his brother's
estates and titles, but to the political position which Hamilton had

occupied. Whilst fighting gallantly for the King at the Battle of
Worcester on September 3rd 1651, where he led a troop of three
hundred horse raised from the Hamilton estates, a bullet smashed
his leg and he was taken prisoner. His death nine days later saved
him from his brother's fate, for the English Parliament had already
ordered that he be tried and brought to justice as an example.[22]
On his death the Earl of Abercorn became heir-male of the
House of Hamilton, asserting claim to the Duchy of Châtelherault. The English honours, along with the title Earl of
Cambridge (since Hamilton's death so odious to the family),
became extinct, and the Earldom of Arran became dormant; but
the other Scottish titles and estates devolved, according to the
patent of 1643, upon Lady Anne. Her portrait by David Scougal
reveals a slender young woman with intelligent dark eyes, closely
resembling her father. Hamilton, anxious to keep the honours and
property in the family, had hoped she would marry Abercorn's
eldest son, Lord Paisley, but an ugly feud over ownership rights
developed between them, and Paisley married beneath himself.[23]
In 1656 Lady Anne married William Douglas, second son of
the Marquis of Douglas, and on her petition at the Restoration he
became third Duke of Hamilton for his lifetime. Hamilton's other
daughter, Lady Susanna, married John Kennedy, seventh Earl of
Cassillis, in December 1668.

Under the Commonwealth the fortunes of the family sank to a
low ebb: their debts amounted to over £112,000 and their estates
were seized, awarded to General Monk and others, and later
sold.[24] So bleak was the situation that in July 1654 Baillie could
write:

> Our nobility well nigh are wracked. Dukes Hamilton,
> the one execute, the other slain; their estates forfault;
> one part of it gifted to English soldiers; the rest will
> not pay the debt; little left to the heretrix; almost the
> whole name undone with debt.[25]

In 1655, Lanark's widow, Elizabeth, finding it difficult to
support herself and her four daughters on the annual pension of
£400 granted to her by Parliament, made an ill-advised marriage
with Thomas Dalmahoy, a family retainer who had been Lanark's
gentleman of the horse. He refused to assume financial responsibility for her daughters and on her death in 1659 he bitterly con-

tested their claims to her property.[26] However, he prospered, and after the Restoration he sat for many years as Member of Parliament for Guildford under the patronage of the Duke of York, later King James II.

By the end of 1656 Duchess Anne* and her husband had paid in full a fine of £9,000 necessary to regain the forfeited estates, and in 1662 Charles II gave them £15,000, the amount he and his father had owed Hamilton.[27] Anne and her sister were understandably anxious that Hamilton's death should be avenged, and in June 1660 they petitioned the House of Lords that those who had sent their father to the block "be proceeded against and brought to condign punishment".[28] Two months later, in August, their uncle Lord Denbigh was invited by the Lords to nominate one of Hamilton's judges for execution. For reasons best known to himself he chose one already dead, William Wyberd, and on being pressed to name another he declined.[29] Perhaps he remembered Hamilton's plea that "my death be not laid to their charge" and believed he was best serving his brother-in-law by honouring that wish. But Anne and Susanna had a compensation of sorts in May 1661, when Argyll was executed for high treason. The great statesman of the Covenant, who had gloated over the destruction of his three principal rivals—Hamilton, Huntly and Montrose—had come to a violent end himself.

Anne, Duchess of Hamilton, outlived her sister, her husband, and her eldest son, the fourth duke, who was killed in a duel with Lord Mohun in 1712. A staunch Presbyterian who seems to have inherited some of the strong-mindedness of her paternal grandmother, she died in October 1716, aged eighty-five, an unrelenting opponent of the Act of Union.[30]

* She was, of course, a duchess in her own right.

EPILOGUE

There were few who loved Hamilton; there were many who hated him. In the popular mind, the efforts of the Whig historians notwithstanding, an aura of heroism and romance surrounds the memories of King Charles and his followers. Several who died in the royal cause, whether they fell on the field, like Falkland, or suffered on the scaffold, like Montrose, captured the imaginations of men. Not so Hamilton. To the Royalists themselves he was no hero, and in an age still steeped in witchcraft, many among them professed to believe an old tale that a fortune-teller had told him that the King would die a violent death and he would succeed him, but whereas he thought the man meant on the throne, he meant on the scaffold.[1] Thus to the Royalists Hamilton was a despicable rogue, a treacherous opportunist whose ultimate sacrifice was merely just retribution and could not redeem him.[2]

Their opinion was reflected in a derogatory pamphlet by Marchamont Nedham, appearing a month after Hamilton's execution:

> He that three kingdoms made one flame
> Blasted their beauty, burnt the frame
> Himself now here in ashes lies
> A part of this great sacrifice. . . .
> 'Twas he that first alarmed the Kirk
> To this prepost'rous bloody work,
> Upon the King's to place Christ's throne,
> A step and foot-stool to his own;
> Taught Zeal a hundred tumbling tricks,
> And Scriptures twined with politics,
> The Pulpit made a juggler's box,
> Set Law and Gospel in the stocks. . . .
> 'Twas he patched up the new divine,
> Part Calvin, and part Cataline,
> Could too transform (without a spell)

Satan into a Gabriel;
Just like those pictures which we paint,
On this side fiend, on that side saint,
Both this, and that, and ev'rything
He was; for, and against the King;
Rather than he his ends would miss,
Betrayed his master with a kiss,
And buried in one common fate
The glories of our Church and State. . . .[3]

But, that April of 1649, the Cromwellian government, perhaps fearing that even Hamilton might be lauded as a martyr, ordered all material pertaining to his life and death confiscated and destroyed.[4] In 1659 a satire appeared which proved that in the decade following his death popular hatred of Hamilton had not abated. It ended:

A traitor I lived, and a traitor I died,
And yet with both parties I never complied;
'Tis strange, you will say, but here is the reason,
I true was to neither, so suffered for treason.[5]

"Time", Hamilton had once written to Charles, "will make appear the faithfulness of your majesty's most loyal subject and humblest servant."[6] Yet even Burnet's painstaking apologia could not arrest the calumny attached to the duke's memory. According to Sir Philip Warwick, who of course knew Hamilton, whereas Burnet did not, the bishop "hath represented this great man by a light which few others, either of his own nation or ours, discovered him by".[7] But as C. V. Wedgwood has pointed out, "the fierce indictments of contemporary opinion have long since lost their force".[8] Indeed, the only important later commentator to lay the blame for Charles' troubles squarely at Hamilton's feet was Mark Napier, but he was biased by reason of his own descent from Montrose's sister. Still, Alison Wilson's verdict on Hamilton in Scott's *Old Mortality* shows how deep-rooted has been the popular opinion of him, and his memory has further suffered by the treatment in at least one modern historical novel which quite unjustly portrays him as a foolish and effeminate fop.[9]

Of Hamilton, then, what are we to conclude? Was he a good or an evil genius? It is tolerably certain that he was neither. Stated quite simply, he was a man who tried to serve two masters. He failed, and from the tragi-comedy of his life he emerges as a kind of anti-hero. His crime was not treachery but weakness. Though not a physical coward, he was certainly a moral one. Trapped between his allegiance to Charles and his own stake in Scotland, he tried to reconcile the consequent dilemma with the pursuit of self-interest. With little concern for opposing ideologies, his was essentially a moderate mind. On almost every issue he could appreciate both sides of the argument, and was rarely zealous about either. If absolute monarchy and Episcopacy were threatened, then, in the interests of peace, they would have to be modified. Because of all this he was pragmatic; beyond an uneasy expediency and the advocacy of compromise solutions he had no well-calculated plans or long-term goals. He lacked that force, statesmanship and vision which set his great contemporaries, Strafford, Argyll and Montrose, head and shoulders above him. As a politician he was myopic and vacillating, and therefore was neither astute nor successful.

"He was so far", says Burnet, "from flattering himself with the hopes of great success in any of his undertakings that he rather apprehended himself under some inauspicious star, that crossed all his attempts, which made him in his latter years long for some secret retirement out of the business."[10] The fault, however, lay not in his stars, but in himself. It was his misfortune, as it proved that of Charles, that he did not appreciate the limits of his own ability. He was unsuited both by temperament and capacity to the part he had been called upon to play. He failed to come to terms with any of his environments. He was uprooted from Scotland and rootless in England, and in many ways as unsuited to the Court as he was to the council chamber and the battlefield. In his concern for financial profit and disregard for religious controversy he was, it could be argued, ahead of his time, a man better suited to the nineteenth century than to the seventeenth, or at any rate a man more suited to play the merchant than the politician.

And yet it might not be too fantastic to observe that, had circumstance settled him on the throne of Scotland in place of Charles, he would have proved a not unsuccessful king. His appreciation of the realities of Scottish politics, his readiness to compromise and his lack of personal arrogance would in all likelihood have allowed him to reach an acceptable arrangement with the disruptive forces within the kingdom. An unknown contemporary may have been more perceptive than he realised when he idly commented "I make no question but if the duke could be King of Scotland, his tender conscience might without the help of divines, be persuaded to digest with a moderate Episcopacy. . . ."[11]

When all the evidence is considered, the best epitaph on Hamilton the public figure still seems to be that of Clarendon:

> His natural darkness and reservation in his discourse
> made him to be thought a wise man, and his having
> been in command under the King of Sweden, and his
> continual discourse of battles and fortifications made
> him to be thought a soldier. And both these mistakes
> were the cause that made him to be looked upon as a
> worse and more dangerous man than in truth he
> deserved to be.[12]

As for Hamilton the private individual, it is difficult for us, now, to judge a fitting verdict. But perhaps those who knew him well would have concurred in the opinion of Sir James Turner, who knew him but briefly, during the Preston campaign, and there formed the following favourable impression: "[He] was a person of excellent qualities, of a great understanding, and good expressions, courteous, affable, humane; so merciful that he was but a bad judiciary . . . one of the best masters to vassals and tenants that our kingdom afforded."[13]

One thing, at least, is certain. By the manner of his end, James Duke of Hamilton atoned in part for the disastrous policies which had helped, however unwittingly, to bring King Charles to his doom. He may not always have lived for the King's cause, but he certainly died for it, a man with no taste for martyrdom who nevertheless became a martyr.

THE TREATY OF CARISBROOKE
26th December 1647

His Majesty giving belief to the professions of those who have entered into the League and Covenant, and that their intentions are real for preservation of His Majesty's person and authority according to their allegiance, and no ways to diminish his just power and greatness, His Majesty, so soon as he can with freedom, honour and safety be present in a free Parliament, is content to confirm the said League and Covenant by Act of Parliament in both Kingdoms, for security of all who have taken or shall take the said Covenant, provided that none who is unwilling shall be constrained to take it. His Majesty will likewise confirm by Act of Parliament in England, Presbyterian government, the directory for worship, and Assembly of Divines at Westminster for three years, so that His Majesty and his household be not hindered from using that form of Divine Service he hath formerly practised, and that a free debate and consultation be had with the Divines at Westminster, twenty of His Majesty's nomination being added unto them, and with such as shall be sent from the Church of Scotland, whereby it may be determined by His Majesty and the two Houses how the Church government, after the said three years, shall be fully established as is most agreeable to the word of God: that an effectual course shall be taken by Act of Parliament, and all other ways needful or expedient, for suppressing the opinions and practices of Anti-Trinitarians, Anabaptists, Antinomians, Arminians, Familists, Brownists, Separatists, Independents, Libertines, and Seekers, and generally for suppressing all blasphemy, heresy, schism, and all such scandalous or either doctrines and practices as are contrary to the light of nature, or to the known principles of Christianity, whether concerning faith, worship, or conversation, and to the power of Godliness, or which may be destructive to order and government, and to the peace of the Church and kingdom: that

in the next session of Parliament after that the kingdom of
Scotland shall declare for His Majesty in pursuance of this
Agreement, he shall in person or by commission confirm the
League and Covenant according to the first Article.
Concerning the Acts passed in the last triennial Parliament
of his kingdom of Scotland, and the Committees appointed
by the same, His Majesty is content then also to give
assurance by Act of Parliament that neither he nor his
successors shall quarrel, call in question, or command the
contrary of any of them, nor question any for giving
obedience to the same; and whereas after the return of the
Scottish army to Scotland, the Houses of Parliament of
England did resolve and appoint the army under command of
Sir Thomas Fairfax to disband, and they having entered into
an engagement to the contrary, His Majesty was carried away
from Holdenby [Holmby] against his will by a party of the
said army, and detained in their power until he was forced to
fly from amongst them to the Isle of Wight, and since that
time His Majesty and the Commissioners of the kingdom of
Scotland have earnestly pressed that His Majesty might come
to London in safety, honour and freedom for a personal
treaty with the two Houses and the Commissioners of the
Parliament of Scotland, which hath not been granted: and
whereas the said army hath in a violent manner forced away
divers members of both Houses from the discharge of their
trust, and possessed themselves of the City of London and all
the strengths and garrisons of the kingdom, and, through
the power and influence of the said army and their adherents,
Propositions and Bills have been sent to His Majesty without
the advice and consent of the kingdom of Scotland, contrary
to the Treaty between the kingdoms, which are destructive to
religion, His Majesty's just rights, the privileges of
Parliament, and liberty of the subject, from which
Propositions and Bills the said Scottish Commissioners have
dissented in the name of the kingdom of Scotland; and,
forasmuch as His Majesty is willing to give satisfaction
concerning the settling of religion and other matter in
difference, as is expressed in this Agreement, the kingdom of
Scotland doth oblige and engage themselves first in a
peaceable way and manner to endeavour that His Majesty

may come to London in safety, honour and freedom for a personal treaty with the Houses of Parliament and the Commissioners of Scotland upon such Propositions as His Majesty shall think fit to make; and that for this end all armies may be disbanded, and that in case this shall not be granted, that Declarations shall be emitted by the Kingdom of Scotland in pursuance of this Agreement, against the unjust proceedings of the two Houses of Parliament towards His Majesty and the Kingdom of Scotland, wherein they shall assert the right which belongs to the Crown in the power of the militia, the Great Seal, bestowing of honours and offices of trust, choice of Privy Councillors, the right of the King's negative voice in Parliament, and that the Queen's Majesty, the Prince, and the rest of the royal issue, ought to remain where His Majesty shall think fit, in either of the kingdoms, with safety, honour and freedom; and that upon the issuing of the said Declarations, that an army shall be sent from Scotland into England, for preservation and establishment of religion, for defence of His Majesty's person and authority, and restoring him to his government, to the just rights of the Crown and his full revenues, for defence of the privileges of Parliament and liberties of the subject, for making a firm union between the kingdoms, under His Majesty and his posterity, and settling a lasting peace; in pursuance whereof the Kingdom of Scotland will endeavour that there may be a free and full Parliament in England, and that His Majesty may be with them in honour, safety and freedom, and that a speedy period be set to this present Parliament, and that the said army shall be upon the march before the said peaceable message and Declaration be delivered to the House; and it is further agreed that all such in the Kingdoms of England and Ireland, as shall join with the Kingdom of Scotland in pursuance of this Agreement, shall be protected by His Majesty in their persons and estates; and that all such His Majesty's subjects in England and Ireland as shall join with him in pursuance of this Agreement may come to the Scotch army and join with them, or else put themselves into other bodies in England and Wales for prosecution of the same ends as the King's Majesty shall think fit, and that all such shall be protected by the Kingdom

of Scotland and their army in their persons and estates, and
where any injury or wrong done to them therein, that they
shall be careful to see them fully repaired so far as is in their
power to do, and likewise, where any injury or wrong is done
to those that join with the Kingdom of Scotland, His
Majesty shall be careful for their full reparation; that His
Majesty or any by his authority or knowledge shall not make
nor admit of any cessation, pacification nor agreement for
peace whatsoever, nor of any Treaty, Propositions, Bills or
any other ways for that end, with the Houses of Parliament
or any army or party in England and Ireland, without the
advice and consent of the Kingdom of Scotland; nor having
their authority shall either make or admit of any of these any
manner of way with any whatsoever without His Majesty's
advice and consent; that, upon the settling of a peace, there
be an Act of Oblivion to be agreed on by His Majesty and
both his Parliaments of both kingdoms; that His Majesty,
the Prince, or both shall come into Scotland upon the
invitation of that kingdom and their declaration that they
shall be in safety, freedom and honour, when possibly they
can come with safety and conveniency; and that His Majesty
shall contribute his utmost endeavours both at home and
abroad for assisting the Kingdom of Scotland in carrying
on this war by sea and land, and for their supply by monies,
arms, ammunition, and all other things requisite, as also for
guarding the coasts of Scotland with ships, and protecting all
Scottish merchants in the free exercise of trade and commerce
with other nations; and His Majesty is very willing and doth
authorise the Scots army to possess themselves of Berwick,
Carlisle, Newcastle-upon-Tyne, Tynemouth, and Hartlepool,
for to be places of retreat and magazine, and, when the peace
of the kingdom is settled, the Kingdom of Scotland shall
remove their forces, and deliver back again the said towns and
castles; that, according to the Large Treaty, payment may be
made of the remainder of the Brotherly Assistance which yet
rests unpaid; and likewise of the £200,000 due upon the late
Treaty made with the Houses of Parliament for the return of
the Scots army, as also that payment shall be made to the
Kingdom of Scotland for the charge and expense of their army
in this future war, together with due recompense for the

losses which they shall sustain therein: that due satisfaction, according to the Treaty on that behalf between the kingdoms, shall be made to the Scottish army in Ireland, out of the land of that kingdom and otherwise; that His Majesty, according to the intention of his father, shall endeavour a complete union of the kingdoms, so as they may be one under His Majesty and his posterity; and, if that cannot be speedily affected, that all liberties, privileges, concerning commerce, traffic, and manufactories peculiar to the subjects of either nation, shall be common to the subjects of both kingdoms without distinction; and that there be a communication of mutual capacity of all other privileges of the subject in the two kingdoms; that a competent number of ships shall be yearly assigned and appointed out of His Majesty's navy, which shall attend the coast of Scotland for a guard and freedom of trade to his subjects of that nation; that His Majesty doth declare that his successors as well as himself are obliged to the performances of the Articles and conditions of this Agreement; that His Majesty shall not be obliged to the performance of the aforesaid articles until the Kingdom of Scotland shall declare for him in pursuance of this Agreement, and that the whole Articles and conditions aforesaid shall be finished, perfected and performed before the return of the Scots army; and that when they return into Scotland at the same time, *simul et semel*, all arms be disbanded in England.

CARISBROOKE, the 26th of December.

Charles Rex:

We do declare and oblige ourselves *in verbo principis*, that the Kingdom of Scotland engaging to perform the written articles, we shall perform our part therein as is above expressed in the said Articles.

At Carisbrooke Castle, the 26th of December.

CHARLES R.

We whose names are underwritten, do hereby engage ourselves upon our honour, faith and conscience, and all that is dearest to honest men, to endeavour to the utmost of our powers that the Kingdom of Scotland shall engage to perform the within written conditions in so far as it relates to them, His Majesty engaging to perform his part in the aforesaid Articles; and we are most confident that the Kingdom of Scotland will do the same, and we are most willing upon the protecting of the said Agreement, to hazard our lives and fortunes in pursuance thereof. By the clause of confirming Presbyterian government by Act of Parliament, His Majesty hath declared to us that he is neither obliged to desire the settling of Presbyterian government, nor to present a Bill for that effect; and we likewise understand that no person whatsoever suffer in his estate or corporal punishment for not submitting to Presbyterian government, His Majesty understanding that this shall not extend to those that are mentioned in the clause against toleration.

This was declared in the presence of Lord Loudoun, Lord Lauderdale, Lord Lanerick [Lanark], and the King took them as witnesses and not assenters, December 27.

LOUDOUN, LAUDERDALE, LANERICK.

ADDITIONAL ARTICLES OF THE ENGAGEMENT

Charles Rex:

His Majesty, out of the natural affection he bears to his ancient and native kingdom, and to demonstrate how sensible he is of their affection expressed to him in the time of his extremity, and how heartily desirous he is to put marks of his grace and favour upon his subjects of that nation which may remain to all posterity, doth declare that he is resolved:

That Scottish men equally with English be employed by His Majesty and his successors, in foreign negotiations and treaties in all time coming;

That a considerable and competent number of Scotsmen be upon His Majesty's Council, and his successors' in England,

and so reciprocally the same number of Englishmen upon
His Majesty's Council in Scotland.

That Scottish men, according to the number and
proportion (of a third part in number and quality be
employed) in places of trust and offices about His Majesty's
person, the Queen's Majesty, the Prince and the rest of the
royal issue, and their families in all time coming.

That His Majesty and the Prince, or at least one of them,
shall reside in Scotland frequently as their occasions can
permit—whereby their subjects of that kingdom may be
known unto them.

THE ARTICLES OF CAPITULATION, UTTOXETER
25th August 1648

1. That James, Duke of Hamilton, his grace, with the rest of the officers and soldiers under his command, now at Uttoxeter, shall render themselves up prisoners of war, with their horses, arms, and all other provisions of war, and baggage, whatsoever (except what is mentioned in the ensuing articles) to Major-General Lambert, or such as he shall appoint, without spoil, concealment, or embezzlement, by four of the clock this afternoon, upon Uttoxeter heath, or some convenient field near to it.

2. That the Duke of Hamilton, with all officers and soldiers of the said Scottish forces at Uttoxeter, shall have their lives and safety of their persons assured to them, and shall not be pillaged or stripped of their wearing clothes, or what they have about them, or otherwise wronged, beaten or abused, upon the delivering up of their arms, or afterwards, and shall have civil usage during the time of their imprisonment.

3. That all field-officers, and captains of horse in command, shall have each of them a horse provided to ride on, to such places as shall be appointed by Major-General Lambert for their stay; each colonel in command to have one horse for his servant to ride with him, and each commission-officer that is sick or wounded, and not able to go on foot, to have one horse provided for himself to ride on, and that a safe convoy shall be provided to conduct the prisoners to the places they shall be sent to; and if any that are sick or wounded do desire it, they may have liberty to stay at Uttoxeter till further order from Major-General Lambert.

4. That the said Duke of Hamilton shall have six of his servants, such as he shall choose, allowed to wait on him, and each of them an horse to ride with him, till they come to the

place of stay, and have none of their wearing clothes, or what they have about them, taken from them.

5. That all treasure and plate remaining in the Scottish army at Uttoxeter shall be delivered up to such persons as Major-General Lambert shall appoint.

Signed,

ROB. LILBURN   WILLIAM LOCKHART

HEZEKIAH HAYNS   JAMES FOULES

EDWARD MANWARING   JAMES TURNER

Genealogical Table A:
THE HOUSE OF HAMILTON

James II = Marie of Gueldres
1437-1460

Princess Mary = (1) Thomas Boyd, Earl of Arran, d. ca. 1472
b. 1452   (2) James, 1st Lord Hamilton, b. ca. 1415 d. 1479
d. ca. 1488

James, 2nd Lord Hamilton = (1) Elizabeth Home
b. ca. 1475 d. 1529   (2) Janet Beaton

James, 3rd Lord Hamilton, = Lady Margaret Douglas
2nd Earl of Arran, Duke of
Chatelherault, d. 1575

James, 4th Lord Hamilton, 3rd Earl of Arran 1538-1609

Gavin d. young

John, 1st Marquis of Hamilton b. ca. 1542 d. 1604 = Lady Margaret Lyon

David d. young

Claud, Lord Paisley b. ca. 1546 d. 1621

HOUSE OF ABERCORN

Lady Anne Cunningham = James, 2nd Marquis of Hamilton 1589-1625   ▷ Anna Stewart

other issue

William, cr. Earl of Lanark; later 2nd Duke of Hamilton 1616-1651 = Elizabeth Maxwell   b 1619-d

Anne d. 1632 = 7th Earl of Eglinton

Margaret = Earl of John Crawford-Lindsay

Mary d. 1633 = Master of Drumlanrig

James, 3rd Marquis and 1st Duke of Hamilton 1606-1649 = Mary Feilding   Ex, d 1637 TB   ▷ Euphemia Ham, 14th

John d. young

James, Lord Polmont 1647-1648

Anne

Elizabeth

Margaret

Mary

Anne 1632-1716 = William Douglas, Earl of Selkirk

Susanna 1633-1694 = 7th Earl of Cassillis

Diana d. young

issue

issue

Charles, Earl of Arran 1634-1640

James 1635-1639

William 1636-1638

Henrietta Mary 1631-1632

1637

Margaret m Lord Belhaven

Mary

Note Pg 259

Genealogical Table B:
THE SCOTTISH SUCCESSION

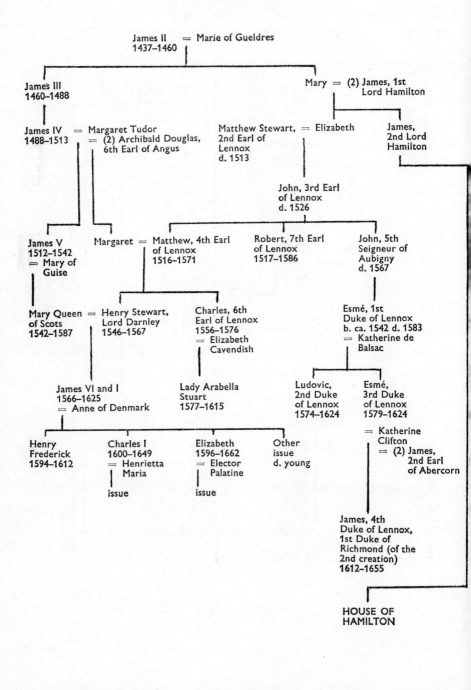

REFERENCES AND NOTES

REFERENCES AND NOTES TO CHAPTER ONE

1. William Maitland of Lethington to Cecil, Dec. 26th 1561, in J. Bain (ed.), *Calendar of State Papers relating to Mary Queen of Scots, 1547–1603* (Edinburgh, 1898), p. 1053.
2. J. Craigie (ed.), *The Basilikon Doron of King James VI* (Edinburgh, 1944), vol. 1 (text), p. 83.
3. Isobel F. Grant, *Social and Economic Development of Scotland before 1603* (Edinburgh, 1930), p. 311.
4. *Basilikon Doron*, vol. 1, p. 71.
5. W. L. Mathieson, *Politics and Religion in Scotland, 1550–1695* (Glasgow, 1902), vol. 1, p. 29.
6. *Basilikon Doron*, vol. 1, p. 79.
7. Speech of King James VI and I to the House of Commons, July 7th 1604; cited in D. H. Willson, "King James I and Anglo-Scottish Unity", in W. A. Aiken and B. D. Henning, *Conflict in Stuart England* (London, 1960), pp. 45–6.
8. David Mathew, *Scotland under Charles I* (London, 1955), p. 235.
9. *Ibid.*, p. 152.
10. *Complete Peerage* (London, 1926), vol. 1, pp. 465–8.
11. 1st Marquis of Hamilton to James VI and I, undated, in *H.M.C., Hamilton MSS* (London, 1887), p. 68.
12. 2nd Marquis of Hamilton to James VI and I, March 1st 1608, in James Maidment (ed.), *Letters and State Papers during the reign of King James the Sixth* (Edinburgh, 1838), pp. 125–7.
13. *Calendar of State Papers Venetian, 1607–1610*, pp. 408–9.
14. Lionello to the Doge, Sept. 8th 1617, *C.S.P.Ven. 1617–1619*, p. 5.
15. Fenton to Mar, Sept. 18th 1617, *H.M.C., Mar and Kellie MSS, Supp.* (London, 1930), p. 80; Sir Philip Warwick, *Memoirs of the Reign of King Charles I* (London, 1702), p. 111.
16. James VI to I to the 2nd Marquis of Hamilton, August 2nd 1621, in Maidment, *op. cit.*, p. 340.
17. D. Calderwood, *History of the Kirk of Scotland (1524–1625)* (Edinburgh, 1842–59), vol. 7, p. 506.
18. 2nd Marquis of Hamilton to Buckingham, undated, in Godfrey Goodman, *The Court of King James the First* (London, 1839), vol. 2, p. 247.
19. I am indebted for this information to Mr. J. R. Maddicott, Librarian and Archivist of Exeter College, Oxford; cf. A. Clark, *Register of the University of Oxford* (Oxford, 1887), vol. 2, pt. 1, p. 282, which wrongly gives the date of Arran's admission as July 10th 1621.

20.   In F. W. Fairholt, *Poems and Songs relating to George Duke of Buckingham* (London, 1851), p. 10.

21.   Kellie to Mar, June 20th 1622, *H.M.C., Mar and Kellie MSS, Supp.*, p. 122; Chamberlain to Carleton, June 22nd 1622, in Thomas Birch (ed.), *Court and Times of James I* (London, 1848), p. 316. Compare this date with the incorrect one, 1620, given by Burnet, and copied by others.

22.   See G. Roberts (ed.), *Diary of Walter Yonge* (London, 1848), pp. 44–5.

23.   Mar to Kellie, March 14th 1623, *H.M.C., Mar and Kellie MSS, Supp.*, p. 157.

24.   Kellie to Mar, Jan. 2nd 1624, *H.M.C., Mar and Kellie MSS, Supp.*, p. 189.

REFERENCES AND NOTES TO CHAPTER TWO

1.   Letter of Rev. Joseph Mead, March 4th 1625, in Birch, *op. cit.*, vol. 2, p. 503.

2.   Chamberlain to Carleton, Nov. 14th 1618, *C.S.P.D. 1611–18*, p. 595.

3.   Kellie to Mar, March 9th 1625, *H.M.C., Mar and Kellie MSS, Supp.*, p. 222; cf. Mead's letter in Birch, *op. cit.*, vol. 2, p. 503, which states that Arran could not be with his father before he died.

4.   *C.S.P.Ven. 1623–25*, p. 617 and p. 621.

5.   Kellie to Mar, March 10th 1625, *H.M.C., Mar and Kellie MSS, Supp.*, p. 225.

6.   Chamberlain to Carleton, March 12th 1625, in Birch, *op. cit.*, vol. 2, pp. 504–5; Kellie to Mar, March 9th 1625, *H.M.C., Mar and Kellie MSS, Supp.*, p. 223.

7.   *Dictionary of National Biography*, vol. 24, p. 178.

8.   Warwick, *op. cit.*, p. 111.

9.   Conway to Lord Treasurer Ley, April 22nd 1625, *C.S.P.D. 1625–26*, p. 12.

10.   C. V. Wedgwood, *The King's Peace, 1637–1641* (London, 1955), p. 64; Peter Heylyn, *Cyprianus Anglicus* (London, 1668), p. 145.

11.   Edward Hyde, Earl of Clarendon, *History of the Rebellion and Civil Wars in England*, ed. by W. Dunn Macray (Oxford, 1888), vol. 4, p. 490.

12.   George Eglisham, *The Forerunner of Revenge*, in *Somers Tracts* (London, 1811), vol. 5, pp. 437–9.

13.   *C.S.P.D. 1619–23*, p. 116.

14.   Contarini to the Doge, Oct. 30th 1626, *C.S.P.Ven. 1625–26*, p. 594; same to the same, Nov. 6th 1626, *C.S.P.Ven. 1626–28*, pp. 5–6.

15.   *R.P.C.S. 1625–27*, pp. 81–2.

16.   Clarendon, *op. cit.*, vol. 1, p. 145.

17.   *R.P.C.S. 1625–27*, p. cv and pp. 397–8 and note.

18. Charles to Hamilton, Dec. 22nd 1626, in C. Rogers (ed.), *The Earl of Stirling's Register of Royal Letters, 1615–1635* (Edinburgh, 1885), vol. I, p. 110.

19. Charles to Advocates, Dec. 27th 1626, in Rogers, *ibid.*, vol. I, pp. 110, 113–14.

20. *R.P.C.S. 1625–27*, p. clxxvii and pp. clxxxii–clxxxiii.

21. Contarini to the Doge, March 26th 1627, *C.S.P.Ven. 1626–28*, p. 161.

22. *R.C.P.S. 1625–27*, pp. 567–8.

23. Gilbert Burnet, *Memoirs of the Lives . . . of James and William, Dukes of Hamilton* (Oxford, 1852), p. 3.

24. *R.C.P.S. 1625–27*, p. 574n.

25. Charles to Hamilton, Feb. 12th 1628, in Rogers, *op. cit.*, vol. I, p. 252.

26. *R.C.P.S. 1625–27*, p. 630.

27. Burnet, *op. cit.*, p. 4.

28. Verses on Buckingham's Assassination, *C.S.P.D. 1625–49*, p. 291.

29. Charles to Hamilton, Sept. 25th 1628, in Burnet, *op. cit.*, p. 4.

30. Goring to Carlisle, Sept. 16th 1628, *C.S.P.D. 1625–49*, p. 294; Sir Robert Aiken to Carlisle, Sept. 29th 1628, *ibid.*, pp. 295–6.

31. Mead to Stuteville, Nov. 1st 1628, in Birch, *op. cit.*, vol. I, p. 419. See also Beaulieu to Puckering, Oct. 30th 1628, *ibid.*, p. 415, where Hamilton's reluctance is similarly stressed.

32. Burnet, *op. cit.*, p. 5.

33. Mark Napier, *Memoirs of the Marquis of Montrose* (Edinburgh, 1856), vol. I, p. 349.

34. Elizabeth of Bohemia to Hamilton, *H.M.C., Hamilton MSS, Supp.*, p. 15. Burnet refers to the eldest daughter as Mary, but her full names were Henrietta Mary, and her family called her Henrietta: see *H.M.C., 4th Report, Pt. I* (London, 1874), p. 259. Henrietta was born in February 1631 and died the following year; Anne (or Anna) was born in January 1632, Susanna (or Susan) in 1633, Charles in November 1634, James in 1635 and William in 1636. See Rosalind K. Marshall, *The Days of Duchess Anne* (London, 1973), p. 14 and p. 236.

35. Burnet, *op. cit.*, p. 517.

36. *Ibid.*, p. 517.

REFERENCES AND NOTES TO CHAPTER THREE

1. M. Roberts, *Gustavus Adolphus* (London, 1958), vol. 2, pp. 414–15.

2. Thomas Carew, *Poems* (Oxford, 1949), p. 77, quoted in Wedgwood, *op. cit.*, p. 21.

3. Burnet, *op. cit.*, p. 7.

4. See S. R. Gardiner, *The Personal Government of Charles I* (London, 1877), vol. I, pp. 245–7; also J. W. Hales, *The Political Element in Massinger*, Contemporary Review, Aug. 1876.

5. Elizabeth of Bohemia to Hamilton, Nov. 19th 1632, *H.M.C.*, *Hamilton MSS, Supp.*, p. 26.
6. See Williams to Arran, Sept. 17th 1622, *C.S.P.D. 1619–23*, p. 448.
7. Hamilton to Sutherland, May 13th 1631, *H.M.C.*, *1st Report* (London, 1870), p. 178.
8. Burnet, *op. cit.*, pp. 8–9.
9. *Ibid.*, pp. 11–12.
10. Beaulieu to Puckering, May 25th 1631, in Birch, *op. cit.*, vol. 2, p. 122.
11. *H.M.C.*, *Mar and Kellie MSS* (London, 1904), p. 182; Marchamont Nedham, *Digitus Dei* (London, 1649), p. 6.
12. Marchamont Nedham, *The Manifold practices and attempts of the Hamiltons . . . to get the Crown of Scotland, etc.* (London, 1648), pp. 8–11; cf. Heylyn, *op. cit.*, p. 371.
13. Nedham, *ibid.*, pp. 14–15.
14. *H.M.C.*, *Mar and Kellie MSS*, pp. 181–4.
15. Burnet, *op. cit.*, p. 17.
16. *H.M.C.*, *Mar and Kellie MSS*, pp. 184–91; *R.P.C.S. 1630–32*, p. 263.
17. John Rushworth, *Historical Collections* (London, 1859), vol. 2, pp. 112–123; *H.M.C.*, *Mar and Kellie MSS*, p. 191n.
18. *R.P.C.S. 1630–32*, p. 263; *R.P.C.S. 1633–35*, p. 139.
19. Soranzo to the Doge, July 4th 1631, *C.S.P.Ven. 1629–32*, p. 523.
20. Thomas Barrington to Lady Barrington, June 24th 1631, *H.M.C.*, *7th Report* (London, 1879), p. 547.
21. *C.S.P.D. 1631–33*, p. 95.
22. *Ibid.*, p. 106.
23. *Ibid.*, p. 109.
24. Burnet, *op. cit.*, p. 5.
25. Soranzo to the Doge, Oct. 3rd 1631, *C.S.P.Ven. 1629–32*, pp. 550–1.
26. Rushworth, *op. cit.*, vol. 1, p. 107 and pp. 129–130; Roberts, *op. cit.*, vol. 2, p. 609.
27. Burnet, *op. cit.*, p. 21.
28. Roberts, *op. cit.*, vol. 2, p. 609.
29. Soranzo's despatch, Nov. 14th 1631, *C.S.P.Ven. 1629–32*, pp. 561–2, and Soranzo and Gussoni to the Doge, Feb. 6th 1632, *ibid.*, p. 584.
30. Pory to Puckering, Dec. 1st 1631, in Birch, *op. cit.*, vol. 1, p. 148.
31. Rushworth, *op. cit.*, vol. 1, p. 107 and pp. 129–30.
32. Charles to Hamilton, Sept. 21st 1631, Burnet, *op. cit.*, p. 24.
33. *H.M.C.*, *Hamilton MSS* (London, 1887), p. 74.
34. *C.S.P.D. 1631–33*, pp. 202–3.
35. *Ibid.*, p. 279.
36. Charles to Hamilton, Dec. 31st 1631, Burnet, *op. cit.*, p. 27.
37. Bulstrode Whitelocke, *A Journal of the Swedish Embassy in the years 1653 and 1654* (London, 1855), vol. 1, p. 313.
38. Roberts, *op. cit.*, vol. 2, p. 610; Rushworth, *op. cit.*, vol. 1, pp. 130–2.

39. Burnet, *op. cit.*, p. 27; *H.M.C., Hamilton MSS*, p. 78.
40. Charles to Hamilton, Aug. 1st 1632, Burnet, *op. cit.*, pp. 29–30.
41. Burnet, *ibid.*, p. 30.
42. *Ibid.*, p. 31.
43. Charles to Hamilton, Sept. 24th 1632, *ibid.*, p. 31.
44. Clifford to Clifton, Oct. 20th 1632, *H.M.C., Hamilton Supp.*, p. 406; Beaulieu to Puckering, Oct. 18th 1632, in Birch, *op. cit.*, vol. 2, p. 184.

REFERENCES AND NOTES TO CHAPTER FOUR

1. Warwick, *op. cit.*, pp. 118–19.
2. Guzzoni to the Doge, Oct. 29th 1632, *C.S.P.Ven. 1629–32*, p. 18.
3. Soranzo's despatch, Jan. 18th 1633, quoted in Gardiner, *op. cit.*, vol. 1, p. 222.
4. Clarendon, *op. cit.*, vol. 4, p. 490.
5. See, for example, Stanhope to Wentworth, Nov. 13th 1638, in William Knowler (ed.), *The Earl of Strafford's Letters and Despatches* (Dublin, 1740), vol. 2, pp. 237–8.
6. Clarendon, *op. cit.*, vol. 4, p. 491.
7. Warwick, *op. cit.*, p. 111.
8. Stanhope to Wentworth, Nov. 13th 1638, in Knowler, *op. cit.*, vol. 2, p. 237.
9. Alexander Peterkin, *Records of the Kirk of Scotland* (Edinburgh, 1838), vol. 1, p. 145.
10. *England's Black Tribunall* (London, 1737), p. 102.
11. Clarendon, *op. cit.*, vol. 4, p. 491.
12. Warwick, *op. cit.*, p. 114.
13. Clarendon, *The Life of Edward, Earl of Clarendon* (Oxford, 1727), vol. 1, p. 13.
14. Burnet, *History of his Own Time* (London, 1838), vol. 1, pp. 65–6 and note.
15. James Balfour, *Historical Works* (Edinburgh, 1824), vol. 2, p. 199.
16. John Spalding, *The History of the Troubles* (Edinburgh, 1828), vol. 1, p. 34.
17. Burnet, *Lives*, p. 33.
18. *R.P.C.S. 1633–35*, pp. 271–3 and pp. 305–16.
19. Heylyn, *op. cit.*, pp. 371–3.
20. Garrard to Wentworth, Feb. 17th 1637, in Knowler, *op. cit.*, vol. 2, p. 148.
21. Clarendon, *Rebellion*, vol. 5, p. 191.
22. *Ibid.*, vol. 1, p. 107.
23. Gardiner, in *Dictionary of National Biography*, vol. 24, p. 180.
24. *C.S.P.D. 1655–56*, p. 362; *Complete Peerage*, vol. 1, pp. 465–8. At that time a livre was worth 10½ pence.
25. Guistinian to the Doge, Nov. 8th 1641, *C.S.P.Ven. 1640–42*, p. 235.

26. Garrard to Wentworth, April 28th 1637, in Knowler, *op. cit.*, vol. 2, p. 72.
27. *C.S.P. Colonial 1574–1660*, pp. 195, 204–5 and 256.
28. *R.P.C.S. 1633–35*, p. 305.
29. *C.S.P. Ireland 1633–1647*, pp. 152 and 242.
30. Gardiner, *History of England ... 1603–42* (London, 1883–1884), vol. 7, p. 178, and vol. 8, pp. 286–7; *The Vintners' Answer to some scandalous pamphlets* (London, 1642); Rushworth, *op. cit.*, vol. 3, p. 277; Garrard to Wentworth, Jan. 8th 1636, in Knowler, *op. cit.*, vol. 1, p. 507.
31. See E. Waterhouse, Paintings from Venice for Seventeenth Century England, *Italian Studies*, May 1952, pp. 720–21.
32. Hamilton to Feilding, Feb. 12th 1636, *H.M.C. 4th Report*, Pt. 1, p. 257.
33. Burnet, *op. cit.*, p. 29.
34. Hamilton to Feilding, July 17th 1637, *H.M.C. 4th Report*, Pt. 1, p. 258.

REFERENCE AND NOTES TO CHAPTER FIVE

1. Balfour, *op. cit.*, vol. 2, p. 199.
2. *R.P.C.S. 1629–30*, pp. 364–6; Father Andrew Leslie to Father General, Oct. 2nd 1635, quoted in W. Forbes Leith, *Memoirs of the Scottish Catholics* (London, 1909), vol. 1, p. 172.
3. Balfour, *op. cit.*, vol. 2, p. 142.
4. *Ibid.*, vol. 2, p. 131.
5. See G. Donaldson (ed.), *Scottish Historical Documents* (Edinburgh, 1970), pp. 191–4; William Cobbett (ed.), *State Trials* (London, 1809), vol. 3, pp. 603–7 and 629; John Row, *History of the Kirk of Scotland* (Edinburgh, 1842), pp. 376–81.
6. Cobbett, *op. cit.*, vol. 3, pp. 597–8.
7. Row, *op. cit.*, p. 384.
8. Burnet, *Own Time*, vol. 1, p. 14.
9. *Ibid.*, vol. 1, p. 15.
10. Spalding, *op. cit.*, vol. 1, p. 47.
11. Anon. to Lanark, April 4th 1648, *Hamilton Papers* (London, 1880), p. 173.
12. Burnet, *op. cit.*, vol. 1, p. 15.
13. *R.P.C.S. 1637*, pp. 483–4 and 490.
14. Robert Baillie, *Letters and Journals* (Edinburgh, 1841–1842), vol. 1, p. 21 and p. 41.
15. Traquair to Hamilton, Oct. 19th 1637, *Hardwicke State Papers* (London, 1778), vol. 2, p. 95.
16. *Ibid.*, vol. 2, pp. 96–7.
17. Cited in Mary Coates, *Social Life in Stuart England* (London, 1924), p. 75.
18. Wedgwood, *op. cit.*, p. 196.

19. Rothes, *A Relation of the Proceedings concerning the Affairs of the Kirk* (Edinburgh, 1830), p. 65; *R.P.C.S. 1638*, pp. 3–4.

20. Rothes, *op. cit.*, p. 43.

21. Traquair to Hamilton, Feb. 26th 1638, *Hardwicke State Papers*, vol. 2, pp. 99–100.

22. See Donaldson, *op. cit.*, pp. 194–201; Gardiner, *Constitutional Documents of the Puritan Revolution, 1625–1660* (Oxford, 1906), pp. 124–34.

23. Warriston, *Diary . . . 1632–1639* (Edinburgh, 1911), vol. 1, pp. 322–3.

24. See, for example, Montrose, Rothes and Cassillis to Lennox, Morton and Hamilton, April 28th 1638, *H.M.C., Hamilton MSS, Supp.*, pp. 45–6, and Burnet, *Lives*, pp. 50–3.

25. Baillie, *op. cit.*, vol. 1, p. 99.

26. *England's Black Tribunal*, pp. 103–4 and p. 106.

27. Traquair and others to Hamilton, March 5th 1638, Burnet, *op. cit.*, p. 48.

28. Traquair to Hamilton, March 5th 1638, *Hardwicke State Papers*, vol. 2, p. 101.

29. Baillie, *op. cit.*, vol. 1, p. 74.

30. Rothes, *op. cit.*, pp. 62–3.

31. Clarendon, *op. cit.*, vol. 1, p. 169.

32. Patrick Gordon, *A Short Abridgement of Britane's Distemper* (Aberdeen, 1844), pp. 56–7.

33. Walter Balcanquall, *A Large Declaration concerning the Late Tumults in Scotland* (London, 1639), p. 77.

34. Baillie, *op. cit.*, vol. 1, p. 75.

35. Hamilton to Charles, June 24th 1638, *Hamilton Papers*, p. 16.

36. Traquair to Hamilton, Oct. 19th 1637, *Hardwicke State Papers*, vol. 2, pp. 96–7.

37. Burnet, *op. cit.*, p. 62.

38. *Ibid.*, pp. 62–5.

39. Hamilton to Dowager Marchioness of Hamilton, May 22nd 1638, *H.M.C., Hamilton MSS, Supp.*, p. 38.

40. Garrard to Wentworth, May 10th 1638, Knowler, *op. cit.*, vol. 2, p. 165.

41. Dorothea Townshend, *The Life and Letters of Endymion Porter* (London, 1897), p. 165.

42. Edmund Waller, *Thirsis, Galatea* (1638); quoted in full in G. Thorn Drury (ed.), *The Poems of Edmund Waller* (London, 1893), pp. 40–2.

43. Hamilton to Dowager Marchioness of Hamilton, May 22nd 1638, quoted in Marshall, *op. cit.*, p. 16.

44. Burnet, *op. cit.*, p. 530.

45. *C.S.P.D. 1637–38*, p. 526.

REFERENCES AND NOTES TO CHAPTER SIX

1.　John Hacket, *Life of Archbishop Williams* (London, 1693), p. 443.
2.　*C.S.P.D. 1637–38*, p. 534.
3.　Zonca to the Doge and Senate, May 21st 1638, *C.S.P.Ven. 1636–39*, pp. 411–12.
4.　Baillie, *op. cit.*, vol. 1, p. 80.
5.　Rothes, *op. cit.*, pp. 102–3.
6.　*Ibid.*, pp. 102–3.
7.　*H.M.C., Hamilton MSS, Supp.*, p. 55.
8.　*Ibid.*, p. 55.
9.　Hamilton to Charles, June 9th 1638, *Hamilton Papers*, p. 8.
10.　Baillie, *op. cit.*, vol. 1, p. 82.
11.　Hamilton to Charles, June 7th 1638, *Hamilton Papers*, pp. 3–7.
12.　Baillie, *op. cit.*, vol. 1, p. 83.
13.　James Gordon, *History of Scots Affairs* (Aberdeen, 1857), vol. 1, pp. 68–9.
14.　Baillie, *op. cit.*, vol. 1, p. 84.
15.　Rothes, *op. cit.*, p. 116; Balfour, *op. cit.*, vol. 2, pp. 265–6.
16.　Burnet, *op. cit.*, pp. 69–70.
17.　Baillie, *op. cit.*, vol. 1, p. 84.
18.　*Ibid.*, vol. 1, p. 85.
19.　Hamilton to Charles, June 9th 1638, *Hamilton Papers*, p. 8.
20.　Charles to Hamilton, June 13th 1638, Burnet, *op. cit.*, p. 72.
21.　Rothes, *op. cit.*, pp. 121–2.
22.　Hamilton to Charles, June 15th 1638, *Hamilton Papers*, p. 13; Hamilton to Charles, June 29th 1638, *ibid.*, p. 19.
23.　Rothes, *op. cit.*, p. 116.
24.　*Ibid.*, p. 123.
25.　Hamilton to Charles, June 15th 1638, *Hamilton Papers*, pp. 12–13.
26.　Wentworth to Vane, April 16th 1638, Knowler, *op. cit.*, vol. 2, p. 325.
27.　Charles to Hamilton, June 20th 1638, Burnet, *op. cit.*, pp. 75–6.
28.　Charles to Hamilton, June 25th 1638, *ibid.*, p. 76.
29.　Bishop of Ross to Hamilton, June 26th 1638, Burnet, *op. cit.*, pp. 78–80.
30.　Hamilton to Charles, June 24th 1638, *Hamilton Papers*, p. 15.
31.　Burnet, *op. cit.*, p. 77.
32.　Baillie, *op. cit.*, vol. 1, p. 80.
33.　Rothes, *op. cit.*, pp. 166–7.
34.　*Ibid.*, pp. 166–7.
35.　Charles to Hamilton, June 29th 1638, Burnet, *op. cit.*, pp. 77–8.
36.　*Ibid.*, p. 81.
37.　Henry Guthry, *Memoirs* (Glasgow, 1747), pp. 40–41.
38.　*Ibid.*, pp. 40–41.
39.　The most spirited defence of all Hamilton's dubious remarks and

actions, including this episode, is to be found in Sir James Turner, *Memoirs of his Own Life and Times* (Edinburgh, 1829), pp. 231–46; on p. 234 he asks, "would any but a fool, or a mad man, have told out his treacherous thoughts to a number of men, of whom he neither had, or sought a promise of silence?"

40. Burnet, *op. cit.*, p. 324.
41. Charles to Hamilton, June 11th 1638, *ibid.*, p. 70.

REFERENCES AND NOTES TO CHAPTER SEVEN

1. *An misseif letter parrafraist in mitter*, in C. H. Firth, "Ballads on the Bishops' Wars, 1638–40", *Scottish Historical Review*, April 1906, pp. 260–1.
2. Baillie, *op. cit.*, vol. 1, p. 93.
3. *H.M.C.*, *6th Report*, *Pt. I* (London, 1877), p. 284; Laud to Wentworth, July 30th 1638, Laud, *Works* (Oxford, 1840), vol. 7, p. 468.
4. See Donaldson, *op. cit.*, pp. 150–153; Burnet, *op. cit.*, p. 91.
5. *Ibid.*, p. 83.
6. *Ibid.*, p. 84.
7. John Forbes *et al.*, *General Demands Concerning the Late Covenant* (Edinburgh, 1838), p. 10; Allan R. Schleich, *The Public Life and Character of . . . Hamilton, 1628–1644* (Nebraska, 1959), p. 82.
8. Baillie, *op. cit.*, vol. 1, pp. 91–2.
9. Hamilton to the "professors and preachers of Aberdeen", Aug. 10th 1638, in Spalding, *op. cit.*, vol. 1, pp. 99–100.
10. *Ibid.*, pp. 102–5.
11. Col. Alexander Hamilton to Hamilton, Aug. 14th 1638, *H.M.C.*, *Hamilton MSS, Supp.*, p. 49.
12. Baillie, *op. cit.*, vol. 1, pp. 98–9.
13. Hamilton to Charles, Aug. 11th 1638, *Hamilton Papers*, p. 22.
14. Burnet, *op. cit.*, p. 88.
15. Charles to Privy Council of Scotland, July 30th 1638, *ibid.*, p. 84.
16. Burnet, *ibid.*, p. 88.
17. Balcanquall, *op. cit.*, pp. 113–14; cf. James Gordon, *op. cit.*, vol. 1, p. 98.
18. Baillie, *op. cit.*, vol. 1, p. 99; cf. Warriston, *op. cit.*, vol. 1, p. 374; Balcanquall, *op. cit.*, pp. 116–17.
19. James Gordon, *op. cit.*, vol. 1, p. 101; Burnet, *op. cit.*, p. 89; Warriston, *op. cit.*, vol. 1, p. 374.
20. G. Donaldson, *Scotland: James V to James VII* (Edinburgh, 1965), p. 320.
21. Burnet, *op. cit.*, pp. 88–9 and 91.
22. *Ibid.*, pp. 92–5.
23. Church to Feilding, Sept. 6th 1638, *H.M.C.*, *Denbigh MSS* (London, 1911), p. 60.

24. Burnet, *op. cit.*, p. 100; Stanhope to Wentworth, Nov. 13th 1638, Knowler, *op. cit.*, vol. 2, p. 237.
25. Hamilton to Charles, Sept. 17th 1638, *Hamilton Papers*, p. 25.
26. Burnet, *op. cit.*, p. 103.
27. Balcanquall, *op. cit.*, p. 145.
28. Hamilton to Charles, Sept. 24th 1638, *Hamilton Papers*, p. 26.
29. Hamilton to the Rothes, Sept. 24th 1638, in Balcanquall, *op. cit.*, p. 202.
30. Guthry, *op. cit.*, p. 37.
31. James Gordon, *op. cit.*, vol. 1, p. 118.
32. Spalding, *op. cit.*, vol. 1, p. 74.
33. Charles to Hamilton, Oct. 9th 1638, Burnet, *op. cit.*, p. 108.
34. Hamilton to Charles, Oct. 15th 1638, *Hamilton Papers*, pp. 43-4.
35. Charles to Hamilton, Oct. 9th 1638, Burnet, *op. cit.*, p. 108.
36. Hamilton to Charles, Oct. 5th 1638, *Hamilton Papers*, p. 38.
37. Hamilton to Charles, Oct. 14th 1638, *ibid.*, pp. 40-1.
38. Examination of Ensign Willoughby, Jan. 9th 1639, Knowler, *op. cit.*, vol. 2, p. 274.
39. Hamilton to Charles, June 29th 1638, *Hamilton Papers*, p. 18; same to the same, Nov. 2nd 1638, *ibid.*, p. 54; Burnet, *op. cit.*, pp. 81-2.
40. Charles to Wentworth, Oct. 22nd 1638, Knowler, *op. cit.*, vol. 2, p. 228.
41. Hamilton to Huntly, Oct. 25th 1638, *H.M.C.*, *6th Report, Pt. I* (London, 1877), p. 720. This letter is unaddressed, and the editor of the *H.M.C. Report* concludes that Lorne was the recipient; it is clear to me, however, that it was written to Huntly.
42. Sir Thomas Hope, *Diary . . . 1633-1646* (Edinburgh, 1843), p. 807.
43. Hamilton to Charles, Nov. 12th 1638, *Hamilton Papers*, p. 56.
44. *Ibid.*, p. 56; see also *ibid.*, p. 56-7n.
45. Hamilton to Charles, Nov. 12th 1638, *ibid.*, p. 56.
46. See P. Hume Brown (ed.), *Early Travellers in Scotland* (Edinburgh, 1891), pp. 132-58.
47. Hamilton to Charles, *Hardwicke State Papers*, vol. 2, p. 114.
48. Baillie, *op. cit.*, vol. 1, p. 105; Charles to Hamilton, Oct. 29th, 1638, Burnet, *op. cit.*, p. 112.
49. *Hamilton Papers*, pp. 46-9.
50. Donaldson, *op. cit.*, p. 321.
51. Baillie, *op. cit.*, vol. 1, p. 123.
52. *Ibid.*
53. *Ibid.*, pp. 124-5.
54. Hamilton to Charles, Nov. 22nd 1638, *Hamilton Papers*, p. 59.
55. *Ibid.*, p. 59.
56. Burnet, *op. cit.*, p. 119; Baillie, *op. cit.*, vol. I, pp. 122-4.
57. Burnet, *op. cit.*, p. 127; James Gordon, *op. cit.*, vol. I, p. 141; Balcanquall, *op. cit.*, p. 237; Warriston, *op. cit.*, vol. 1, p. 401.
58. James Gordon, *op. cit.*, vol. 1, p. 152; Balcanquall, *op. cit.*, p. 242.

59. Hamilton to Charles, Nov. 27th 1638, *Hardwicke State Papers*, vol. 2, pp. 113–15.
60. Isaac D'Israeli, *Commentaries on the Life and Reign of Charles the First* (London, 1851), vol. 2, pp. 215–40.
61. Hamilton to Charles, Dec. 1st 1638, *Hamilton Papers*, p. 62.
62. Burnet, *op. cit.*, pp. 128–30.
63. Alexander Peterkin, *Records of the Kirk of Scotland* (Edinburgh, 1838), vol. 1, pp. 143–5.
64. Balcanquall, *op. cit.*, p. 284.
65. Peterkin, *op. cit.*, vol. 1, p. 186.
66. Balcanquall, *op. cit.*, p. 284.
67. *R.P.C.S. 1638–1643*, p. 91.
68. Hamilton to Charles, Dec. 17th 1638, *Hamilton Papers*, p. 67.
69. Charles to Hamilton, Dec. 7th 1638, Burnet, *op. cit.*, p. 136.

REFERENCES AND NOTES TO CHAPTER EIGHT

1. Northumberland to Wentworth, January 29th 1639, Knowler, *op. cit.*, vol. 2, p. 276.
2. William Davenport, *The Plot*, in C. H. Firth, "Ballads on the Bishops' Wars, 1638–40", *Scottish Historical Review*, April 1906, p. 247.
3. *Chicke Chake for the Anti-Covenanters* (1639), in James Maidment (ed.), *A book of Scotish pasquils, 1568–1715* (Edinburgh, 1868), pp. 75–6.
4. C. V. Wedgwood, *The Sense of the Past* (New York, 1960), p. 192.
5. Burnet, *op. cit.*, pp. 143–4.
6. Gardiner, *History of England*, vol. 9, p. 7.
7. Hamilton to Charles, April 18th 1639, *Hamilton Papers*, pp. 74–6.
8. Hamilton to Charles, April 10th 1639, Burnet, *op. cit.*, p. 156.
9. Charles to Hamilton, April 23rd 1639, *ibid.*, p. 156.
10. *Ibid.*, p. 157.
11. *C.S.P.D. 1639*, p. 146.
12. *Ibid.*, p. 146.
13. Heylyn, *op. cit.*, p. 387.
14. Burnet, *op. cit.*, p. 151; Baillie, *op. cit.*, vol. 1, p. 99; Charles to Hamilton, April 2nd 1639, in James O. Halliwell, *Letters of the Kings of England* (London, 1848), vol. 2, p. 313.
15. Hamilton to Provost, Magistrates and Council of the City of Edinburgh, May 2nd 1639, Peterkin, *op. cit.*, vol. 1, p. 215.
16. *Ibid.*, vol. 1, p. 222.
17. Hamilton to Charles, May 7th 1639, *Hamilton Papers*, p. 79.
18. Norgate to Read, May 16th 1639, *C.S.P.D. 1639*, p. 180.
19. Hamilton to Charles, May 14th 1639, *Hamilton Papers*, p. 81.
20. During the next six years the Campbells laid the island waste, causing great hardship to the population; in 1646 an uprising

broke out by islanders loyal to Hamilton. See Robert McLellan, *The Isle of Arran* (New York, 1970), pp. 133–6.

21. Burnet, *op. cit.*, pp. 158–9.
22. Hamilton to Rothes, undated, *ibid.*, p. 160.
23. Rothes to Hamilton, May 13th 1639, *ibid.*, p. 163; cf. *C.S.P.D. 1639*, p. 191.
24. Hamilton to Rothes, May 17th 1639, Burnet, *op. cit.*, pp. 164–5.
25. Napier, *Montrose and the Covenanters*, vol. 1, p. 275; Burnet, *op. cit.*, p. 167.
26. *C.S.P.D. 1639*, p. 226.
27. Burnet, *op. cit.*, pp. 165–6 and 168–71.
28. Hamilton to Charles, May 26th 1639, *Hamilton Papers*, pp. 86–7.
29. Guthry, *op. cit.*, p. 48; Burnet, *op. cit.*, p. 330.
30. Charles to Hamilton, May 13th 1639, Burnet, *op. cit.*, p. 173.
31. Hamilton to Charles, May 31st 1639, *Hamilton Papers*, p. 90.
32. Hamilton to Charles, May 28th 1639, *ibid.*, p. 89.
33. See Napier, *op. cit.*, vol. 1, pp. 256–62.
34. Patrick Gordon, *op. cit.*, p. 18.
35. Charles to Hamilton, May 29th 1639, Burnet, *op. cit.*, p. 173.
36. Hamilton to Charles, May 31st 1639, *Hamilton Papers*, p. 91.
37. Rossingham to Conway, May 8th 1639, *C.S.P.D., 1639* p. 140.
38. Argyll to Holland, May 22nd 1639, *C.S.P.D. 1639*, pp. 208–9.
39. Hamilton to Charles, May 14th 1639, *Hamilton Papers*, p. 81.
40. Charles to Hamilton, June 4th 1639, Burnet, *op. cit.*, p. 175.
41. Rothes to Murray, August 1639, *Hamilton Papers*, p. 99.
42. Baillie, *op. cit.*, vol. 1, p. 220.
43. Johnston of Warriston, *Diary . . . 1639*, edited by G. N. Paul (Edinburgh, 1896), pp. 87–8.
44. Cf. *Diary of the Duke of Rutland*, in *H.M.C., 12th Report, vol. I, Rutland MSS* (London, 1888), p. 514.
45. Spalding, *op. cit.*, vol. 1, p. 218.
46. Burnet, *op. cit.*, pp. 178–80; see also *His Majesty's Declaration concerning his proceedings with his subjects of Scotland since the Pacification in the Camp near Berwick* (London, 1640).
47. Temple to Leicester, June 20th 1639, in Arthur Collins (ed.), *Letters and Memorials of State* (London, 1746), p. 603.
48. Burnet, *op. cit.*, p. 144; *C.S.P.D. 1639*, p. 355.

REFERENCES AND NOTES TO CHAPTER NINE

1. Burnet, *op. cit.*, p. 183.
2. *C.S.P.D. 1639*, p. 432.
3. Warriston, *op. cit.*, pp. 92–3; Schleich, *op. cit.*, p. 183; Burnet, *op. cit.*, p. 205.
4. Hamilton to Charles, July 8th 1639, Burnet, *op. cit.*, pp. 184–7.
5. *Ibid.*, p. 184
6. *C.S.P.D. 1639*, p. 396.

7. De Vic to Windebanke, July 21st 1639, *C.S.P.D. 1639*, p. 409.
8. Traquair to Hamilton, July 12th and July 13th 1639, *Hamilton Papers*, pp. 94–6; Boroughs to Windebanke, July 26th 1639, *C.S.P.D. 1639*, pp. 407–8.
9. *Hardwicke State Papers*, vol. 2, pp. 141–2.
10. Burnet, *op. cit.*, p. 188.
11. Warriston, *op. cit.*, pp. 73–6.
12. Charles to Wentworth, July 27th 1639, Knowler, *op. cit.*, vol. 2, p. 374.
13. *H.M.C., 3rd Report* (London, 1872), p. 79.
14. Lennox to Traquair, August 12th 1639, *H.M.C., 9th Report* (London, 1883), pp. 260–61.
15. Hamilton to Traquair, August 16th 1639, in J. Aiton, *Life and Times of Alexander Henderson* (London, 1836), pp. 418–19.
16. Lindsay to Hamilton, August 16th 1639, *Hamilton Papers*, p. 101.
17. Hamilton to Lindsay, August 20th 1639, *H.M.C., Hamilton MSS*, p. 109.
18. Gardiner, *History of England . . . 1603–42*, vol. 9, p. 53.
19. Wentworth to Radcliffe, Sept. 21st 1639, in T. D. Whitaker, *The Life . . . of Sir George Radcliffe* (London, 1810), pp. 180–81.
20. Wedgwood, *The King's Peace*, p. 287.
21. Hope, *op. cit.*, p. 110; Northumberland to Leicester, Oct. 17th 1639, in Collins, *op. cit.*, p. 614; Baillie, *op. cit.*, vol. I, p. 274; *H.M.C., 3rd Report*, p. 79; Guthry, *op. cit.*, p. 56; William Sanderson, *A compleat History* (London, 1658), p. 256.
22. Burnet, *op. cit.*, p. 204.
23. *C.S.P.Ven. 1640–42*, p. 12; Knowler, *op. cit.*, p. 431.
24. John Nalson (ed.), *An Impartiall Collection of the Great Affairs of State* (London, 1682–1683), vol. 2, p. 86.
25. Collins, *op. cit.*, p. 609.
26. Traquair to Hamilton, Jan. 27th 1640, *C.S.P.D. 1639–40*, p. 383.
27. Spalding, *op. cit.*, vol. 1, p. 182.
28. Hamilton to Lindsay, March 2nd 1640, Burnet, *op. cit.*, pp. 207–8.
29. Baillie, *op. cit.*, vol. 1, p. 109; Balfour, *op. cit.*, vol. 3, p. 76; *C.S.P.D. 1639–40*, p. 610.
30. Nalson, *op. cit.*, vol. 1, p. 376.
31. Burnet, *op. cit.*, pp. 210–11; *H.M.C., Hamilton MSS*, p. 146.
32. Burnet, *op. cit.*, pp. 348 and 519.
33. Mary was brought up with his legitimate daughters at Hamilton Palace. The date of her birth is unknown, but her mother appears to have been Euphemia Hamilton. Dr. Rosalind Marshall has kindly provided me with this information.
34. *H.M.C., Hamilton, MSS*, p. 56.

REFERENCES AND NOTES TO CHAPTER TEN

1. *H.M.C., De L'Isle MSS*, vol. 6 (London, 1966), p. 270.
2. Clarendon, *Rebellion*, vol. 1, p. 199.
3. *C.S.P.D. 1640*, pp. 590–91.
4. Loudoun to Hamilton, August 20th 1640, *C.S.P.D. 1640*, pp. 610–11.
5. Mark Napier, *Memorials of Montrose* (Glasgow, 1848), vol. 1, p. 267.
6. *Ibid.*, pp. 154–5.
7. Napier, *Montrose and the Covenanters* (London, 1838), vol. 2, pp. 383–4.
8. Vane to Windebank, August 23rd 1640, *C.S.P.D. 1640*, p. 620; Wedgwood, *The King's Peace*, pp. 347–8.
9. *Acts of the Parliament of Scotland* (Edinburgh, 1814–75), vol. 5, p. 286).
10. Baillie, *op. cit.*, vol. 2, p. 403.
11. *C.S.P.D. 1640-41*, pp. 9–10.
12. Maidment, *op. cit.*, p. 95.
13. *C.S.P.Ven. 1640–42*, p. 75.
14. Clarendon, *op. cit.*, vol. 1, pp. 200–201.
15. Northumberland to Leicester, July 22nd 1640, in Collins, *op. cit.*, p. 657.
16. Guistinian to the Doge, Nov. 30th 1640, *C.S.P.Ven. 1640–42*, p. 98.
17. See Schleich, *op. cit.*, p. 222.
18. Wedgwood, *op. cit.*, p. 355.
19. Baillie, *op. cit.*, vol. 1, p. 277.
20. *Ibid.*, p. 304.
21. Clarendon, *op. cit.*, vol. 1, p. 362.
22. Northumberland to Leicester, Dec. 31st 1640, in Collins, *op. cit.*, p. 666.
23. Northumberland to Leicester, Dec. 5th 1639, *H.M.C., 3rd Report* (London, 1872), pp. 78–9.
24. Perez Zagorin, *The Court and the Country* (London, 1969), pp. 207–14.
25. Clarendon, *op. cit.*, vol. 4, p. 362.
26. Baillie, *op. cit.*, vol. 1, p. 305.
27. Wedgwood, *Strafford, 1593–1641* (London, 1935), p. 305.
28. J. P. Cooper, "The Fortune of Thomas Wentworth, Earl of Strafford", *Economic History Review*, Dec. 1958, p. 247.
29. Baillie, *op. cit.*, vol. 1, pp. 310–11.
30. Strafford to Hamilton, April 24th 1641, Burnet, *op. cit.*, pp. 232–3.
31. Wedgwood, *The King's Peace*, pp. 427–8.

REFERENCES AND NOTES TO CHAPTER ELEVEN

1. Clarendon, *op. cit.*, vol. 1, pp. 361–2.
2. Napier, *Memorials of Montrose*, vol. 1, p. 267.
3. Napier, *Montrose and the Covenanters*, vol. 2, pp. 441, 455 and 485–6.
4. Statement of Walter Stewart, June 9th 1641, *ibid.*, vol. 2, p. 453.
5. Bere to Pennington, July 8th 1641, *C.S.P.D. 1641–43*, p. 46.
6. Nicholas to Pennington, July 15th 1641, *C.S.P.D. 1641–43*, p. 53.
7. Balfour, *op. cit.*, vol. 3, p. 45.
8. *Ibid.*, p. 45.
9. Bere to Pennington, August 30th 1641, *C.S.P.D. 1641–43*, p. 110.
10. *A.P.S.*, vol. 5, p. 655; see Webb to Nicholas, Sept. 21st 1641, in G. F. Warner (ed.), *The Nicholas Papers* (London, 1886), vol. 1, p. 49.
11. Balfour, *op. cit.*, vol. 3, pp. 95–9; Baillie, *op. cit.*, vol. 1, p. 190.
12. Spalding, *op. cit.*, vol. 1, pp. 338–9.
13. Porter to Nicholas, Sept. 7th 1641, *Nicholas Papers*, vol. 1, p. 40.
14. Wemyss to Ormonde, Sept. 25th 1641, Thomas Carte (ed.), *Ormonde Papers* (London, 1739), vol. 1, p. 4.
15. *Hardwicke State Papers*, vol. 2, p. 299.
16. Spalding, *op. cit.*, vol. 1, pp. 343–4; Baillie, *op. cit.*, vol. 1, p. 391.
17. *Ibid.*, p. 391; *A.P.S.*, vol. 5, p. 366.
18. See *H.M.C.*, *4th Report*, pp. 163–70.
19. *Ibid.*, p. 168.
20. *Hardwicke State Papers*, vol. 2, p. 301.
21. Hamilton to Charles, Oct. 12th 1641, in Helen C. Foxcroft, "An early recension of Burnet's memoirs of the Dukes of Hamilton", *English Historical Review*, 24, July 1909, p. 539.
22. Balfour, *op. cit.*, vol. 3, p. 95.
23. *Ibid.*
24. *Ibid.*
25. *Ibid.*, pp. 96, 99 and 108.
26. *Hardwicke State Papers*, vol. 2, p. 302; cf. p. 299.
27. Hamilton to Charles, Oct. 22nd 1641, *Hamilton Papers*, pp. 103–5.
28. Hamilton to Charles, Oct. 23rd 1641, *ibid.*, p. 106.
29. Hamilton to Feilding, Nov. 4th 1641, *H.M.C.*, *4th Report*, Pt. I, p. 258.
30. Nicholas to Charles, Nov. 8th 1641, in John Evelyn, *Diary*, ed. by W. Bray (London, 1879), vol. 4, p. 107.
31. *A Scottish Journey*, in *Scottish History Society Miscellany* (Edinburgh, 1904), vol. 2, p. 287; for a Royalist view of the Incident, holding Hamilton mainly responsible, see Spalding, *op. cit.*, vol. 2, pp. 74–9.
32. Baillie, *op. cit.*, vol. 1, p. 393.

33.   See *The Marquess Hamilton's speech* ... *Nov. 6th 1641* (Edinburgh, 1641).

34.   Nicholas to Charles, Nov. 12th 1641, in Evelyn, *op. cit.*, vol. 4, p. 134.

35.   Guistinian to the Doge, Nov. 8th 1641, *C.S.P.Ven. 1640–42*, p. 236.

36.   *Ibid.*, p. 235.

REFERENCES AND NOTES TO CHAPTER TWELVE

1.   *H.M.C., Hamilton MSS, Supp.*, p. 55.

2.   Schleich, *op. cit.*, p. 268; Hawkins to Leicester, Oct. 24th 1639, *H.M.C., De L'Isle MSS*, vol. 6 (London, 1966), p. 198.

3.   Nedham, *Digitus Dei*, p. 13.

4.   Gardiner, *History of England* ... *1603–42*, vol. 10, p. 142.

5.   Sir John Scot of Scotstarvet, *The Staggering State of Scots Statesmen*, in Trans. R.H.S., new ser. (London, 1872), vol. 1, p. 360.

6.   Wedgwood, *The King's War* (London, 1958), p. 74.

7.   Hamilton to Murray, April 7th 1642, Burnet, *op. cit.*, pp. 246–7.

8.   Henrietta Maria to Charles, in Mary Anne Everett Green (ed.), *Letters of Queen Henrietta Maria* (London, 1857), p. 56.

9.   Hamilton to Argyll, March 24th 1642, *Hardwicke State Papers, Supp.*, p. 27.

10.   See George Montague to Lord Montague, April 14th 1642, in *H.M.C., Buccleuch and Queensbury MSS* (London, 1899), vol. 1, p. 298; Everett Green, *op. cit.*, pp. 60–63; *R.P.C.S. 1638–43*, p. 261.

11.   Burnet, *op. cit.*, p. 248.

12.   Baillie, *op. cit.*, vol. 2, p. 44.

13.   Danvers to Row, July 18th 1642, *C.S.P.D. 1641–43*, p. 356. From that time onwards Lady Anne resided with her grandmother, the Dowager Marchioness of Hamilton.

14.   Baillie, *op. cit.*, vol. 2, p. 46.

15.   Burnet, *op. cit.*, p. 251; Spalding, *op. cit.*, vol. 2, p. 69.

16.   Burnet, *op. cit.*, p. 250.

17.   *Ibid.*; Spalding, *op. cit.*, vol. 2, p. 59.

18.   Burnet, *op. cit.*, p. 250.

19.   *Ibid.*, p. 254.

20.   Murray to Lanark, Sept. 10th 1642, *ibid.*, p. 253.

21.   Lanark to Murray, Aug. 31st 1642, *ibid.*, p. 255.

22.   Burnet, *ibid.*, p. 256.

23.   *Ibid.*, p. 257.

24.   Charles to Hamilton, Oct. 27th 1642, *ibid.*, p. 258.

25.   *Complete Peerage*, vol. 1, pp. 465–8.

26.   Burnet, *op. cit.*, pp. 259f. The Marquis of Douglas hoped to

retrieve his family's French Duchy of Touraine: see Browne to
Nicholas, Jan. 23rd 1643, Evelyn, *Diary*, vol. 4, p. 331.

27.   Burnet, *op. cit.*, pp. 261–2; Pickering to Pym, Dec. 28th 1642,
      H.M.C., *Hamilton MSS*, *Supp.*, pp. 62–3.
28.   Charles to Hamilton, Dec. 29th 1642, Burnet, *op. cit.*, pp. 262–3.
29.   Baillie, *op. cit.*, vol. 2, p. 38.
30.   Charles to Hamilton, Dec. 2nd 1642, Burnet, *op. cit.*, pp. 259–60.
31.   Pickering to Pym, Dec. 28th 1642, *H.M.C.*, *Hamilton MSS*, *Supp.*,
      p. 63.
32.   Burnet, *op. cit.*, pp. 263–7.
32.   Burnet, *op. cit.*, pp. 263–7.
33.   *H.M.C.*, *Hamilton MSS*, *Supp.*, p. 65; Burnet, *op. cit.*, p. 268.
34.   *H.M.C.*, *Hamilton MSS*, *Supp.*, pp. 65–7.
35.   Baillie, *op. cit.*, vol. 2, pp. 64–5.
36.   Burnet, *op. cit.*, p. 270.
37.   *Ibid.*, p. 269.

REFERENCES AND NOTES TO CHAPTER THIRTEEN

1.   Burnet, *op. cit.*, p. 271; Hope, *op. cit.*, p. 185.
2.   Burnet, *op. cit.*, p. 271.
3.   Poyntz to Ormonde, June 1st 1643, Carte, *op. cit.*, vol. 1, p. 19.
4.   Burnet, *op. cit.*, pp. 271–2.
5.   "Some Lines on the killing of ye Earle of Newcastle's sonne's
     dogg by ye Marquess Hamilton, in the Queen's Garden at
     Yorke", in Maidment, *op. cit.*, pp. 108–9.
6.   Charles to Henrietta, March 12th 1643, in Everett Green, *op.
     cit.*, p. 174.
7.   He was created Duke of Hamilton, Marquis of Clydesdale, Earl
     of Arran and Cambridge, Lord Aven and Innerdale, with remain-
     der to himself and his male heirs, whom failing, to his brother
     and his male issue, whom failing, to his eldest daughter and her
     male heirs bearing the name and arms of Hamilton, whom failing,
     to his nearest lawful heirs. See *Complete Peerage*, vol. 6, p. 260.
8.   Baillie, *op. cit.*, vol. 2, p. 64.
9.   Poyntz to Ormonde, June 1st 1643, Carte, *op. cit.*, vol. 1, p. 19.
10. Hamilton to Charles, April 21st 1643, Burnet, *op. cit.*, pp. 275–6.
11. Henrietta to Hamilton, Mary 28th 1643, in Everett Green, *op. cit.*,
     pp. 214–15; for Henrietta's hostility to Hamilton at this time, see
     Agostini's despatch, April 3rd 1643, *C.S.P.Ven. 1642–43*, p. 259.
12. Baillie, *op. cit.*, vol. 2, p. 67; Poyntz to Ormonde, June 1st 1643,
     Carte, *op. cit.*, vol. 1, pp. 19–20; G. Wishart, *Memoirs of . . .
     Montrose* (Edinburgh, 1893), pp. 31–3.
13. Baillie, *op. cit.*, vol. 2, p. 68.
14. Burnet, *op. cit.*, pp. 281–282 and 288–9.
15. Charles to the Privy Council of Scotland, May 22nd 1643, Burnet,
     op. cit., p. 294.

16. Charles to Lanark, May 29th 1643, *ibid.*, p. 336.
17. *ibid.*, pp. 295–6.
18. See *ibid.*, pp. 282–7; *R.P.C.S. 1638–43*, pp. 429–34.
19. Hamilton to Jermyn, June 5th 1643, Burnet, *op. cit.*, p. 291.
20. Hamilton to Henrietta, June 5th 1643, *ibid.*, pp. 292–3.
21. Baillie, *op. cit.*, vol. 2, pp. 72–3; Spalding, *op. cit.*, vol. 2, pp. 128–9.
22. Wishart, *op. cit.*, p. 29.
23. Montrose, *My dear and only love* (1643).
24. Hamilton to Henrietta, June 10th 1643, Burnet, *op. cit.*, pp. 293–4.
25. Baillie, *op. cit.*, vol. 2, p. 100.
26. Burnet, *op. cit.*, p. 298.
27. *Ibid.*, pp. 296–7 and 337; Baillie, *op. cit.*, vol. 2, pp. 76–7.
28. Spalding, *op. cit.*, vol. 2, p. 145.
29. See Gardiner, *Constitutional Documents*, pp. 267–71.
30. Burnet, *op. cit.*, p. 305.
31. *Ibid.*, p. 308.
32. Rushworth, *op. cit.*, vol. 5, pp. 482–3.
33. *Ibid.*, vol. 5, p. 482; Warwick, *op. cit.*, p. 297.
34. Henrietta to Hamilton, Aug. 28th 1643, in Everett Green, *op. cit.*, pp. 226–7.
35. Spalding, *op. cit.*, vol. 2, p. 153.
36. Burnet, *op. cit.*, p. 308; Charles to Hamilton, Sept. 28th 1643, *ibid.*, p. 316.
37. Baillie, *op cit.*, vol. 1, p. 399; Hamilton pledged 1000 merks towards the new library.
38. Burnet, *op. cit.*, p. 319; Spalding, *op. cit.*, vol. 2, 169.
39. Hamilton to Charles, Oct. 24th 1643, Burnet, *op. cit.*, pp. 318–19.
40. *Ibid.*, p. 320.
41. Baillie, *op. cit.*, vol. 2, p. 103.
42. Burnet, *op. cit.*, p. 321; *H.M.C.*, *2nd Report* (London, 1871), p. 169.
43. Agostini to the Doge, Dec. 25th 1643, *C.S.P.Ven. 1643–47*, p. 52; Spalding, *op. cit.*, vol. 2, pp. 171–2 and p. 299.
44. Burnet, *op. cit.*, pp. 324–6.
45. Baillie, *op. cit.*, vol. 2, p. 125.

REFERENCES AND NOTES TO CHAPTER FOURTEEN

1. Burnet, *op. cit.*, p. 346.
2. Baillie, *op. cit.*, vol. 2, p. 125.
3. *Ibid.*, vol. 2, p. 139.
4. *Ibid.*, vol. 2, p. 138; Guthry, *op. cit.*, p. 131; H. W. Meikle, *Correspondence of the Scots Commissioners in London* (London, 1917), p. 6.
5. Burnet, *Own Time*, vol. 1, p. 22.
6. Baillie, *op. cit.*, vol. 2, p. 125.

7. Robert Menteth, *History of the Troubles* (London, 1735), p. 168; *A.P.S.*, vol. 6, p. 181.
8. Clarendon, *Rebellion*, vol. 4, p. 146 and p. 149.
9. Burnet, *Lives*, p. 349.
10. Robert Wodrow, *Analecta* (Glasgow, 1842), vol. 1, pp. 160–61.
11. Burnet, *Own Time*, vol. 1, p. 68.
12. Baillie, *op. cit.*, vol. 3, p. 201.
13. Clarendon, *op. cit.*, vol. 4, pp. 142–6.
14. *Ibid.*, vol. 4, pp. 150–51.
15. Jean de Montereul, *Diplomatic Correspondence*, edited by J. G. Fotheringham (Edinburgh, 1898–99), vol. 1, p. 203.
16. Clarendon, *op. cit.*, vol. 4, p. 151; Cowley to Culpepper, April 20th 1646, in O. Ogle and W. H. Bliss (eds.), *Calendar of Clarendon State Papers* (Oxford, 1872), vol. 1, p. 313.
17. Walsingham to Digby, August 8th 1645, *C.S.P.D. 1645–47*, p. 53.
18. *Calendar of Clarendon State Papers*, vol. 1, p. 273; Culpepper to Hyde, May 5th 1646, *ibid.*, vol. 1, p. 315.
19. Clarendon, *op. cit.*, vol. 4, p. 149.

REFERENCES AND NOTES TO CHAPTER FIFTEEN

1. Lanark to Hamilton, May 26th 1646, *H.M.C.*, *Hamilton MSS, Supp.*, p. 70.
2. Clarendon, *op. cit.*, vol. 4, p. 292.
3. Burnet, *Lives*, pp. 210–11.
4. *Lords Journals*, VIII, pp. 4216 and 4222.
5. *C.S.P.D. 1655–56*, p. 128.
6. Charles to Henrietta, April 6th 1646, *Charles in 1646*, p. 32.
7. Moray to Hamilton, Nov. 14th 1646, *Hamilton Papers*, p. 124.
8. Montereul, *op. cit.*, vol. 1, pp. 126 and 177; Warwick, *op. cit.*, p. 327.
9. *Lords Journals*, VIII, pp. 392–3.
10. Guthry, *op. cit.*, pp. 181–2.
11. Burnet, *op. cit.*, pp. 359–62.
12. Montereul, *op. cit.*, vol. 1, p. 236.
13. Burnet, *op. cit.*, p. 362.
14. Rushworth, *op. cit.*, vol. 4, pp. 56–7.
15. Burnet, *op. cit.*, p. 362.
16. *Ibid.*, pp. 365–7.
17. Charles to Henrietta, May 4th 1646, *Charles in 1646*, p. 86.
18. Burnet, *op. cit.*, p. 367.
19. *Ibid.*, pp. 368–9.
20. Charles to Henrietta, Sept. 14th 1646, *Charles in 1646*, pp. 64–5.
21. Burnet, *op. cit.*, p. 372.
22. Henrietta to Hamilton, Sept. 22nd 1646, in Everett Green, *op. cit.*, p. 322; Burnet, *op. cit.*, p. 374.
23. Charles to Hamilton, Sept. 26th 1646, *ibid.*, p. 372.

24.	*Ibid.*, p. 373.
25.	Hamilton to Charles, Oct. 6th 1646, *ibid.*, pp. 374–5.
26.	Warwick, *op. cit.*, pp. 324–5.
27.	Lanark to Charles, Dec. 17th 1646, Burnet, *op. cit.*, pp. 390–91.
28.	Lanark to Charles, Dec. 22nd 1646, *ibid.*, pp. 392–3.
29.	*Ibid.*, p. 396.
30.	*Ibid.*,
31.	Moray to Hamilton, Dec. 12th 1646. *Hamilton Papers*, p. 136.
32.	*A.P.S.*, vol. 6, pt. 1, pp. 772–3.

REFERENCES AND NOTES TO CHAPTER SIXTEEN

1.	Clarendon, *op. cit.*, vol. 5, p. 6.
2.	Montereul, *op. cit.*, vol. 2, pp. 51, 428 and 498; Guthry, *op. cit.*, p. 102.
3.	Montereul, *op. cit.*, vol. 2, p. 289.
4.	*Ibid.*, p. 288.
5.	H.M.C., *Hamilton MSS*, p. 56.
6.	Montereul, *op. cit.*, vol. 2, p. 255.
7.	*Ibid.*, p. 275.
8.	Gardiner, *Constitutional Documents*, pp. 347–53.
9.	Donaldson, *Scotland: James V to James VII*, p. 337.
10.	Burnet, *Own Time*, vol. 1, p. 64.
11.	A. MacDonald (ed.), *Letters to the Argyll Family* (Edinburgh, 1839), p. 40.
12.	Montereul, *op. cit.*, vol. 2, pp. 407–8.
13.	Rushworth, *op. cit.*, vol. 7, p. 197; quoted in Gardiner, *History of the Great Civil War*, vol. 3, p. 422.
14.	Clarendon, *op. cit.*, vol. 4, p. 414.
15.	Anon. to Lanark, March 21st 1648, *Hamilton Papers*, p. 169.
16.	Patrick Gordon, *op. cit.*, p. 208.
17.	Burnet, *Lives*, p. 438.
18.	*Ibid.*, p. 439.
19.	*Calendar of Clarendon State Papers*, vol. 1, p. 419.
20.	Montereul, *op. cit.*, vol. 2, p. 459.
21.	Guthry, *op. cit.*, p. 229.
22.	H.M.C., *Hamilton MSS, Supp.*, p. 58.
23.	Cromwell to the Committee at York, August 23rd 1648, Carlyle, *op. cit.*, vol. 1, p. 346.
24.	Clarendon, *op. cit.*, vol. 4, p. 347.
25.	Byron to Lanark, March 10th 1648, *Hamilton Papers*, p. 166.
26.	Musgrave to Lanark, June 14th 1648, *ibid.*, p. 213.
27.	Anon. to Lanark, Feb. 20th 1648, *Hamilton Papers Addenda*, p. 7.
28.	Anon. to Lanark, June 1648, *Hamilton Papers*, pp. 205–6.
29.	Guthry, *op. cit.*, pp. 225–7; Burnet, *op. cit.*, p. 527.
30.	Donaldson, *op. cit.*, p. 337.
31.	Burnet, *op. cit.*, p. 432.

32. Turner, *op. cit.*, pp. 57–8.
33. Hamilton to Lambert, July 6th 1648, Sanderson, *op. cit.*, p. 1072.
34. Lambert to Hamilton, July 8th 1648, *ibid.*

REFERENCES AND NOTES TO CHAPTER SEVENTEEN

1. Turner, *op. cit.*, p. 70.
2. Thomas May, *A Breviary of the History of the Parliament of England*, in Francis Maseres (ed.), *Select Tracts relating to the Civil Wars in England* (London, 1815), vol. 1, p. 122.
3. Bulstrode Whitelocke, *Memorials of English Affairs* (Oxford, 1853), vol. 2, p. 359; see *The Declaration of James, Duke of Hamilton, etc.* (Edinburgh, 1648).
4. Burnet, *op. cit.*, p. 519.
5. *Remains Historical and Literary connected with the Palatine Counties of Lancaster and Chester* (Manchester, 1909), p. 251.
6. Hamilton to Langdale, August 7th 1648, quoted in Gardiner, *History of the Great Civil War* (London, 1886–91), vol. 3, p. 422.
7. *Remains Historical and Literary*, pp. 252–3.
8. *Ibid.*
9. John Hodgson, *Autobiography* (Edinburgh, 1806), pp. 114–15.
10. Turner, *op. cit.*, pp. 61–2.
11. Hodgson, *op. cit.*, pp. 114–15; Thomas Carlyle, *Letters and Speeches of Oliver Cromwell*, ed. by S. C. Lomas (London, 1904), vol. 1, p. 326.
12. *Ibid.*, vol. 2, p. 215.
13. See Cromwell to St. John, Sept. 1st 1648, *ibid.*, vol. 1, p. 350.
14. Burnet, *op. cit.*, p. 455.
15. Cromwell to the Committee of Lancashire, August 17th 1648, Carlyle, *op. cit.*, vol. 1, p. 329.
16. *Remains Historical and Literary*, pp. 268–70.
17. *Ibid.*

REFERENCES AND NOTES TO CHAPTER EIGHTEEN

1. E. Broxap, *The Great Civil War in Lancashire (1642–1651)* (Manchester, 1910), p. 166.
2. *Remains Historical and Literary*, pp. 268–70; Clarendon, *op. cit.*, vol. 4, p. 369; but compare Langdale to Lanark, August 1st 1648, from Appleby, declaring that Hamilton "is as careful of me, and all those under my command, as they were his own, furnishing us with arms and ammunition, and upon all occasions with his own forces to assist us" (Burnet, *op. cit.*, p. 452).
3. Cromwell to Lenthall, August 20th 1648, Carlyle, *op. cit.*, vol. 1, p. 338.
4. Turner, *op. cit.*, p. 64.

5.   Cromwell to Lenthall, August 20th 1648, Carlyle, *op. cit.*, vol. 1, pp. 338–9.
6.   *Ibid.*, vol. 1, p. 340.
7.   *Ibid.*
8.   *Ibid.*
9.   *Ibid.*, vol. 1, p. 341.
10.   *Ibid.*, vol. 1, p. 340.
11.   Burnet, *op. cit.*, p. 458; Carlyle, *ibid.*, vol. 1, p. 341.
12.   *Ibid.*, vol. 1, p. 342.
13.   Burnet, *op. cit.*, p. 459.
14.   Turner, *op. cit.*, p. 71.
15.   *Ibid.*, p. 70.
16.   Burnet, *op. cit.*, p. 459.
17.   *Ibid.*, p. 461.
18.   *Ibid.*, p. 462.
19.   *Ibid.*, p. 461.
20.   Edmund Ludlow, *Memoirs*, ed. by C. H. Firth (Oxford, 1894), vol. 2, p. 202. Ludlow claims that Hamilton surrendered to Colonel Wayte of the Leicestershire militia, just as Grey arrived upon the scene. Cf. Wayte's own evidence, Burnet, *op. cit.*, p. 493. Lucy Hutchinson, in *Memoirs of the Life of Colonel Hutchinson* (London, 1806), p. 289, asserts that Hamilton surrendered to Grey. It is noteworthy that on September 23rd 1648 the latter received Parliament's thanks for taking the duke prisoner, and at the same time Majors Smithson and Evans were awarded £100 each for the parts they played in apprehending him. See Whitelocke, *op. cit.*, vol. 2, p. 393.
21.   Burnet, *op. cit.*, pp. 461–2.
22.   Turner, *op. cit.*, p. 76.

REFERENCES AND NOTES TO CHAPTER NINETEEN

1. Edmund Ludlow, *Memoirs*, ed. by C. H. Firth (Oxford, 1894), vol. 1, p. 203.
2.   See, for example, Nedham, *Digitus Dei*, pp. 22–4; *H.M.C., De L'Isle MSS*, p. 574.
3.   Burnet, *op. cit.*, p. 463.
4.   Quoted in Gardiner, *History of the Great Civil War*, vol. 4, p. 206.
5.   Carte, *op. cit.*, vol. 1, p. 177.
6.   Cromwell to Jenner and Ashe, Nov. 20th 1648, Carlyle, *op. cit.*, vol. 1, p. 387.
7.   *Ibid.*, vol. 1, pp. 355–6; John Thurloe, *Collection of State Papers*, ed. by T. Birch (London, 1742), vol. 1, pp. 101–2; *Commons Journals*, V, p. 685.
8.   Cromwell to the Committee of Estates, Sept. 16th 1648, Carlyle, *op. cit.*, vol. 1, pp. 360–62.

9. Scots' reply to Cromwell, Sept. 20th 1648, Thurloe, *op. cit.*, vol. 1, p. 102.
10. Cromwell to Lenthall, Oct. 9th 1648, Carlyle, *op. cit.*, vol. 1, p. 380.
11. Thurloe, *op. cit.*, vol. 1, pp. 105–8.
12. *H.M.C.*, *Laing MSS* (London, 1914), vol. 1, pp. 237–8.
13. *A.P.S.*, vol. 6, Pt. 2, pp. 143–7.
14. Balfour, *op. cit.*, vol. 3, p. 377.
15. Nedham, *Digitus Dei*, p. 25.
16. See R. P. Stearns, *The Strenuous Puritan* (Urbana, Ill., 1954), p. 339n; Ludlow, *op. cit.*, vol. 2, p. 202; Turner, *op. cit.*, p. 75.
17. Clement Walker, *An Appendix to the History of Independency* (London, 1661); Nedham, *op. cit.*, p. 26.
18. *Mercurius Elencticus*, Dec. 12th–19th 1648.
19. *Mercurius Pragmaticus*, Dec. 14th and 18th 1648; cf. *Mercurius Melancolicus*, Dec. 25th–Jan. 1st 1648 and *Moderate Intelligencer*, Dec. 19th–29th 1648.
20. Carte, *op. cit.*, vol. 1, p. 202.
21. Burnet, *op. cit.*, p. 483; cf. *H.M.C.*, *Hamilton MSS*, p. 129, which omits the words "being innocent".
22. See David Underdown, *Pride's Purge* (Oxford, 1971), p. 168 and pp. 183–4.
23. Burnet, *op. cit.*, p. 482.
24. *Ibid.*, p. 506.
25. Cromwell and Ireton to Whitchcott, Dec. 22nd 1648, in C. H. Firth (ed.), *The Clarke Papers* (London, 1904), vol. 2, p. 142.
26. Whitelocke, *op. cit.*, vol. 2, pp. 516–17.
27. *Ibid.*
28. Burnet, *op. cit.*, p. 487.
29. *Ibid.*, p. 487; the whole text of his trial, and those of the other accused, is in the library of Worcester College, Oxford.
30. See *Complete Peerage*, vol. 6, p. 260n.
31. Burnet, *op. cit.*, p. 495.
32. *Ibid.*, p. 496.
33. Cromwell to Jenner and Ashe, Nov. 20th 1648, Carlyle, *op. cit.*, vol. 1, p. 387.
34. Burnet, *op. cit.*, p. 496.
35. *Ibid.*, pp. 491–2.
36. *Ibid.*, p. 492.
37. *Ibid.*, pp. 501–2; J. H. Round, "The Case of Lucas and Lisle", *Trans. R.H.S.*, new ser., vol. 8, pp. 154–80 (London, 1894), p. 173.
38. Death Warrant, March 6th 1649, *H.M.C.*, *7th Report* (London, 1879), p. 71.
39. Burnet, *op. cit.*, p. 492.
40. Ludlow, *op. cit.*, vol. 1, pp. 202.
41. Carte, *op. cit.*, vol. 1, p. 247.
42. *Commons Journals*, VI, pp. 159–60.
43. Nedham, *op. cit.*, p. 27.
44. *Clarke Papers*, vol. 2, p. 196.

REFERENCES AND NOTES TO CHAPTER TWENTY

1. Hamilton to his daughters, March 9th 1649, Burnet, *op. cit.*, pp. 505–6.
2. *A true and perfect Copie of a speech delivered by James, Duke of Hamilton in the Chamber at St. James on the 9 of March that morning before he suffered*, (The Hague, 1649): printed in Burnet, *op. cit.*, pp. 506–9.
3. Burnet, *op. cit.*, pp. 508–9.
4. *Ibid.*, p. 509; cf. *H.M.C., Hamilton MSS*, p. 129.
5. Burnet, *op. cit.*, p. 511.
6. Nedham, *Digitus Dei*, p. 27.
7. Clarendon, *Rebellion*, vol. 4, p. 507; *England's Black Tribunall*, pp. 100–102; Menteth, *op. cit.*, p. 502.
8. Whitelocke, *Memorials*, vol. 2, p. 549.
9. *England's Black Tribunall*, p. 102.
10. *Ibid.*
11. *Ibid.*
12. *Ibid.*, p. 105.
13. *Ibid.*; cf. Whitelocke, *op. cit.*, vol. 2, p. 549, who says he saw Hamilton hand the executioner £10.
14. *England's Black Tribunall*, pp. 106–10; in his will Hamilton had laid emphasis on an unostentatious funeral: see *H.M.C., Hamilton MSS*, p. 58.
15. *H.M.C., De L'Isle MSS*, vol. 6, p. 587.
16. Clarendon, *op. cit.*, vol. 5, p. 5.
17. *H.M.C., Hamilton MSS*, p. 58.
18. Hamilton to Lanark, March 8th 1649, Burnet, *op. cit.*, p. 505.
19. Henrietta to Lanark, April 22nd 1649, *ibid.*, p. 527.
20. *H.M.C., Hamilton MSS*, p. 57; if Lanark should die before the marriages of his daughters, he recommended such marital arrangements to the Earl of Crawford-Lindsay, Lord Bargeny, and others.
21. Lanark to Lady Anne, June 10th 1649, Burnet, *op. cit.*, p. 534.
22. See *C.S.P.D. 1651*, p. 423.
23. *H.M.C., Hamilton MSS*, pp. 57–8; *C.S.P.D. 1651*, pp. 16 and 22; *C.S.P.D. 1657–58*, pp. 227–8, 232 and 327; Baillie, *op. cit.*, vol. 3, p. 366.
24. *C.S.P.D. 1655–56*, p. 362; *C.S.P.D. 1656–57*, pp. 157–8.
25. Baillie, *op. cit.*, vol. 3, p. 249.
26. *C.S.P.D. 1660–61*, p. 380.
27. *C.S.P.D. 1658–59*, p. 22; *C.S.P.D. 1661–62*, pp. 324 and 349.
28. *Lords Journals*, XI, p. 78; *H.M.C., 7th Report*, pp. 111–12; *H.M.C., Hamilton MSS, Supp.*, p. 80.
29. Ludlow, *op. cit.*, vol. 2, p. 285.
30. For an excellent life of Anne and a fascinating glimpse into the social affairs of the House of Hamilton, see Marshall, *op. cit.*

REFERENCES AND NOTES TO EPILOGUE

1. Wishart, *op. cit.*, p. 233.

2. But see Clarendon, *Rebellion*, vol. 4, p. 142, where we are told that by his death Hamilton "was not only vindicated in the opinion of many honest men from all the jealousies and aspersions which he had long suffered under, but the proceeding that had been against him was looked upon by many as void of that justice and policy which had been requisite".

3. Nedham, *Digitus Dei*, pp. 29–31; for Sibbald's reaction see Sibbald to Lanark, May 5th 1649, *H.M.C.*, *Hamilton MSS*, *Supp.*, p. 76.

4. *C.S.P.D. 1649–50*, p. 528.

5. *Duke Hamilton's Ghost* (London, 1659).

6. Hamilton to Charles, May 26th 1639, *Hamilton Papers*, p. 87.

7. Warwick, *op. cit.*, p. 111.

8. Wedgwood, *The King's Peace*, p. 213.

9. See, for example, the treatment of Hamilton in Margaret Irwin, *The Proud Servant* (London, 1934), and more especially in Nigel Tranter, *The Young Montrose* (London, 1973).

10. Burnet, *op. cit.*, p. 520.

11. Quoted in Nedham, *Manifold Practices*, pp. 22–3.

12. Clarendon, *op. cit.*, vol. 4, p. 508.

13. Turner, *op. cit.*, pp. 84–5.

SELECT BIBLIOGRAPHY

ABBOTT, W. C. (ed.). *Writings and Speeches of Oliver Cromwell*, vol. I (Cambridge, Mass., 1937)

An Act of the Estates of Scotland in 1643, and Letters of Horning and Rebellion against James Duke of Hamilton, etc., ... with a letter from a person of quality in London to some friends in Scotland, etc. (London, 1648)

Acts of the General Assembly of the Church of Scotland, 1638–1642 (Edinburgh, 1843)

The Acts of the Parliament of Scotland, 12 vols (Edinburgh, 1814–75)

AIKEN, W. A. and HENNING, B. D. (eds.). *Conflict in Stuart England* (London, 1960)

AIKIN, LUCY. *Memoirs of the Court of King Charles the First*, 2 vols (London, 1833)

AIRY, O. (ed.). *The Lauderdale Papers, 1639–1667*, vol. I (London, 1884)

AITON, J. *Life and Times of Alexander Henderson* (Edinburgh, 1836)

AITON, W. *An Inquiry into the Pedigree, Descent, and Public Transactions of the Chiefs of the Hamilton Family, etc.* (Edinburgh, 1827)

ALBION, G. *Charles I and the Court of Rome* (London, 1935)

ANDERSON, J. (*Historical and Genealogical Memoirs of the House of Hamilton* (Edinburgh, 1825)

Another great and bloudy fight in the North, between the forces under the ... Duke of Hambleton ... and the Parliament's forces ... under Major Gen. Lambert ... neer the borders of Yorkshire ... Likewise, sad tydings from Colchester (London, 1648)

AYLMER, G. E. *The King's Servants: the Civil Service of Charles I, 1625–1642* (London, 1961)

BAILLIE, ROBERT. *Letters and Journals*, ed. by David Laing, 3 vols (Edinburgh, 1841–42)

BAIN, J. (ed.). *Calander of State Papers relating to Mary Queen of Scots, 1547–1603*, Vol. I (Edinburgh, 1898)

BALCANQUALL, WALTER. *A Large Declaration concerning the Late Tumults in Scotland, by the King* (London, 1639)

BALFOUR, JAMES. *The Historical Works*, Vols. 2 and 3 (Edinburgh, 1824)

BEATTY, J. L. *Warwick and Holland* (Denver, Colo., 1965)

BELL, ROBERT. *Memorials of the Civil War*, Vol. I (London, 1849)

BIRCH, THOMAS (ed.). *Court and Times of James I*, 2 vols (London, 1848)

BLAIR, ROBERT. *Autobiography* (Edinburgh, 1848)

BOASE, C. W. (ed.). *Registrum Collegii Exoniensis* (Oxford, 1894)

BOROUGH, JOHN. *Notes on the Treaty of Ripon*, ed. by J. B. Bruce (London, 1869)

BRERETON, SIR WILLIAM. *Journal*, ed. by J. C. Hodgson, vol. 2 (London, 1915)

BROWN, P. HUME (ed.). *Early Travellers in Scotland* (Edinburgh, 1891)

BROXAP, E. *The Great Civil War in Lancashire (1642–1651)* (Manchester, 1910)

BRUCE, J. B. (ed.). *Charles I in 1646: Letters of King Charles the First to Queen Henrietta Maria* (London, 1856)

BUCHAN, J. *Montrose* (London, 1928)

——*Oliver Cromwell* (London, 1934)

BURNET, GILBERT, Bishop of Salisbury. *History of His Own Time*, 6 vols (London, 1838)

——*Memoirs of the Lives and Actions of James and William, Dukes of Hamilton and Castle-herald* (Oxford, 1852)

BURTON, J. H. *History of Scotland*, vol. 6.

CALDERWOOD, D. *History of the Kirk of Scotland (1524–1625)*, 8 vols (Edinburgh, 1842–59)

Calendar of State Papers, Colonial

Calendar of State Papers, Domestic

Calendar of State Papers, Ireland

Calendar of State Papers, Venetian

CARLYLE, THOMAS. *Historical Sketches of Notable Persons and Events in the Reigns of James I and Charles I* (London, 1898)

——*Letters and Speeches of Oliver Cromwell*, ed. by S. C. Lomas, 3 vols (London, 1904)

CARTE, THOMAS. *Collection of Original Letters and Papers . . . found among the Duke of Ormonde's Papers*, 2 vols (London, 1739)

CARY, HENRY. *Memorials of the Great Civil War in England, 1646 to 1652* (London, 1842)

CAVENDISH, MARGARET, Duchess of Newcastle. *Life of the Duke of Newcastle*, ed. by C. H. Firth (London, 1886)

CHAMBERLAIN, JOHN. *Letters*, ed. by N. E. McClure (Philadelphia, 1839)

CLARK, A. *Register of the University of Oxford*, vol. 2, Pt. I (Oxford, 1887)

COATE, MARY. *Social Life in Stuart England* (London, 1924)

COATES, W. H. (ed.). *The Journal of Sir Simonds D'Ewes* (New Haven, Conn., 1942)

COBBETT, WILLIAM (ed.). *Complete Collection of State Trials*, vol. 3 (London, 1809)

COLLINS, ARTHUR (ed.). *Letters and Memorials of State . . . from the originals at Penshurst* (London, 1746)

COOPER, J. P. "The Fortune of Thomas Wentworth, Earl of Strafford", *Economic History Review*, Dec. 1958.

CRAIGIE, J. (ed.). *The Basilicon Doron of King James VI*, 2 vols (Edinburgh, 1944)

DALRYMPLE, DAVID (ed.). *Memorials and Letters relating to the History of Britain in the Reign of James the First and Charles the First* (Glasgow, 1776)

DAWSON, W. H. *Cromwell's Understudy: the Life and Times of General John Lambert and the rise and fall of the Protectorate* (London, 1938)

DEWAR, R. "Burnet on the Scottish Troubles", *Scottish Historical Review*, 4, July 1907, pp. 384–98

D'ISRAELI, ISAAC. *Commentaries on the Life and Reign of Charles the First*, 2 vols (London, 1851)

DONALDSON, G. *The Making of the Scottish Prayer Book of 1637* (Edinburgh, 1954)

——*Scotland: James V to James VII* (Edinburgh, 1965)

——(ed.). *Scottish Historical Documents* (Edinburgh, 1970)

DUGDALE, WILLIAM. *A Short View of the Late Troubles* (Oxford, 1681)

Duke Hamilton's conditions for surrendering himself with the officers and souldiers under his Command . . . to the Parliament forces in the County of Stafford; . . . also the taking of Sir Marmaduke Langdale . . . (London, 1648)

Duke Hamilton's ghost, or the underminer countermined (London, 1659)

EGLISHAM, GEORGE. *The Forerunner of Revenge*, in *Somers Tracts*, vol. 5, pp. 437–9 (London, 1811)

——*The humble petition of George Eglisham, Doctor of Physicke, lately one of King James his Physician's Person above the space of Ten Years*, in *Somers Tracts, ibid.*, pp. 439–44.

England's Black Tribunall (London, 1737)

EVELYN, JOHN. *Diary*, ed. by W. Bray, 4 vols (London, 1879)

FAIRFAX, THOMAS. *The Fairfax correspondence: memoirs of the reign of Charles the First*, ed. by G. W. Johnson, 4 vols (London, 1848)

FAIRHOLT, F. W. *Poems and Songs relating to George Duke of Buckingham* (London, 1851)

FIRTH, C. H. "Ballads on the Bishops' Wars, 1638–40", *Scottish Historical Review*, 3, April 1906, pp. 257–73.

FIRTH, C. H. (ed.). *The Clarke Papers*, vol. 2 (London, 1904)

——*Papers relating to Thomas Wentworth, first Earl of Strafford* (London, 1885)

——and RAIT, R. S. (eds.). *Acts and ordinances of the Interregnum, 1642–1660*, 2 vols (London, 1911)

FISCHER, T. A. *The Scots in Germany* (Edinburgh, 1902)

FORBES, JOHN, *et al. General Demands Concerning the Late Covenant: Propounded by the Ministers and Professors of Divinities in Aberdene, together with the Answers of those Reverend Brethren to the said Demands* (Edinburgh, 1638)

FOXCROFT, HELEN C. "An early recension of Burnet's memoirs of the Dukes of Hamilton", *English Historical Review*, 24, July 1909, pp. 510–40

FRASER, Sir WILLIAM. *Chiefs of Grant*, vol. 2 (Edinburgh, 1883)

GARDINER, S. R. *The Fall of the Monarchy of Charles I, 1637–1649*, 2 vols (London, 1882)

——*History of England . . . 1603–42*, 10 vols (London, 1883–84)

——*History of the Great Civil War*, 3 vols (London, 1886–91)

——*The Personal Government of Charles I*, 2 vols (London, 1877)

——(ed.). *Constitutional Documents of the Puritan Revolution, 1625–1660* (Oxford, 1906)

——*The Hamilton Papers . . . relating to the years 1638–1650* (London, 1880)
——*Addenda to the Hamilton Papers* (London, 1893)
GEYL, P. "William II and the Stuarts", *Scottish Historical Review*, 20, April 1923, pp. 190–217.
GOODMAN, GODFREY. *The Court of King James the First*, Vol. 2 (London, 1839)
GORDON, JAMES. *History of Scots Affairs*, 3 vols (Aberdeen, 1857)
GORDON, PATRICK. *A Short Abridgement of Britane's Distemper* (Aberdeen, 1844)
GRANT, ISOBEL F. *Social and Economic Development of Scotland before 1603* (Edinburgh, 1930)
GREEN, MARY ANNE EVERETT (ed.). *Letters of Queen Henrietta Maria* (London, 1857)
GUTHRY, HENRY, Bishop of Dunkeld. *Memoirs* (Glasgow, 1747)
HACKET, JOHN. *Life of Archbishop Williams* (London, 1693)
HALES, J. W. "The Political Element in Massinger", *Contemporary Review*, Aug. 1876.
HALLIWELL, JAMES O. *Letters of the Kings of England*, 2 vols (London, 1848)
HAMILTON, GEORGE. *History of the House of Hamilton* (Edinburgh, 1933)
HAMILTON, JAMES, 3rd Marquis and 1st Duke of Hamilton. *The copy of a letter from Duke Hamilton to the Ministers at Lancaster* (London, (1648)
——*The declaration of Duke Hamilton at the head of his army, upon his joyning with Maj. Gen. Langdale in the North of England, concerning his . . . sovereign Charles King of Great Britain. Likewise . . . Langdale's propositions to the Lord Duke concerning the King's Majesty, and the Duke's answer . . . and the resolution of the Scots Army . . .* (London? 1648)
——*The Declaration of James, Duke of Hamilton* [*concerning the punishment to be enforced against any officer or soldier under his command injuring the person or goods of Englishmen*] (Edinburgh, 1648)
——*An explanation of the meaning of the Oath and Covenant . . .* [*Proclamation, Dec. 8th, 1638*] (Edinburgh? 1639)
——*It will, no doubt, seem strange to see my name in print, etc.* [*The Duke of Hamilton's Vindication of himself, as High Commissioner, against the charges of having accepted the declaration of the Covenant, etc.*] (Edinburgh? 1638)
——*The Marquess Hamilton's speech before the King's most excellent Majesty concerning his return into England spoke in Parliament in Scotland . . . Nov. 6th, 1641* (Edinburgh, 1641)
——*Whereas some have given out that by the act of Councell, which explaineth the Confession of Faith, etc. to be understood . . . as it was then professed . . . when it was made, etc.* (Edinburgh, 1638)
HARGRAVE, FRANCIS. *A Complete Collection of State Trials and Proceedings for High Treason*, vol. 2 (London, 1776)
HEWISON, J. K. *The Covenanters: a History of the Church in Scotland from the Reformation to the Revolution* (Glasgow, 1908)

HEXTER, J. H. *Reign of King Pym* (Cambridge, Mass., 1942)
HEYLYN, PETER. *Cyprianus Anglicus: or, the History of the Life and Death of William Laud* (London, 1668)
HILLIER, GEORGE. *Charles I in the Isle of Wight* (London, 1852)
His Majesty's Declaration concerning his proceedings with his subjects of Scotland since the pacification in the camp near Berwick (London, 1640)
Historical Manuscripts Commission, *First to Ninth Reports* (London, 1870–83)
——*Buccleuch and Queensberry Manuscripts* (London, 1899)
——*Cowper Manuscripts*, vol. 2 (London, 1888)
——*De L'Isle Manuscripts*, vol. 6 (London, 1966)
——*Report on the Manuscripts of the Earl of Denbigh*, vol. 5 (London, 1911)
——*Egmont Manuscripts* (London, 1905)
——*Report on the Manuscripts of the Duke of Hamilton* (London, 1887)
——*Supplementary Report on the Manuscripts of the Duke of Hamilton* (London, 1932)
——*Laing Manuscripts*, vol. I (London, 1914)
——*Mar and Kellie Manuscripts* (London, 1904)
——*Supplementary Report on the Manuscripts of the Earl of Mar and Kellie* (London, 1930)
HODGSON, JOHN. *Autobiography* (Edinburgh, 1806)
HOPE, Sir THOMAS. *Diary . . . 1633–1646* (Edinburgh, 1843)
HUTCHINSON, LUCY. *Memoirs of the Life of Colonel Hutchinson* (London, 1806)
HYDE, EDWARD, Earl of Clarendon. *History of the Rebellion and Civil Wars in England*, ed. by W. Dunn Macray, 6 vols (Oxford, 1888)
——*The Life of Edward, Earl of Clarendon* (Oxford, 1727)
JOHNSTONE OF WARRISTON, ARCHIBALD. *Diary . . . 1632–1639*, ed. by D. H. Fleming, 2 vols (Edinburgh, 1911)
——*Diary . . . 1639*, ed. by G. N. Paul (Edinburgh, 1896)
KNOWLER, WILLIAM (ed.). *The Earl of Strafford's Letters and Despatches*, 2 vols (Dublin, 1740)
LANE, JANE. *The Reign of King Covenant* (London, 1956)
LANG, ANDREW. *History of Scotland*, vol. 3 (New York, 1940)
LAUD, WILLIAM, Archbishop of Canterbury. *Works*, Vols. 3, 4, 7, 8 (Oxford, 1840)
LAW, ROBERT. *Memorialls, or the Memorable Things that fell out . . . from 1638 to 1684*, ed. by C. K. Sharpe (Edinburgh, 1818)
LEITH, W. F. *Memoirs of the Scottish Catholics in the XVIIth and XVIIIth centuries*, 2 vols (London, 1909)
LESLIE, JOHN, Earl of Rothes. *A Relation of the Proceedings Concerning the Affairs of the Kirk of Scotland, from August 1637 to July 1638* (Edinburgh, 1830)
A Letter . . . containing the substance of severall Speeches made by His Majesty, and by duke Hamilton, etc. (London? 1648)
A Letter from Holland; being a true relation of all the proceedings of the

Northern Armies under the command of Duke Hamilton, etc. (Rotterdam, 1648)

LILLY, WILLIAM. *Observations on the Life and Death of King Charles* (London, 1651)

"A Little yet true rehearsal of several passages of affairs, collected by a friend of Doctor Alexander's at Aberdeen", in *Transactions of the Royal History Society*, vol. 5, pp. 353–79 (London, 1877)

A List of the Judges of the high Court of justice for the Tryall of James Earl of Cambridge, Henry Earl of Holland, . . . Arthur Lord Capel . . . appointed by an act of the Commons of England, etc. (London, 1648)

LLOYD, RICHARD. *State Worthies, or, the statesman and favourites of England,* ed. by C. Whitworth, vol. 2 (London, 1766)

LODGE, EDMUND. *Portraits of illustrious personages of Great Britain,* Vol. 3 (London, 1850)

LOUNSBURY, R. G. *The British at Newfoundland, 1634–1763* (New Haven, Conn., 1934)

LUDLOW, EDMUND. *Memoirs,* ed. by C. H. Firth, 2 vols (Oxford, 1894)

MACDONALD, A. (ed.). *Letters to the Argyll Family* (Edinburgh, 1839)

McLELLAN, ROBERT. *The Isle of Arran* (New York, 1970)

McROBERTS, DAVID (ed.). *Essays on the Scottish Reformation, 1513–1625* (Glasgow, 1962)

MAIDMENT, JAMES (ed.). *A Book of Scotish Pasquils, 1568–1715* (Edinburgh, 1868)

——*Letters and State Papers during the reign of King James the Sixth* (Edinburgh, 1838)

MARSHALL, ROSALIND K. *The Days of Duchess Anne* (London, 1973)

——*The House of Hamilton in its Anglo-Scottish setting in the seventeenth century* (unpublished doctoral dissertation, Edinburgh, 1970)

MATHEW, DAVID. *Scotland under Charles I* (London, 1955)

——*The Social Structure of Caroline England* (Oxford, 1948)

MATHIESON, W. L. *Politics and Religion in Scotland, 1550–1695,* 2 vols (Glasgow, 1902)

MAY, THOMAS. *A Breviary of the History of the Parliament of England,* in Francis Maseres, *Select Tracts relating to the Civil Wars in England,* vol. I (London, 1815)

MEIKLE, H. W. *Correspondence of the Scots Commissioners in London* (London, 1917)

MELDRUM, N. *The General Assembly of 1638* (unpublished doctoral dissertation, Edinburgh, 1924)

MENTETH, ROBERT. *The History of the Troubles of Great Britain . . . 1633–50* (London, 1735)

Mercurius Elencticus

Mercurius Pragmaticus

MITCHISON, ROSALIND. *A History of Scotland* (London, 1970)

The Moderate Intelligencer

MONTEREUL, JEAN DE. *Diplomatic Correspondence,* ed. by J. G. Fotheringham, 2 vols (Edinburgh, 1898–99)

MUNRO, ROBERT. *Robert Munro, his Expedition*, vol. 2 (London, 1637)

NALSON, JOHN (ed.). *An Inpartiall Collection of the Great Affairs of State, from the beginning of the Scotch Rebellion to the Murder of Charles I*, 2 vols (London, 1682–83)

NAPIER, MARK. *Memoirs of the Marquis of Montrose*, 2 vols (Edinburgh, 1856)

——*Memorials of Montrose*, 2 vols (Glasgow, 1848)

——*Montrose and the Covenanters*, 2 vols (London, 1838)

National Library of Wales, Calendar of Wynn Papers (Aberystwyth, 1926)

NEDHAM, MARCHAMONT. *Digitus Dei: or, God's Justice upon treachery and treason, exemplified in the life and death of the late James, Duke of Hamilton, being an exact relation of his traitorous practices since the year 1630 . . . whereto is added an epitaph* (London, 1649)

——*The manifold practices and attempts of the Hamiltons, and particularly the present Duke . . . to get the Crown of Scotland, etc.* (London, 1648)

NOTESTEIN, W. "The establishment of the Committee of both King doms", *American Historical Review*, 17, April 1912, pp. 477–95.

OGLE, O. and BLISS, W. H. (eds.). *Calendar of Clarendon State Papers preserved in the Bodleian Library*, vol. I (Oxford, 1872)

ORMEROD, G. (ed.). *Military Proceedings in Lancashire* (Manchester, 1844)

PEACOCK, MABEL G. W. *An index of the Royalists whose estates were confiscated during the Commonwealth* (London, 1879)

PEARL, VALERIE. "The 'Royal Independents' in the English Civil War", in *Transactions of the Royal History Society*, 5th series, vol. 18, pp. 69–96 (London, 1968).

PECK, FRANCIS. *Desiderata Curiosa* (London, 1879)

PETERKIN, ALEXANDER. *Records of the Kirk of Scotland*, 2 vols (Edinburgh, 1838)

POMFRET, THOMAS. *Life of the Countess of Devonshire* (London, 1685)

PORTER, ENDYMION. "A Scottish Journie", in *Scottish History Society Miscellany*, vol. 2 (Edinburgh, 1904)

PRESTWICH, MENNA. *Cranfield: politics and profits under the early Stuarts* (Oxford, 1966)

Register of the Privy Council of Scotland, 2nd ser., 8 vols (Edinburgh, 1899–1908)

Remains Historical and Literary connected with the Palatine Counties of Lancaster and Chester (Manchester, 1909)

ROBERTS, G. (ed.). *Diary of Walter Yonge* (London, 1848)

ROBERTS, M. *Gustavus Adolphus*, 2 vols (London, 1958)

ROBERTSON, A. *The Life of Sir Robert Moray* (London, 1922)

ROBINSON, E. *A Discourse of the Civil War in Lancashire* (London, 1864)

ROGERS, C. "Rehearsal of Events which occurred in the north of Scotland from 1635 to 1645 in relation to the National Covenant", in *Transactions of the Royal History Society*, new ser., vol. 5, pp. 354–79 (London, 1877)

——(ed.). *The Earl of Stirling's Register of Royal Letters, 1615–1635*, 2 vols (Edinburgh, 1885)

ROUND, J. H. "The Case of Lucas and Lisle", in *Transactions of the Royal History Society*, new ser., vol. 8, pp. 154–80 (London, 1894)

ROW, JOHN. *History of the Kirk of Scotland (1588–1637)* (Edinburgh, 1842)

RUSHWORTH, JOHN. *Historical Collections of Private Passages of State*, 8 vols (London, 1859)

——*Trial of Strafford* (London, 1680)

SANDERSON, WILLIAM. *A compleat History of the Life and Reigne of King Charles from his cradle to his grave* (London, 1658)

SCHLEICH, ALLAN R. *The Public Life and Character of James, 3rd Marquis and 1st Duke of Hamilton, 1628–1644* (unpublished doctoral dissertation, Nebraska, 1959)

SCOT OF SCOTSTARVET, Sir JOHN. "The Staggering State of Scots Statesmen from 1550–1650, in *Transactions of the Royal History Society*, new ser., vol. I, pp. 427–512 (London, 1872)

SCOTT, WALTER (ed.). *A collection of scarce and valuable tracts . . . selected from an infinite number . . . in particular that of the late Lord Somers*, vol. 5 (London, 1811)

SCROPE, R. (ed.). *Clarendon State Papers*, vol. 2 (Oxford, 1773)

SMITH, L. PEARSALL. *The Life and Letters of Sir Henry Wotton*, 2 vols. (Oxford, 1907)

SPALDING, JOHN. *The History of the Troubles and Memorable Transactions in Scotland and England, from 1624 to 1645*, 2 vols (Edinburgh, 1828)

SPOTTISWOODE, J. *History of the Church and State of Scotland*, 3 vols (Edinburgh, 1857)

STACE, MACHELL (comp.). *Cromwelliana* (London, 1810)

STEARNS, R. P. *The strenuous Puritan: Hugh Peter, 1598–1660* (Urbana, Ill., 1954)

STEVENSON, D. *The Scottish Revolution, 1637–1644: the triumph of the Covenanters* (Newton Abbot, 1973)

STONE, L. *The Crisis of the Aristocracy, 1558–1641* (Oxford, 1965)

TERRY, C. S. *The Life and Campaigns of Alexander Leslie, first Earl of Leven* (London, 1899)

THURLOE, JOHN. *A Collection of the State Papers of John Thurloe, etc.*, ed. by T. Birch, vol. I (London, 1742)

TOWNSHEND, DOROTHEA. *The Life and Letters of Endymion Porter* (London, 1897)

TURNER, Sir JAMES. *Memoirs of his own Life and Times* (Edinburgh, 1829)

TWEEDIE, W. K. *The Life of John Livingston* (Edinburgh, 1845)

UNDERDOWN, D. *Pride's Purge: politics in the Puritan Revolution* (Oxford, 1971)

WALKER, CLEMENT. *An Appendix to the History of Independency* (London, 1661)

——*Relations and Observations* (London, 1661)

WALTON, J. *The bloudy battel at Preston, etc.* (London, 1648)

WARBURTON, ELIOT. *Memoirs of Prince Rupert and the Cavaliers*, 3 vols (London, 1849)

WARNER, G. F. (ed.). *The Nicholas Papers*, vol. I (London, 1886)

WARWICK, Sir PHILIP. *Memoirs of the Reign of King Charles I* (London, 1702)

WATERHOUSE, E. Paintings from Venice for Seventeenth Century England, *Italian Studies*, 7, May 1952, pp. 1–23.

WEBER, K. *Lucius Cary, second Viscount Falkland* (New York, 1967)

WEDGWOOD, C. V. "Anglo-Scottish Relations, 1603–1642", in *Transactions of the Royal History Society*, 4th ser., vol. 32, pp. 31–48 (London, 1950)

——*The King's Peace, 1637–1641* (London, 1955)

——*The King's War, 1641–1647* (London, 1958)

——*The Sense of the Past* (New York, 1960)

——*Strafford, 1593–1641* (London, 1935 and 1961)

——*The Thirty Years War* (London, 1938)

WHITAKER, T. D. *The Life and Original Correspondence of Sir George Radcliffe* (London, 1910)

WHITELOCKE, BULSTRODE. *A Journal of the Swedish Embassy in the years 1653 and 1654*, vol. I (London, 1855)

——*Memorials of English Affairs*, 4 vols (Oxford, 1853)

WILBRAHAM, R. and LOTHIAN, J. *Three Letters concerning the surrender of many Scottish lords . . . with a list of the names of the lords, knights, colonels, and other officers of Duke Hamilton's army . . . taken prisoners by the Parliament forces under . . . Cromwell, etc.* (Edinburgh? 1648)

WILLCOCK, J. *The Great Marquess: Life and Times of Archibald . . . Marquess of Argyll* (Edinburgh, 1903)

WILLSON, D. H. "King James I and Anglo-Scottish Unity", in W. A. Aiken and B. D. Henning (eds.) *Conflict in Stuart England* (London, 1960)

——*King James VI and I* (New York, 1956)

WILSON, ARTHUR. *The History of Great Britain, being the life and reign of King James the First* (London, 1653)

WILSON, JAMES. *The History of Scottish Affairs* (Perth, 1827)

WISHART, G. *Memoirs of . . . James Graham, Marquis of Montrose* (Edinburgh, 1893)

WODROW, ROBERT. *Analecta*, vol. 1 (Glasgow, 1842)

YORK, PHILIP, Earl of Hardwicke. *Miscellaneous State Papers, from 1501 to 1726*, vol. 2, and *Supplement* (London, 1778)

WOOLRYCH, A. *Battles of the English Civil War* (New York, 1961)

ZAGORIN, PEREZ. *The Court and the Country: the beginning of the English Revolution* (London, 1969)

INDEX

Abell, William, 46
Abercorn, James Hamilton, Earl of, 17, 43, 164, 240
Aberdeen, 74, 79, 96, 103, 104, 166
Abernathy (an ex-Jesuit), 80
Aboyne, James Gordon, Viscount, 103–4, 160
Act of Classes, 221, 238
Act of Union, 241
Alexander, William, Lord, 46
Almond, James, Baron Livingstone of, see Callander, James Livingstone, Earl of
Annan, 195
Annandale, John Murray, Earl of, 129, 152
Anstruther, Sir Robert, 27
Antrim, Katherine Macdonnell, Countess of, 56, 69
Antrim, Randal Macdonnell, Earl of, 68–9, 97, 154, 180
Appleby, 198, 200, 219
Arbroath Abbey, 5, 8, 18, 48
Argyll, Archibald Campbell, 7th Earl of, 11, 57, 79
Argyll, Archibald Campbell, 8th Earl of, later Marquis of, 51, 56, 102, 104, 110, 122, 123, 137, 138, 141, 145, 147, 150, 154, 173, 175, 180, 186, 201, 223, 244, Pl. XIA
  invasion of lands by Antrim, 68, 69
  sacks Brodick Castle, 101
  Character of, 57–8, 182
  committal to Covenant, 64, 68
  and Covenanting Army, 157, 183–4
  and Cromwell, 182, 189, 220
  and "Engagement", 186–9, 191, 193, 194
  Executed, 241
  and General Assembly, 144
  at Glasgow Assembly, 83, 87, 88, 89, 90

Hamilton's, appraisal of, 86
  fears of, 121
  "friendship" with, 127, 129, 140, 143, 156, 182, 185
  life, refuses to intercede for, 231
  and "The Incident", 132–6
  and King's Confession, 78, 79
  and Kirk Party, 181
  and Loudoun's Annuities, 148–149
  created Marquis, 139
  and Morton, 130–1, 142
  proposal to partition Scotland, 118
  and Scottish Privy Council, 148, 153
  and Treasurer's post, 130, 138
Argyll, Archibald Campbell, 9th Earl of, see Lorne, Archibald Campbell, Viscount, later 9th Earl of Argyll
Argyllshire, 97
Arminianism and Jacobus Arminius, 49 & n, 50, 123
Armstrong, Archie, 53
Army, see Covenanting Army; Irish Army; New Model Army; Royalist Army; Scottish Army
Army Council, 231–2
Arnim, Hans Georg von, 25, 32
Arran, Charles Hamilton, Earl of (son) 22, 77, 115
Arran, James Hamilton, 1st Earl of, 7
Arran, James Hamilton, 2nd Earl of, see Châtelherault, James Hamilton, Duke of
Arran, James Hamilton, 3rd Earl of, 8, 9
Arran, Isle of, 7, 9, 17, 97, 101, 267–8
Arundel, Thomas Howard, Earl of, 97, 105, 106
Arundell, Col. Sir John, 164, 165, 167, 169, 170